IMAGES
of America

Tinicum Township, Bucks County

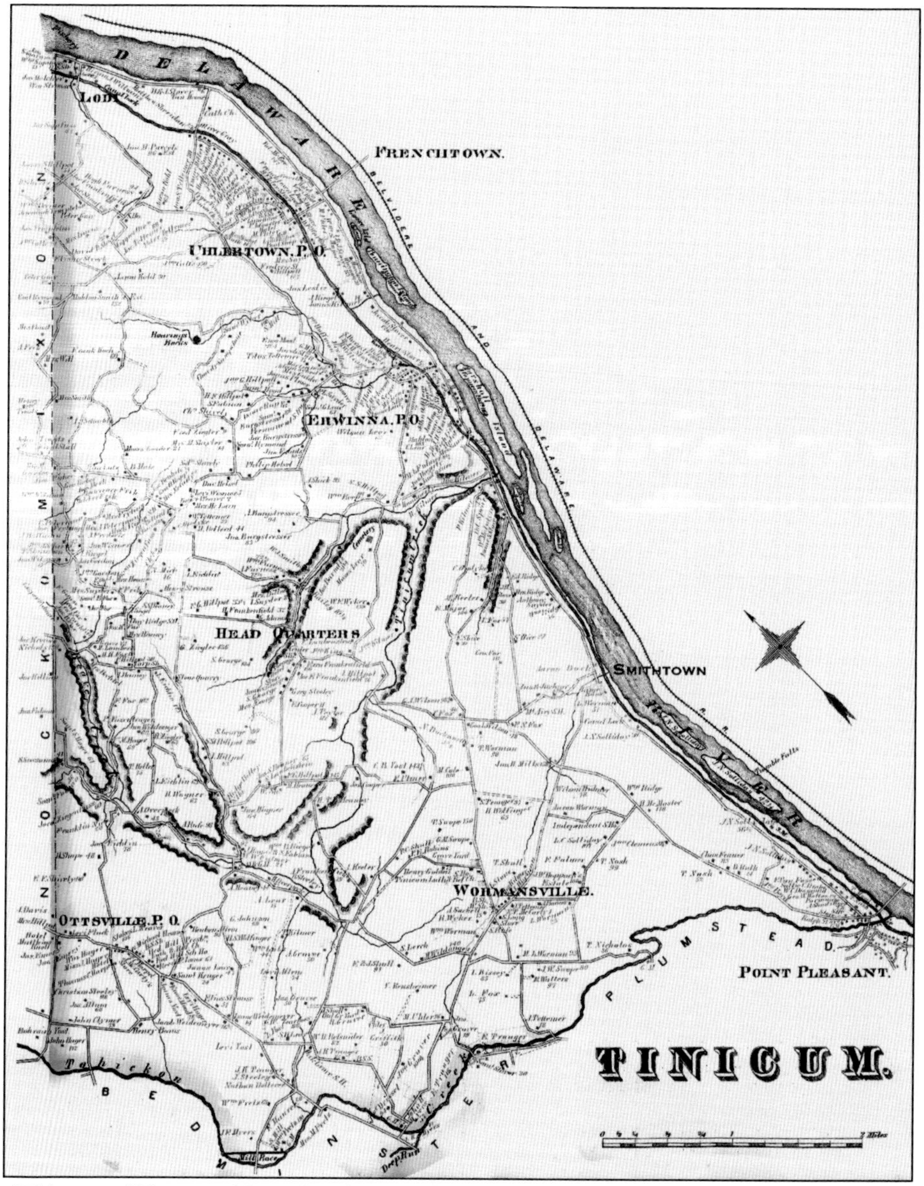

The 1876 map of Tinicum Township locates the villages and hamlets within its 30 square miles. Point Pleasant is at the southeastern tip on the banks of the Delaware River, on the east, and Tohickon Creek, which forms the western boundary of the township. Smithtown, the only hamlet that has disappeared, was just north of Point Pleasant. The hamlet of Wormansville is west of Smithtown. Continuing north along the Delaware shoreline, Erwinna is at midpoint, followed by Uhlerstown, which is opposite Frenchtown, New Jersey. The hamlet of Headquarters (spelled as two words above), or Sundale, developed in the geographic center of the township, between Erwinna and Ottsville. On the western boundary, modern Route 611 passes Ottsville, on the old Durham Road from Philadelphia. (WLC.)

On the cover: Please see page 31. (OVP.)

IMAGES
of America

TINICUM TOWNSHIP, BUCKS COUNTY

Patricia Valentine Whitacre
and Richard A. Plank

ARCADIA
PUBLISHING

ISBN 978-0-7385-5753-3

Published by Arcadia Publishing
Charleston, South Carolina

Printed in the United States of America

Library of Congress Catalog Card Number: 2007934698

For all general information contact Arcadia Publishing at:
Telephone 843-853-2070
Fax 843-853-0044
E-mail sales@arcadiapublishing.com
For customer service and orders:
Toll-Free 1-888-313-2665

Visit us on the Internet at www.arcadiapublishing.com

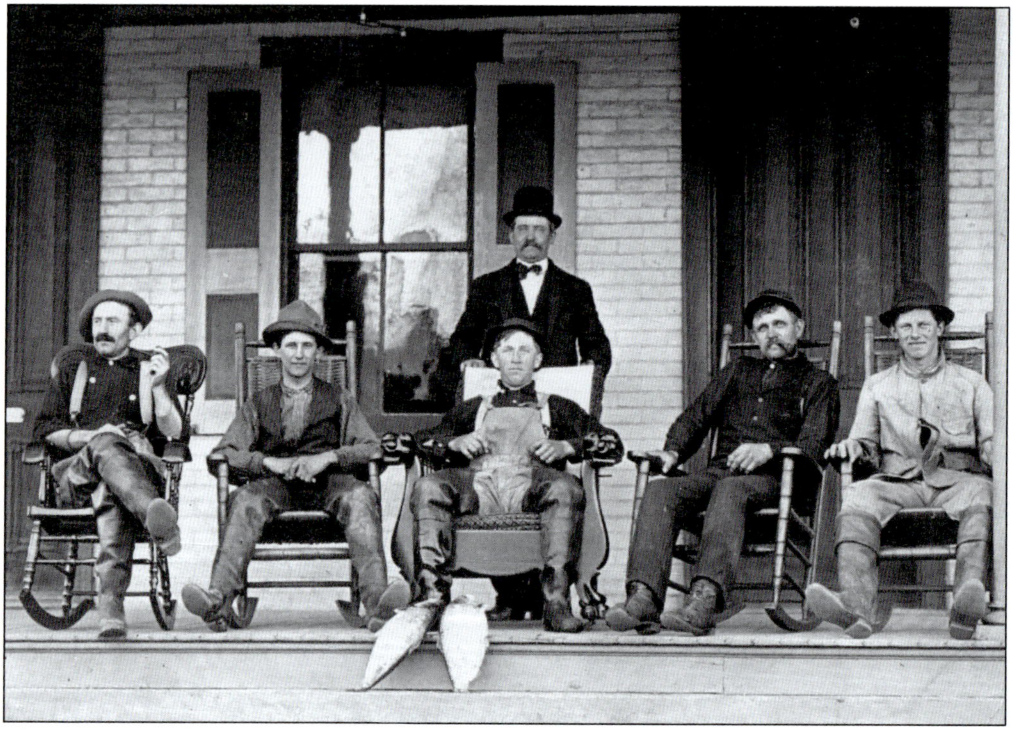

The spring run of shad up the Delaware River has been eagerly anticipated by both anglers and diners for generations. Pictured with their catch, around 1910, on the porch of Shank's Hotel, also known as the Delaware Valley House, at the Uhlerstown-Frenchtown Bridge are, from left to right, Wilson Hager, Grant Weaver, John Tettemer, Leonard Schaible, and Harry Vanselous, with host Newton Shank (standing). (WVR.)

Contents

ACKNOWLEDGMENTS

We offer our sincere appreciation to all who helped compile this history of Tinicum Township. With nine generations of Tinicum roots and a lifetime of service to the community, John Quinby has been invaluable in locating and identifying old photographs. Lynn Scoboria Greening, a graduate of Tinicum's one-room schools, has spent years, with husband Ted, collecting reminiscences and memorabilia in her school district histories. Buck Walter, an eighth-generation resident, shed light on the Point Pleasant area, while Blanche Wehrung and Elsie Heaney sorted the details of the Ottsville area. Les Schuman, Ernie Schaible Jr., and Ebby Ridge clarified Erwinna and Uhlerstown information. The late Lois Anderson featured local history as editor of the *Tinicum Bulletin*, and Violet Gruver Rutter shared childhood memories in her book, *Not That Long Ago.*

We regret that space prevents us from acknowledging all the sources of information and of over 1,200 photographs, from which we selected 233 for this book. Bruce Wallace restored these images to their fullest potential.

The following list of contributors includes the three-letter code that identifies the source of each photograph: Peggy Alexander (ALX), Kathryn Auerbach (KAB), Elsie Weaver Beck (EWB), Sylvia Becker (LCH), Bill Bickel (BBK), Gary Bickel (GBK), Bucks County Department of Parks and Recreation (BCP), Mitchell Bunkin (BNK), Christ Evangelical Lutheran Church (LTC), Charles A. Cooper, D.D.S. (CPR), *Delaware Valley News* (DVN), Laure Duval (LDV), Mary Schaible Fox (FOX), Henry and Hattie Fretz (FTZ), Linda Frey (FRY), Friends of the Delaware Canal (FOC), Allan Goulding (GLD), Lynn Scoboria Greening (LSG), Joan Haas (HAS), Bill Hall (HAL), JoAnn Hamilton (SZP), Robert Hanley (HNL), Elsie Heaney (EWH), Alice Hilbert (HLB), Idarose Huf (HUF), *Intelligencer* (INT), Jackie Kinney (JKN), Richard Kolbe (KLB), Richard Lennox (LNX), David Lord (DLD), Sonja Ridge Mitchell (SRM), Don and Barbara Morris (DBM), Overpeck family (OVP), Grace Weaver Pandy (WVR), Lotus Payer (PYR), Graham Place (PLC), Richard A. Plank (RPK), John and Joan Quinby (QBY), Dorsey Reading (DRD), Jim Reilly (RLY), Diane Schaefer (DTS), Ernie Schaible Jr. (SBL), Walter Schneiderwind (WSW), Les Schuman (LSH), Chris Shivo (SHV), Esther Sigafoos (SIG), Gail Springer (SPR), Harold Steeley (HST), Paul Sterner (PST), Tinicum Civic Association (TCA), Tinicum Township Collection (TTP), Tom Vanderlely (VND), Bruce Wallace (WLC), Walter family (WLT), Henry Weaver (HWV), Linda Wegscheider (VNS), Blanche Wehrung (BWG), Denny Wehrung (DWG), Marylou Wenner (WNR), Bob Whitacre (WHT), Mildred Williams (WMS), and Marcia Yeager (YGR). The Spruance Library of the Bucks County Historical Society (BCHS) provided photographs and the book *A Genealogical Record of the Descendants of Henry Stauffer* by Rev. A. J. Fretz, 1899 (STV).

We hope that this collection of Tinicum images will inspire others to preserve family photographs, and perhaps share them with neighbors in another volume on Tinicum Township, Bucks County.

Introduction

"We wonder if the things we ought to cherish most are slipping from our grasp while we pursue things that really matter least."

Raymond Stover's expression of his family's philosophy might also apply to that of other early Tinicum families. Several descendants of the earliest settlers have contributed photographs and information to this history of the township. A few possess the deeds, written on parchment, by which their ancestors acquired their land two centuries ago. Several have placed permanent easements on their land, guaranteeing that it will forever retain its rural character.

The original inhabitants of the land were the Lenni-Lenape Indians, who lived peacefully with the earliest settlers. They survive in the roots of some local families. The melting pot of Tinicum neighbors began with the earliest Scotch-Irish and English Quakers but was quickly infused by German immigrants, who continued to dominate the population into the 20th century, when others from overseas, and fugitives from America's increasingly crowded cities, chose to live in Tinicum.

Family albums have produced a rich collection of images, which illustrate early farming techniques and machinery, leisure activities, and the architecture of the families' homes and barns. The photographs and captions describing local architecture will help future generations to understand and preserve these features as they adapt historic buildings for modern living. Vintage aircraft from Van Sant Airport continue to fly above Tinicum's historic landscape, adding to the impression that the township is locked in a time warp.

In the 21st century, an age of computers and commuters, few residents make their living as farmers, preferring instead to preserve their land as natural areas, while others lease their fields to area farmers. Recognizing the survival of many native plant communities first documented by early botanists, Bucks County has designated most of Tinicum's 30 square miles as of highest priority for natural areas protection. Meanwhile, modern farmers have expanded the variety of their crops and livestock to include Christmas trees, birdseed, vineyards, and alpacas, and some have adopted organic farming techniques.

The topography that guided early settlement has continued to guide development. The limited groundwater and other natural resources are protected by ordinance. To encourage the preservation of historic buildings, their adaptive reuse for purposes other than their original intent is permitted. Nearly a third of Tinicum's land, so richly described by the images in this book, is now permanently protected from development. This includes both parkland and the private lands whose owners have generously relinquished their development rights. Clearly, the residents of Tinicum continue to follow the Stover philosophy of preserving the heritage of yesterday to leave as a legacy for future generations.

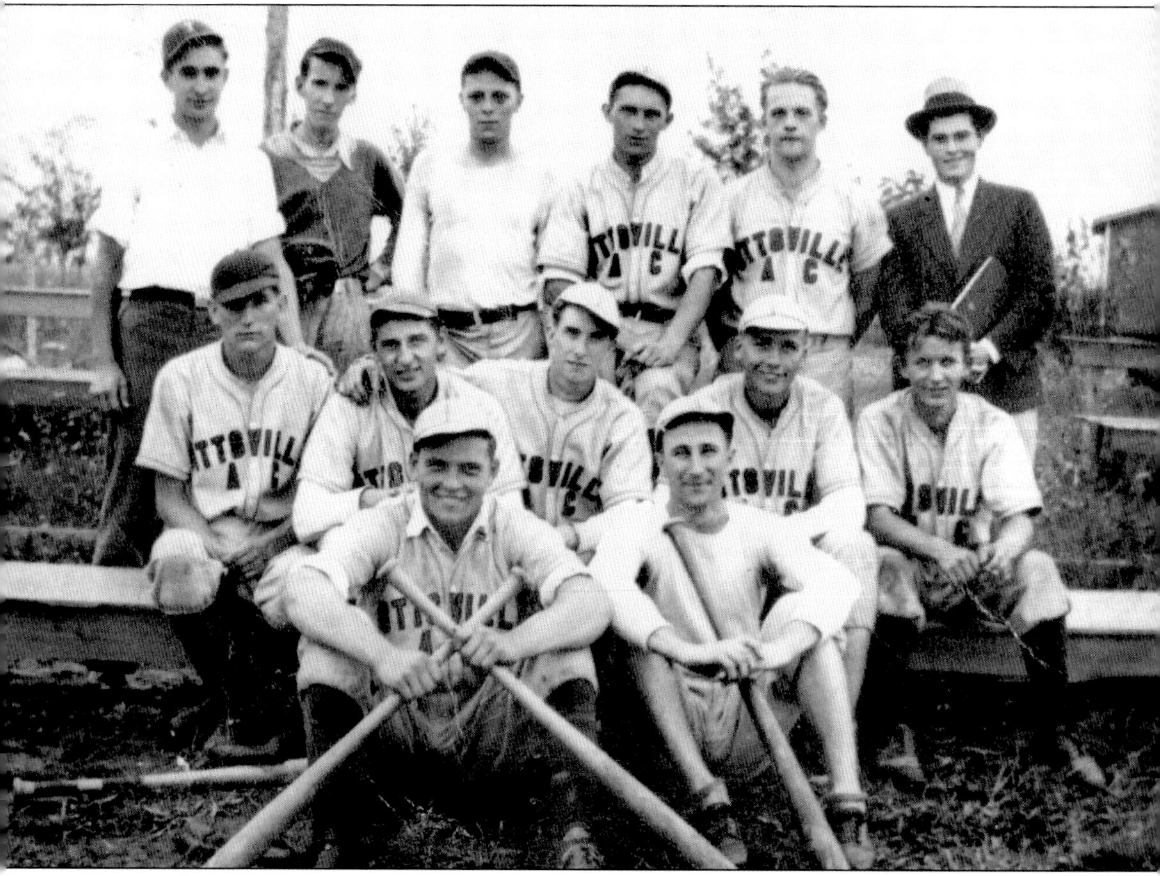

During the Depression, people needed something to give them hope and heroes. Tinicum youths spent hours practicing baseball and making bats by shaving ash branches to shape. They biked to Easton to study newsreels of Babe Ruth. John Schaefer later recalled that when peace was declared after World War II, troops across Europe set up makeshift games of baseball to celebrate. The Ottsville ball field is now woodland, across Route 611 from the post office. In the Erwinna games behind the Stovers' Riverside Farm, hitting a ball into the canal guaranteed a home run. In this 1934 photograph, members of the Ottsville team are, from left to right, (first row) John Schaefer and Pete Sobel; (second row) Quint Sobel, unidentified, Woody Wehrung, Frank Schaefer, and Chet Jesiolowski; (third row) Frank Cech, Dave Logan, unidentified, Gus Dreger, Aaron Trauger, and manager James Arthur. (BWG.)

One

A Melting Pot of Neighbors

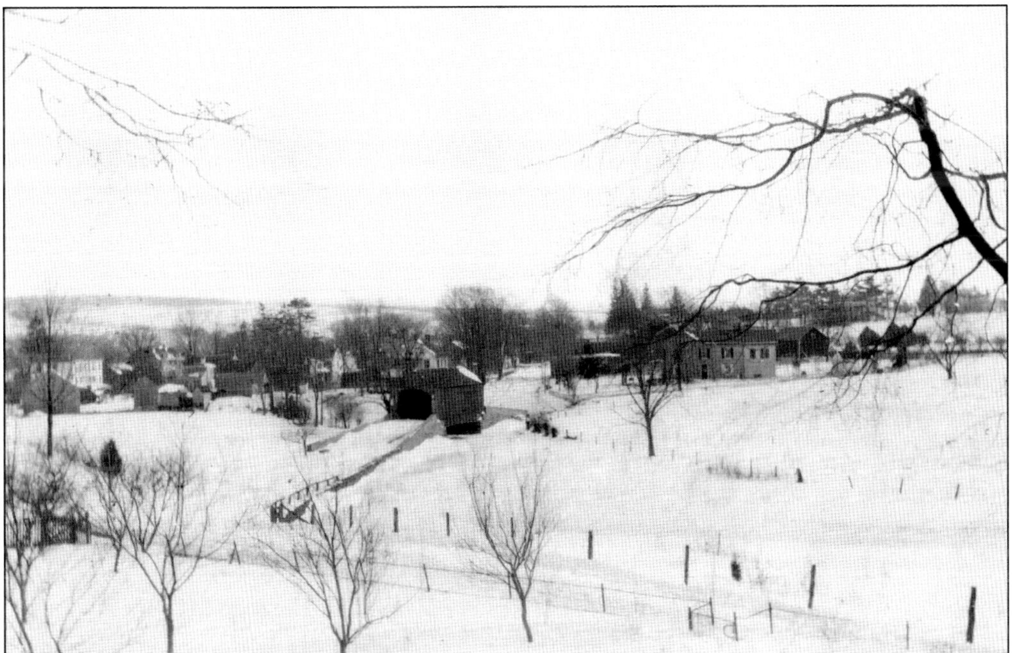

This peaceful 1918 view of Erwinna under a blanket of snow would not have been possible if French businessman E. I. du Pont had accepted Arthur Erwin's 1801 invitation to locate his American gunpowder factory along the Delaware River here. Fortunately, Du Pont chose Wilmington, Delaware, and the early settlers of Tinicum gradually welcomed a variety of neighbors to share their beautiful township. Viewed from above Geigel Hill Road looking south, Erwinna today has seen little change. (LSH.)

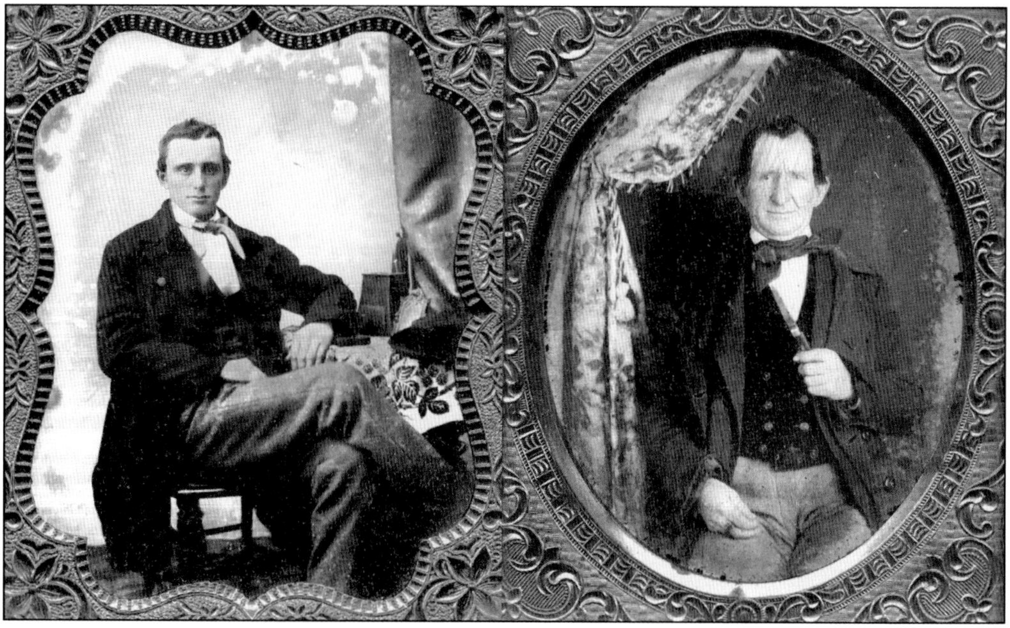

These ambrotypes of Cletus Haney (left) and his father, Samuel Haney, 1808–1890, are rare survivors of an early form of photography, around 1860, that recorded images on fragile glass. The metronome beside Cletus indicates a musical connection, but the meaning of the dagger clutched to the breast of Samuel is a mystery to his descendants. Michael Heany was among the earliest German settlers in Tinicum, buying land in 1745. (EWH.)

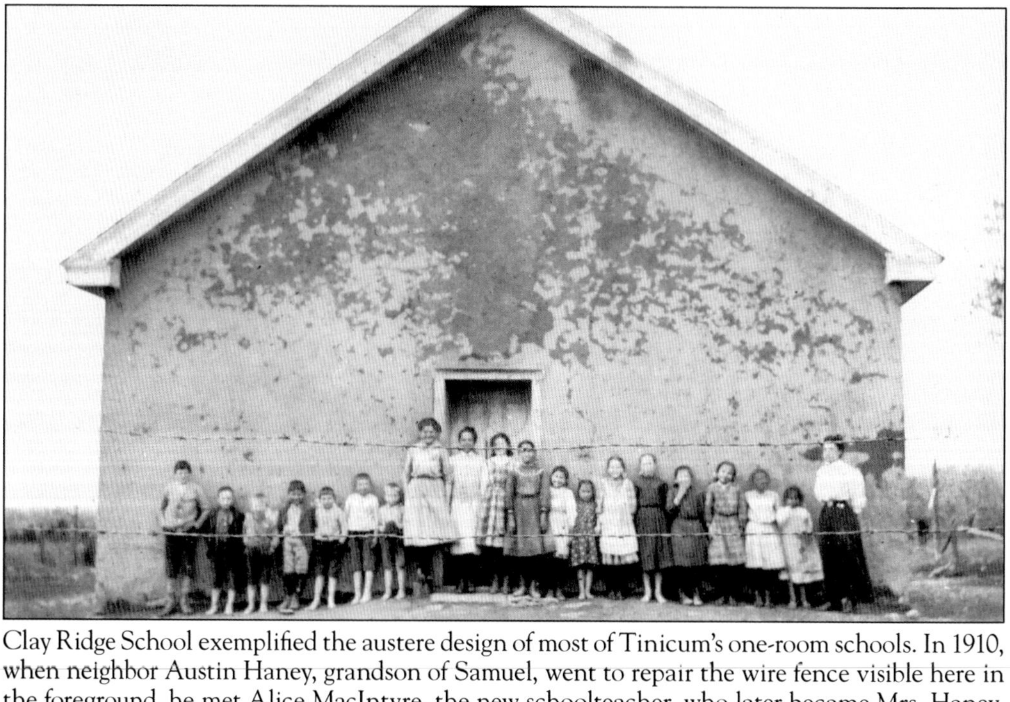

Clay Ridge School exemplified the austere design of most of Tinicum's one-room schools. In 1910, when neighbor Austin Haney, grandson of Samuel, went to repair the wire fence visible here in the foreground, he met Alice MacIntyre, the new schoolteacher, who later became Mrs. Haney. The building survives, with its separate boy and girl outhouses, as a private residence on Geigel Hill Road, opposite Clay Ridge Road. (EWH.)

The tintype, a successor to the ambrotype, was a more affordable and durable form of photography. In this 1892 tintype taken in Point Pleasant are, from left to right, (first row) Adda Shaddinger, Martha (Smith) Shaddinger, and Laura DeWeise; (second row) William Ridge Cooper, M.D., Harry Walter, M.D., and John Willis Walter, M.D. (WLT.)

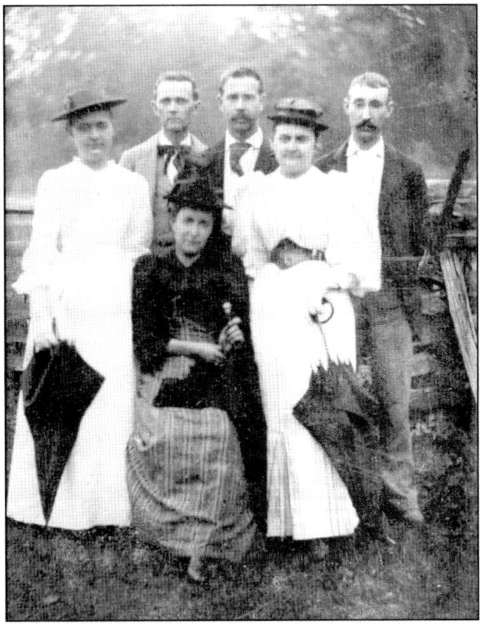

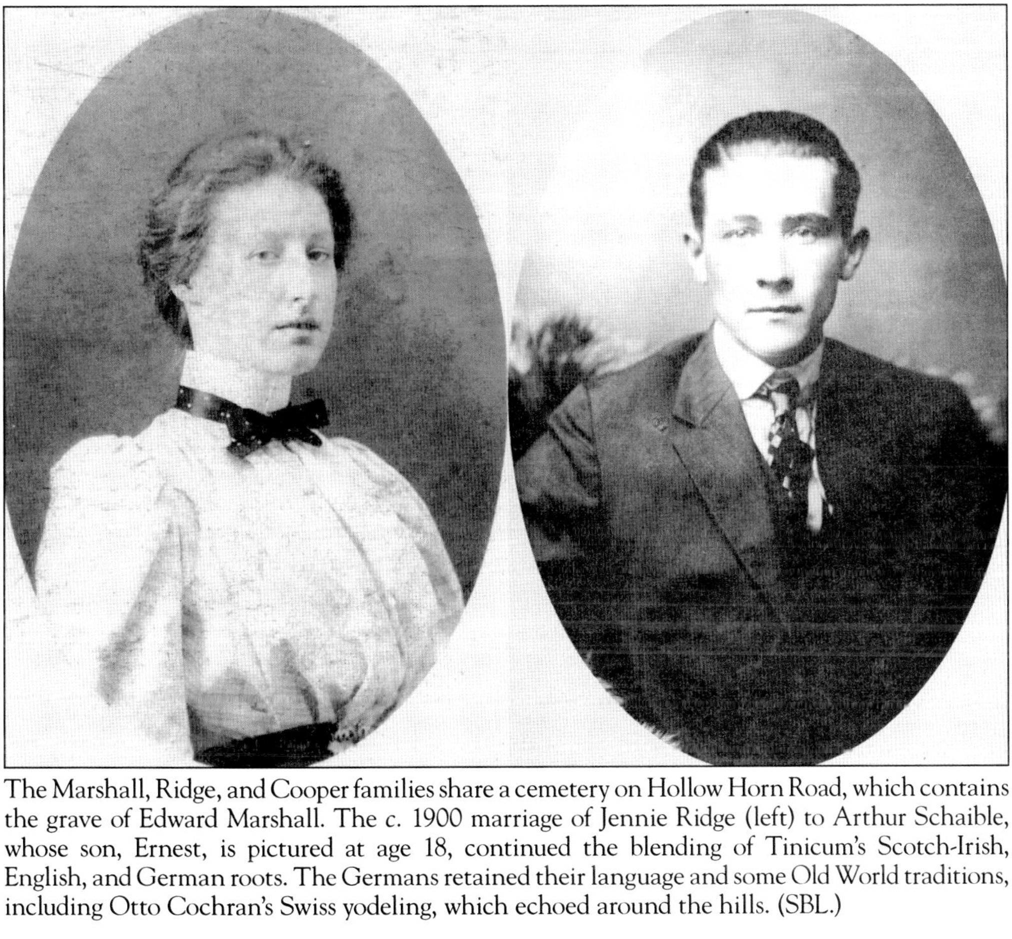

The Marshall, Ridge, and Cooper families share a cemetery on Hollow Horn Road, which contains the grave of Edward Marshall. The c. 1900 marriage of Jennie Ridge (left) to Arthur Schaible, whose son, Ernest, is pictured at age 18, continued the blending of Tinicum's Scotch-Irish, English, and German roots. The Germans retained their language and some Old World traditions, including Otto Cochran's Swiss yodeling, which echoed around the hills. (SBL.)

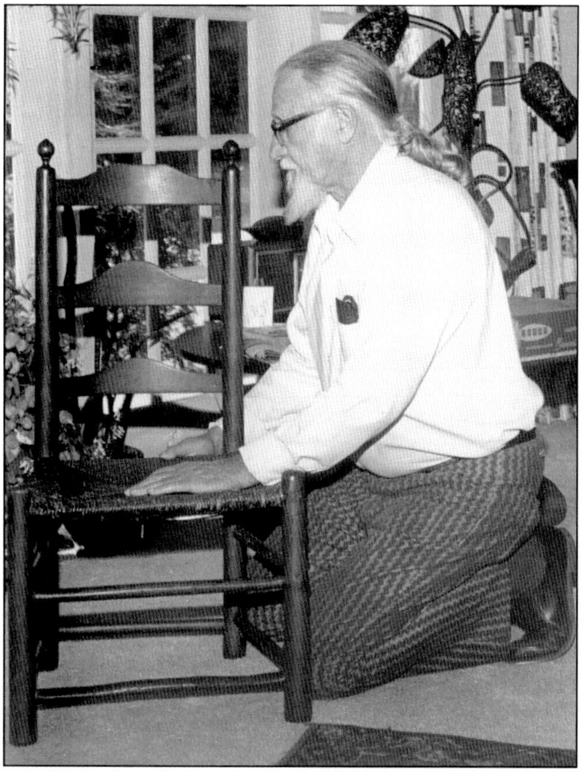

William, Moses, and Edward Marshall signed the 1738 petition for the formation of a township to be called Tennicunk. Edward was one of the walkers of the infamous Walking Purchase of 1737, by which the sons of William Penn cheated the Lenni-Lenapes out of a vast portion of their land. A descendant of the Marshall family, Ernest Schaible Sr. of Uhlerstown, is pictured with this chair, which belonged to Edward and remains in the family. (SBL.)

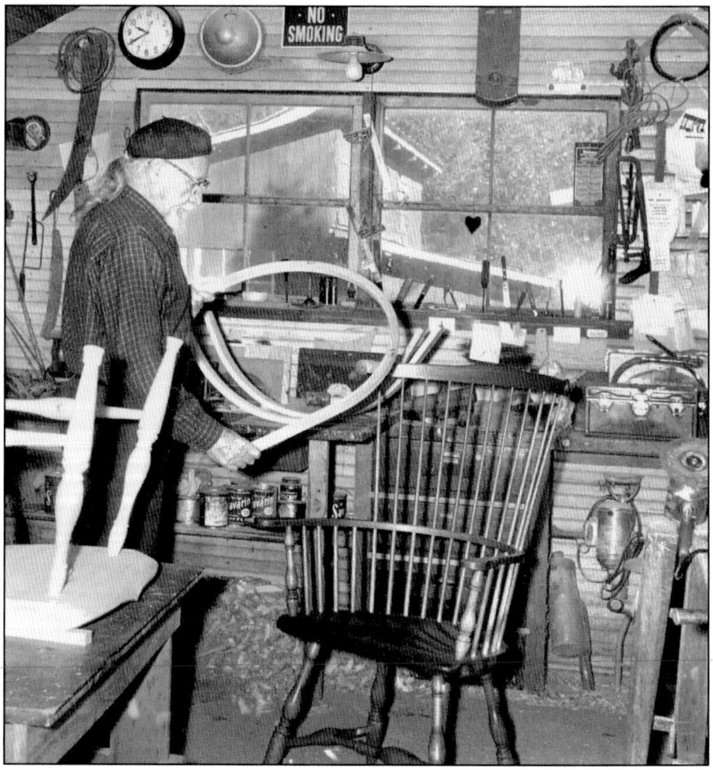

Ernest Schaible Sr., son of Jennie and Arthur, learned the rudiments of carpentry while building houses and canal boats with his father, then honed his skills to become renowned for the authentic restoration of historic buildings, including old stone houses, and fine quality reproductions of antique furniture. He is pictured here in his workshop near Uhlerstown in 1971. (SBL.)

Jim Ridge, shad fisherman, canal worker, and lively fiddle player, left indelible memories with Boy Scouts and patrons of the general store he and his wife, "Aunt Sally," ran for many years near Smithtown. Pictured here on the steps of the store, around 1920, Ridge was the first ranger of Treasure Island Boy Scout Camp, from 1913 to 1928, retiring at age 80. Later his son, Arthur, was a ranger at the camp. (SRM.)

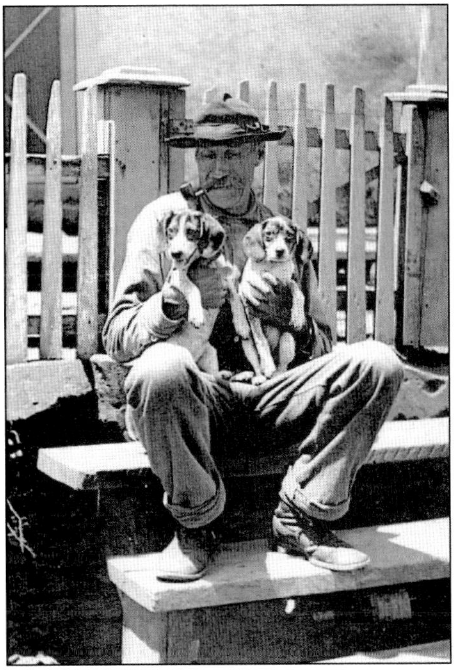

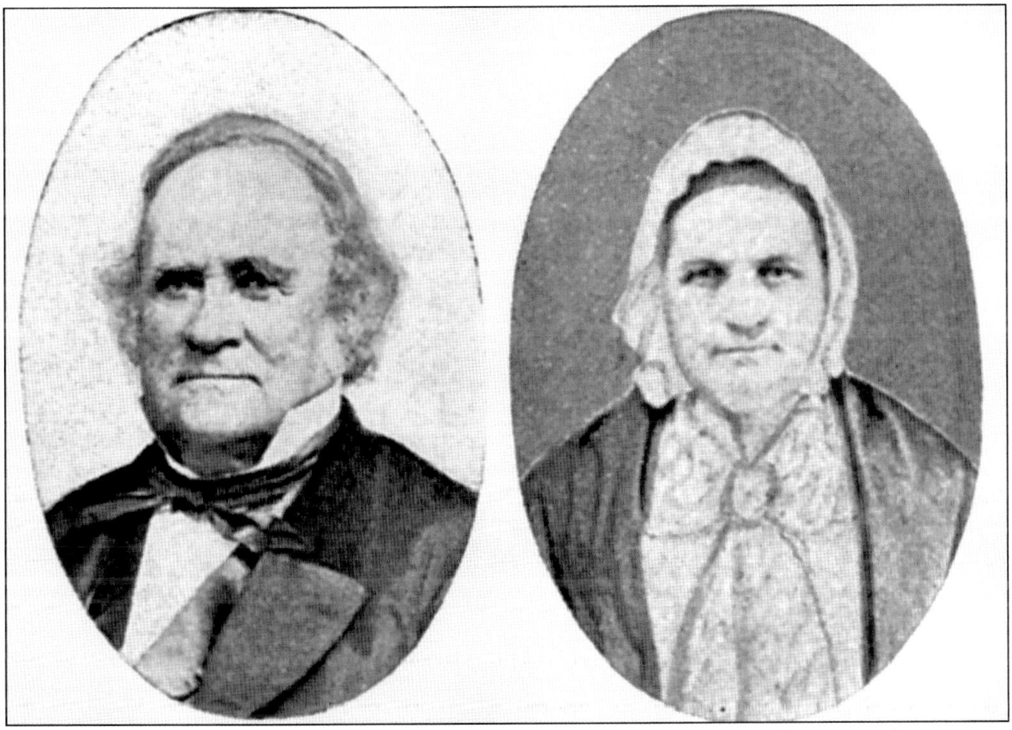

After their 1810 marriage, Henry S. and Barbara Stover lived in Point Pleasant, where Henry first worked at his father's mill. He then bought several mill sites along the Delaware River and creeks, moving to Erwinna in 1832 to build his home and a grist- and sawmill. His sons Jacob and Isaac assumed the business in 1850. Isaac also operated a flax mill near the Erwinna Covered Bridge. (BCHS, STV.)

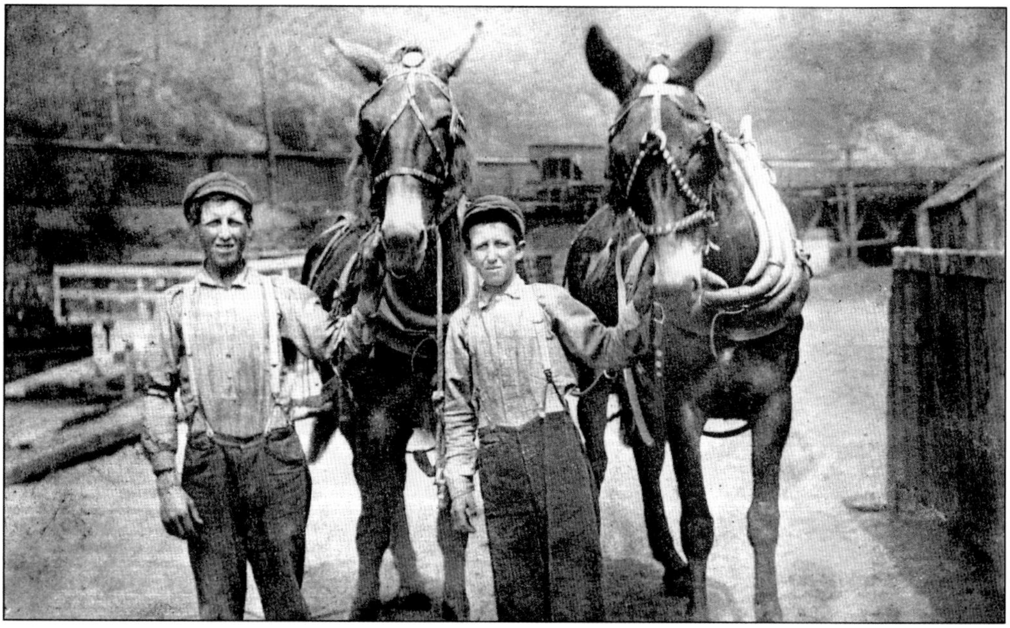

When the Delaware Canal was built in the 1830s, a new wave of settlers from southern Germany joined the melting pot of Tinicum neighbors, adding names like Sigafoos, Bickel, and Freuh/Free. In 1920, Jim Bickel (left) rented his mule team to the canal boat operators. His unidentified younger companion bears a strong family resemblance. Suspenders allowed flexibility in sizes of comfortable, loose-fitting work pants. (BBK.)

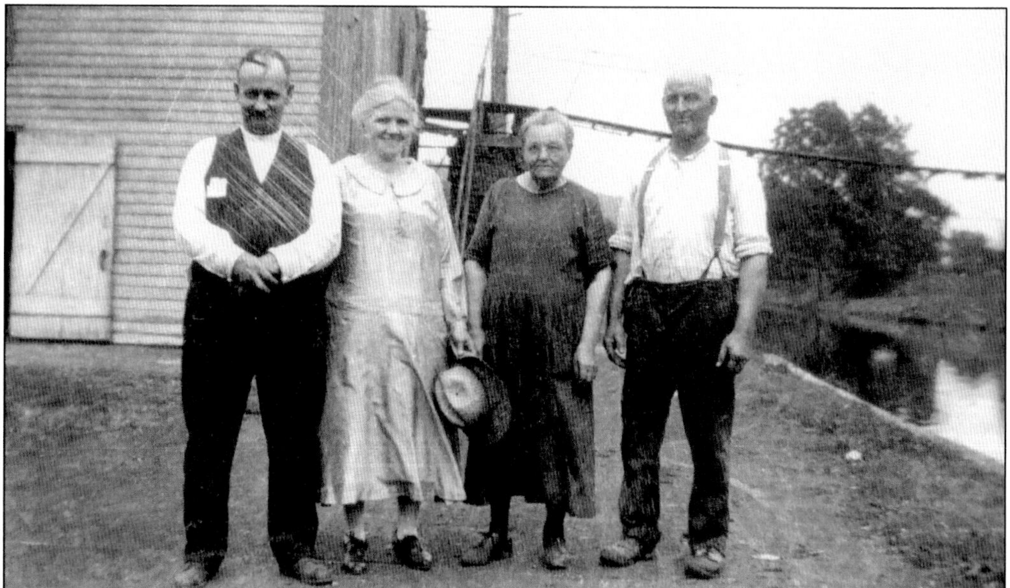

John L. Free was among the last of the Free family members to work on the canal during its century of operation. He owned three canal boats and several boardinghouses along the canal where men and their mules could rest overnight. Standing beside the canal in 1957 are, from left to right, Mahlon and Margaret Free and Rosina Free and her husband, John. A suspended footbridge over the canal is visible behind them. (HAS.)

While many of the later German immigrants to Tinicum settled in the vicinity of the canal, other Germans continued to locate in the interior of the township. George Wehrung arrived in America in 1871, followed by his family in 1886. They settled around 1910 in Ottsville, where son Christian grew up to become the village blacksmith, seen here around 1935. (BWG.)

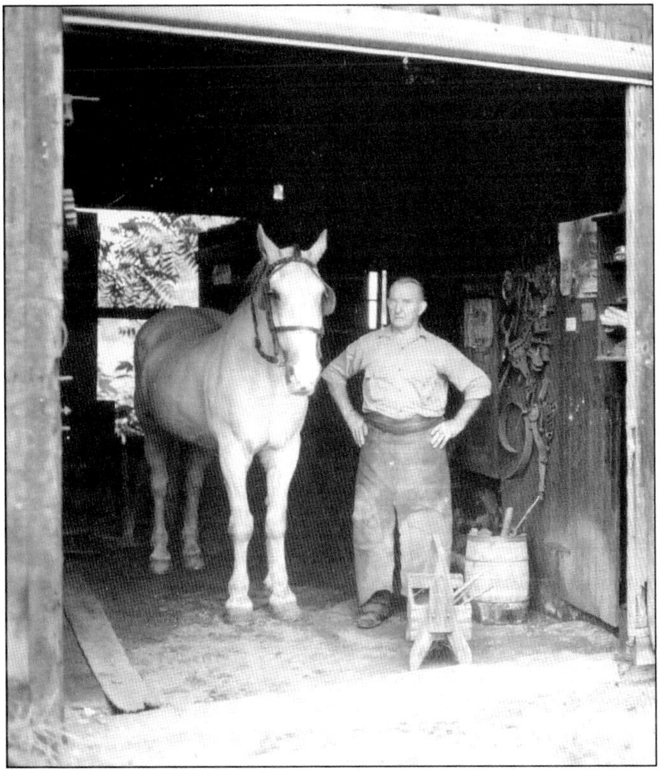

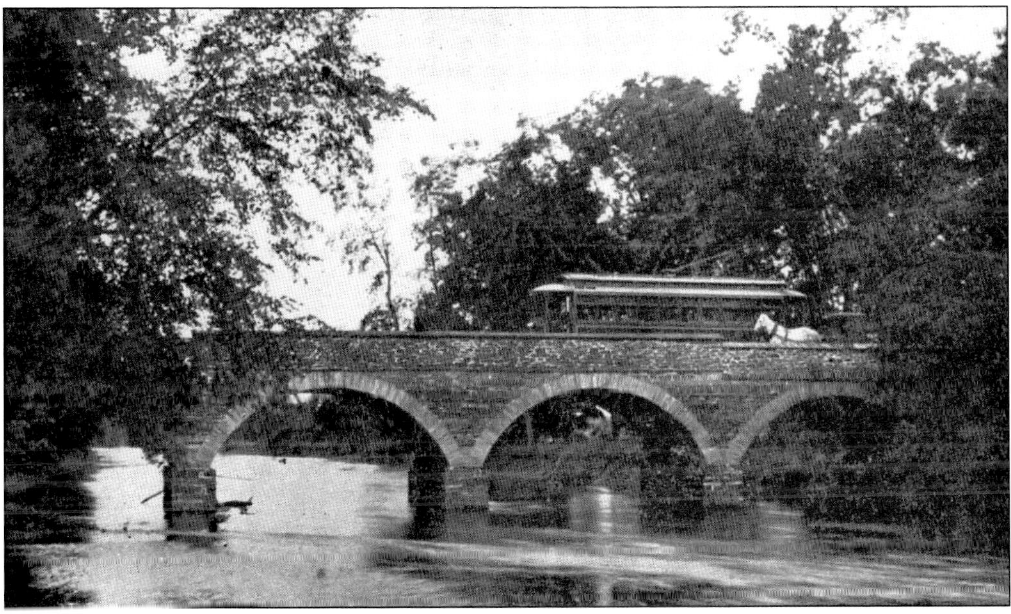

Old and new forms of transportation are reflected in this 1904 advertisement of the Philadelphia and Easton Railway Company. The trolley passes a horse and carriage as they cross over Tohickon Creek along Easton Road, now Route 611, from Bedminster into Tinicum. Now city people could live in Tinicum and work in the city, and residents could shop and attend movies in Easton. (RPK.)

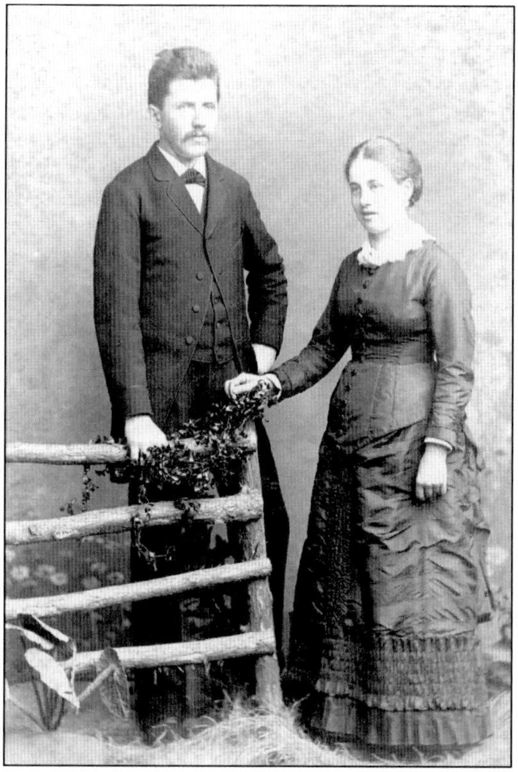

Paul Krebs had been an upholsterer in Dresden, Germany, before moving his business to Philadelphia, where he and Elsbeth were married in 1882. After trolley service was extended through Ottsville in 1904, they moved to a farm on Clay Ridge Road in 1905. (EWH.)

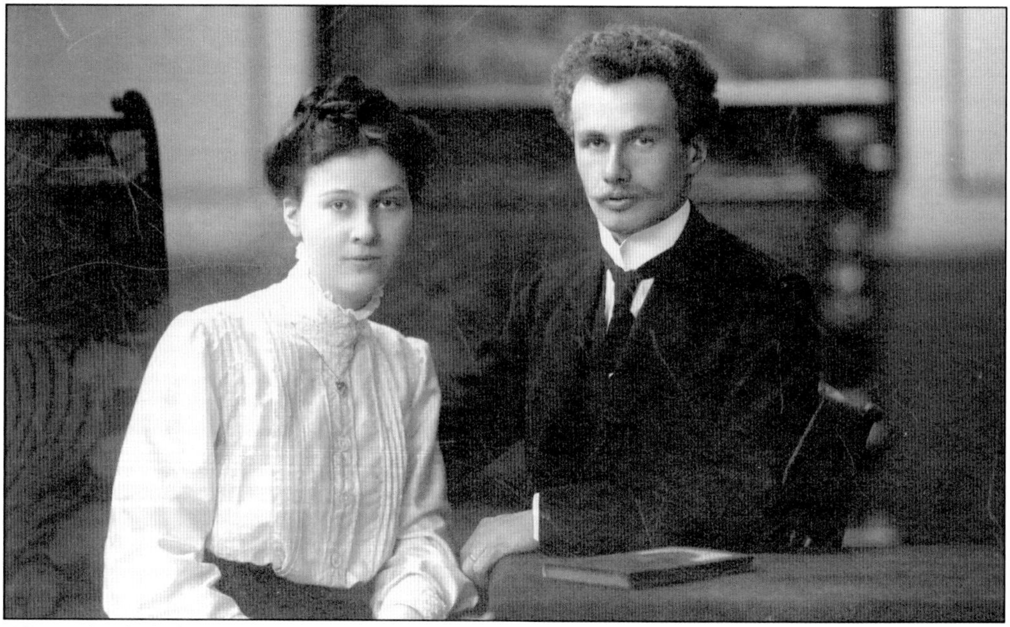

Alexander (Alex) Wittig had first lived in Philadelphia and then returned to his native Leipzig, Germany, in 1910 to bring his fiancée, Felicia, home to Ottsville, after posing for this engagement photograph. They were active members of the community for the next seven decades. Their daughter, Eleanor, is among the 1922 Red Hill School students pictured on page 79 and later was a teacher in Tinicum's one-room schools. (EWH.)

Early in the 20th century, eastern Europeans joined Tinicum's melting pot. Advised to move to the country for his health in 1923, Russian immigrant Andrew Timochenko bought a farm near Ottsville, from which he commuted to Philadelphia to work at Kaplan's Bakery. Before moving to rural life, his Polish-German wife, Ida, sat for this portrait with baby Frances. Andrew's health was restored, and he lived another 60 years to the age of 100. (DTS.)

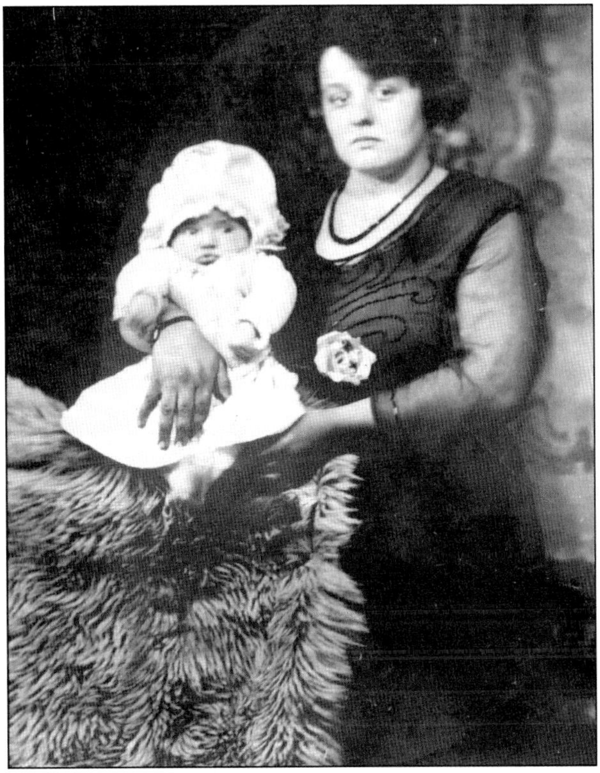

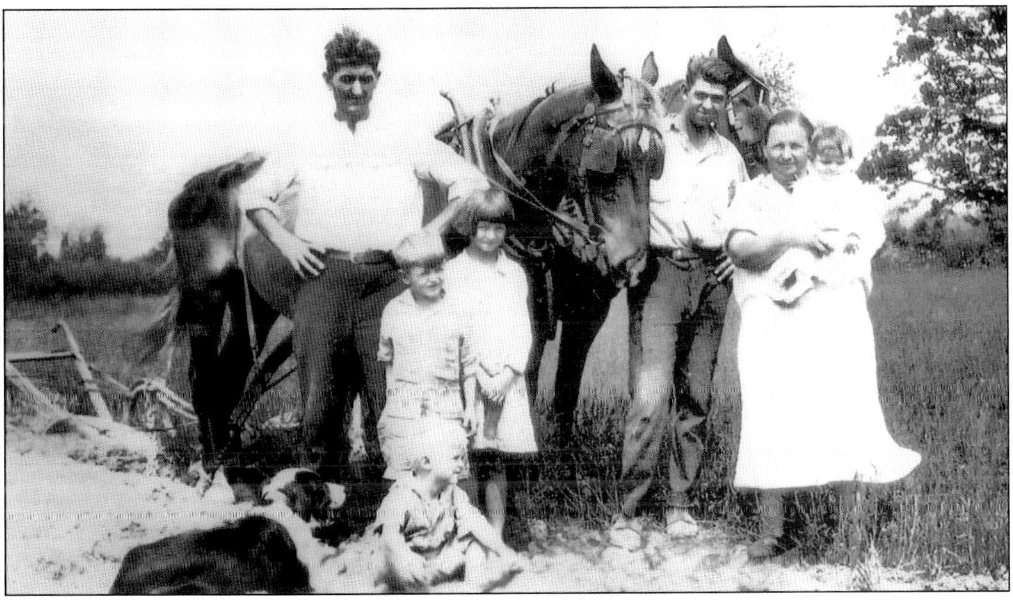

Polish immigrants Joseph and Pruxeta Szczepanski are pictured in 1929 on their Scherman Road farm with their children, from left to right, Stanley (seated), Alex, Clara, teenage son Floyd (who later anglicized his name to Stevens), and Theresa in her mother's arms. Other Tinicum families with eastern European roots include Albanian Sciss; Czechoslovakians Biresch, Sispera, and Dudas; Greek Pablos; Hungarians Horvath and Biro; Lithuanian Sobel; Romanian Gessner; and Yugoslavian Shussler. (SZP, SPR.)

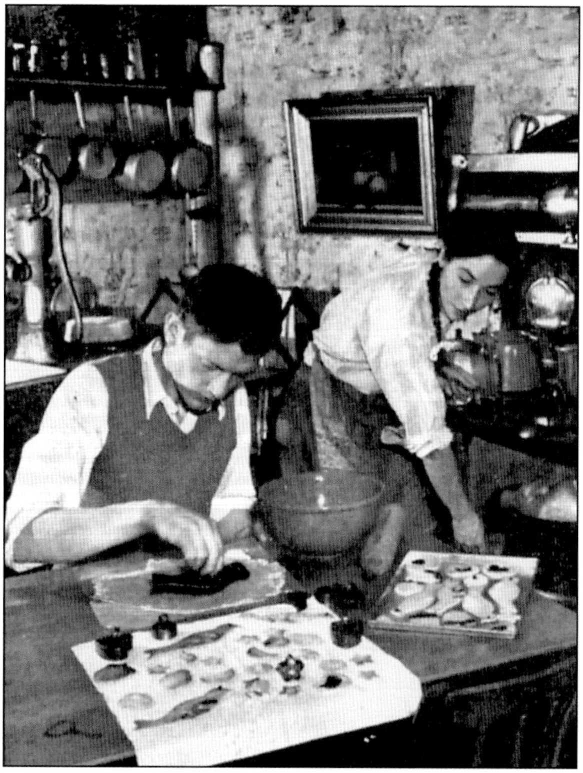

During the Depression, writers and artists discovered that Tinicum's old farms were the perfect quiet haven for practicing their art. Sculptor Charles Rudy, whose works grace many public buildings, directed the completion of the sculpture at Stone Mountain, Georgia. He lived with his wife, Lorraine, on Sheephole Road, with his studio in the adjacent barn. In this *c.* 1940 photograph of their kitchen, he sculpts cookies from cutters he had made. (WLC.)

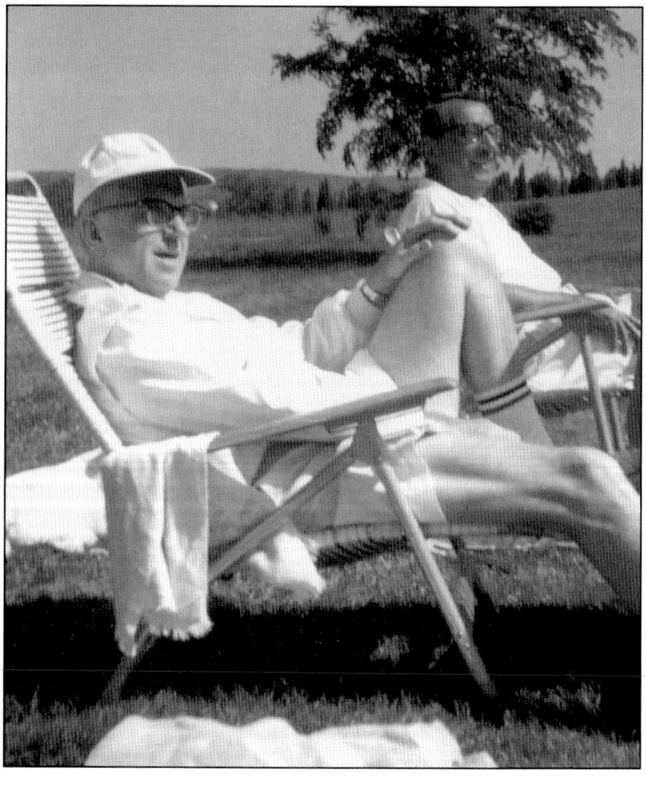

James Michener was planning his home on Red Hill Road in 1949 as the musical *South Pacific*, based on his book, was becoming a Broadway hit. He thereupon decided that he could afford to add a second bathroom. He relaxes here in 1967 after playing tennis with neighbors. On Sheephole Road, writer John Wexley was another longtime resident. His screenplays made stars of unknowns Spencer Tracy and Clark Gable. (PLC.)

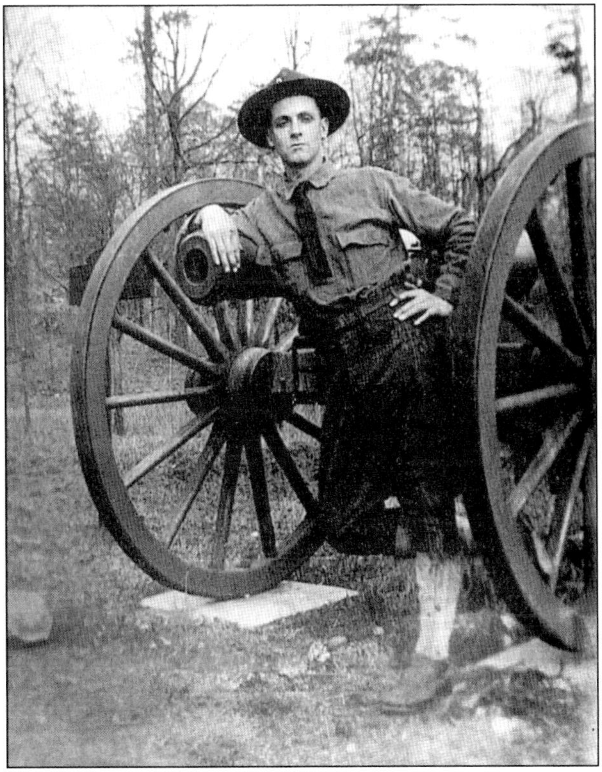

The men of Tinicum have served America in wartime. Arthur Erwin, the wealthy Irish immigrant who founded Erwinna, outfitted soldiers for the militia in the American Revolution. The Upper Tinicum Lutheran Church cemetery alone contains over 90 graves of veterans of the War of 1812, Civil War, and two world wars, including that of Sgt. Clarence J. Weaver, who died in France in 1918 shortly after this photograph was taken. (EWB.)

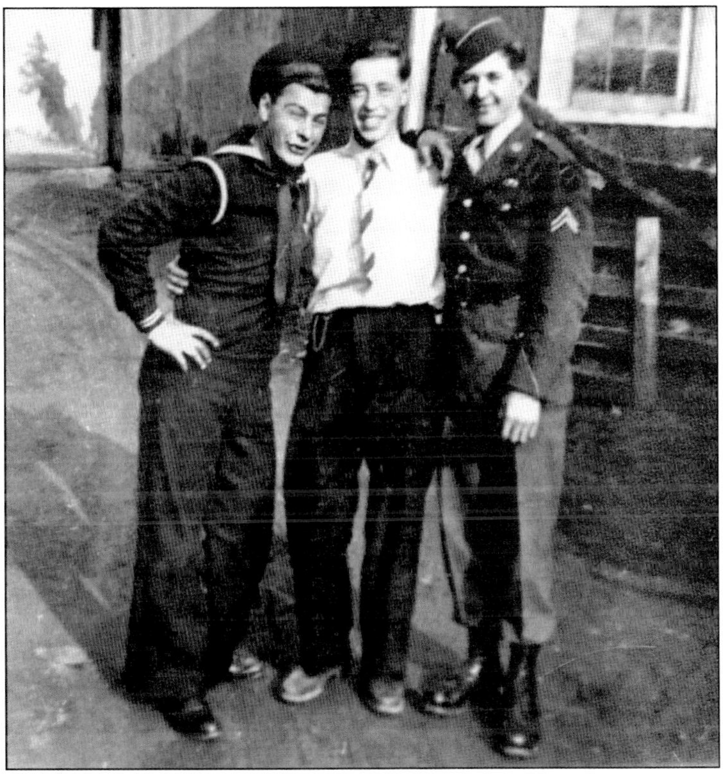

During World War II, one member of a farming family was exempt from the draft to continue to produce food for America and its allies, while his brothers served in the military. In 1942, Lester Bickel (left), who later participated in the D-day invasion, and neighbor Stanley Szczepanski, paratrooper, are home on leave and visiting with civilian farmer Sam Bickel. After his brother's safe return, Sam enlisted in the U.S. Army in 1946. (BBK.)

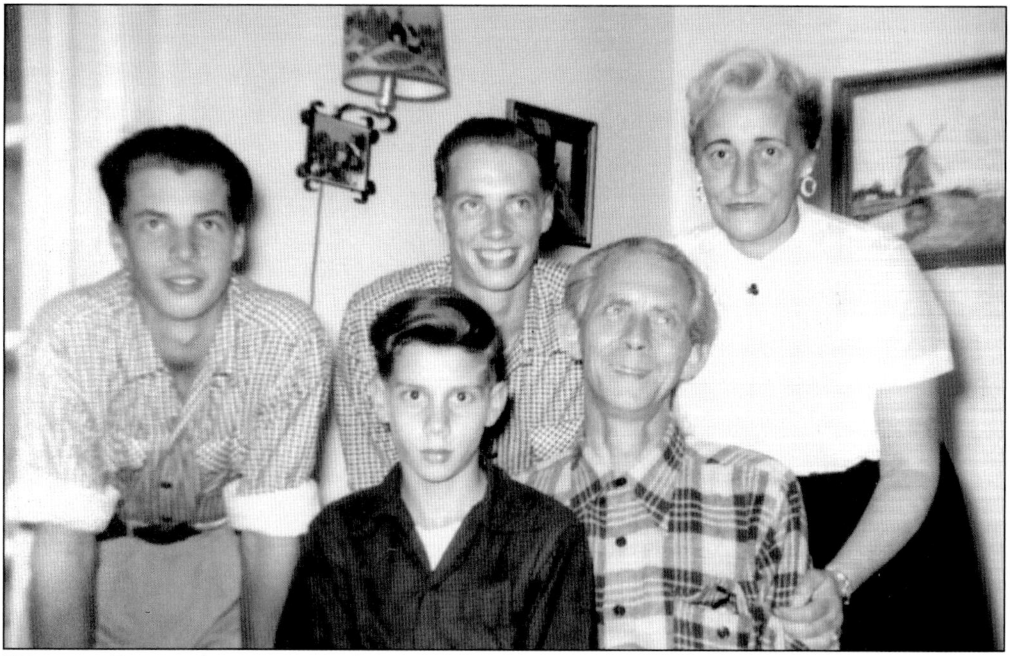

War-torn Europe drove more refugees to America after World War II. Hendrick and Ann Vanderlely brought their sons Tom (seated), Hans (standing left), and Hank from the Netherlands to Ottsville. One of Hendrick's paintings of his homeland is on the wall behind the family in 1953. (VND.)

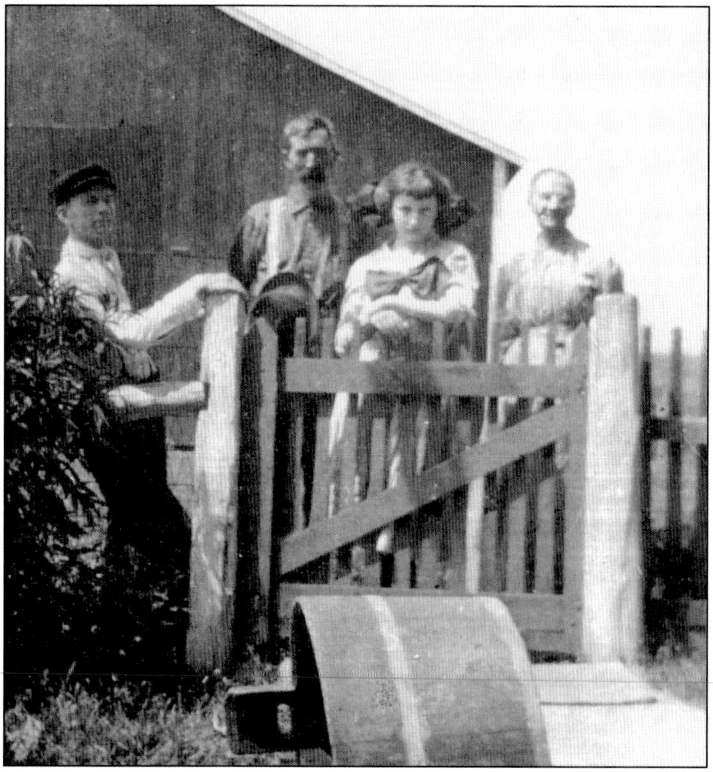

Some early residents continue to make their presence known long after their death. While several apparitions of people have been observed, other manifestations have included flashing lights, footsteps, the smell of cigar smoke, and the movement of objects. Residents of the former Edward Kramer home have seen a tall, bearded man who disappears through a solid wall and resembles the man in this *c.* 1905 photograph of the Kramer family. (HAL.)

Two

THE RURAL WAY OF LIFE

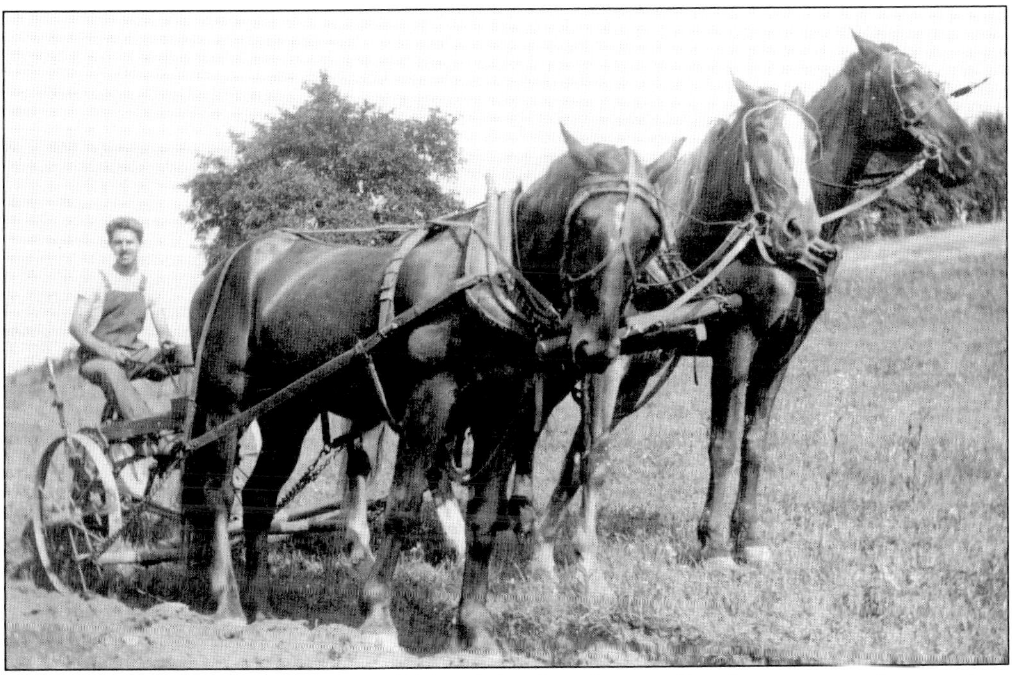

Ernest Schultz of Erwinna, shown in 1914 with his three-horse sulky plow, ran several enterprises. As a dynamiter, he could demolish stumps and boulders, dig ditches, drain swamps, plant trees, regenerate old orchards, and break up hardpan. Nicknamed "Nitro," his business cards read, "You may need a blaster. THAT'S ME." He also ran Valley Sales and Services, which included mechanical repairs and the application of calcium chloride for abatement of road dust. (LSH.)

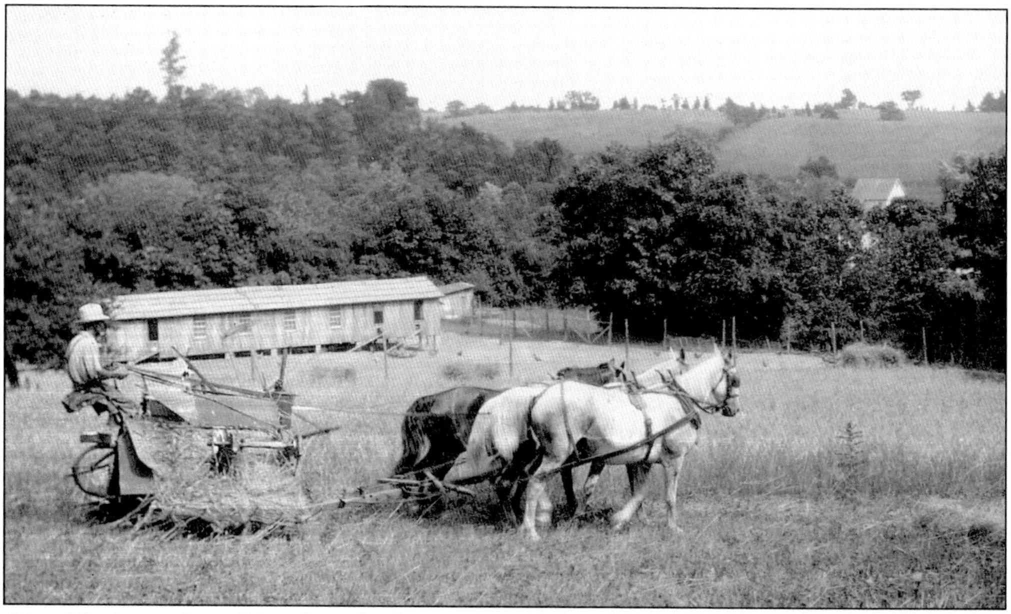

Alex Wittig used a self-binder, which cut grain and tied it into sheaves, saving many hours of hand labor. Woods have now replaced the open fields in this 1928 view, overlooking the Overpecks' butcher and blacksmith shops, which are pictured on page 31. (OVP.)

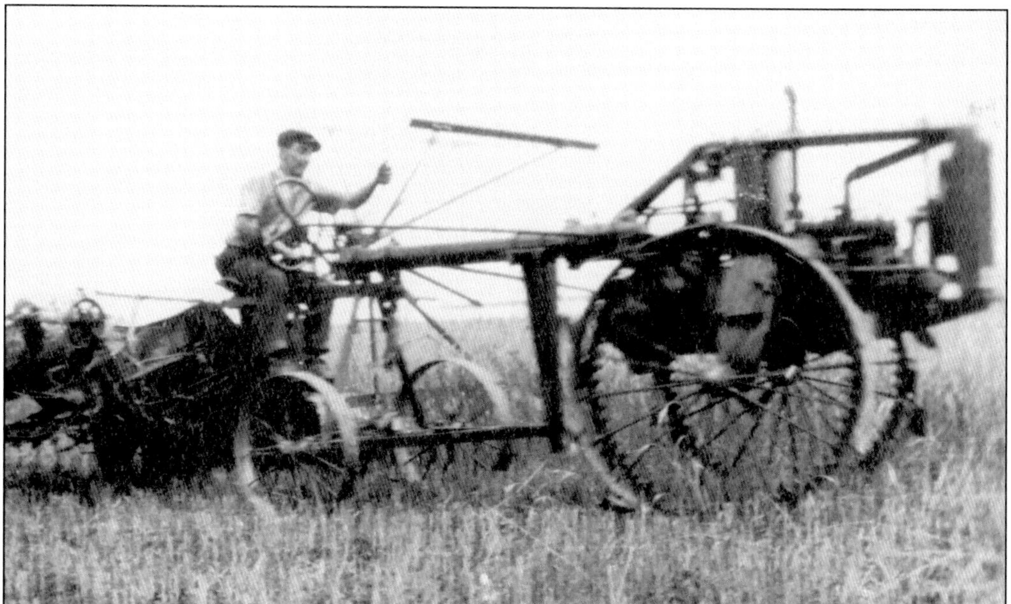

Several early manufacturers of tractors produced a front-end-drive design. This unusual Moline model operated by John Wampfler on the Hugh Weaver farm on Uhlerstown Hill Road, around 1920, is hauling a self-binder. Plows, cultivators, and mowing machines were also sold as attachments to these tractors. The design was discontinued because it proved to be too unstable and dangerous to operate. (EWB.)

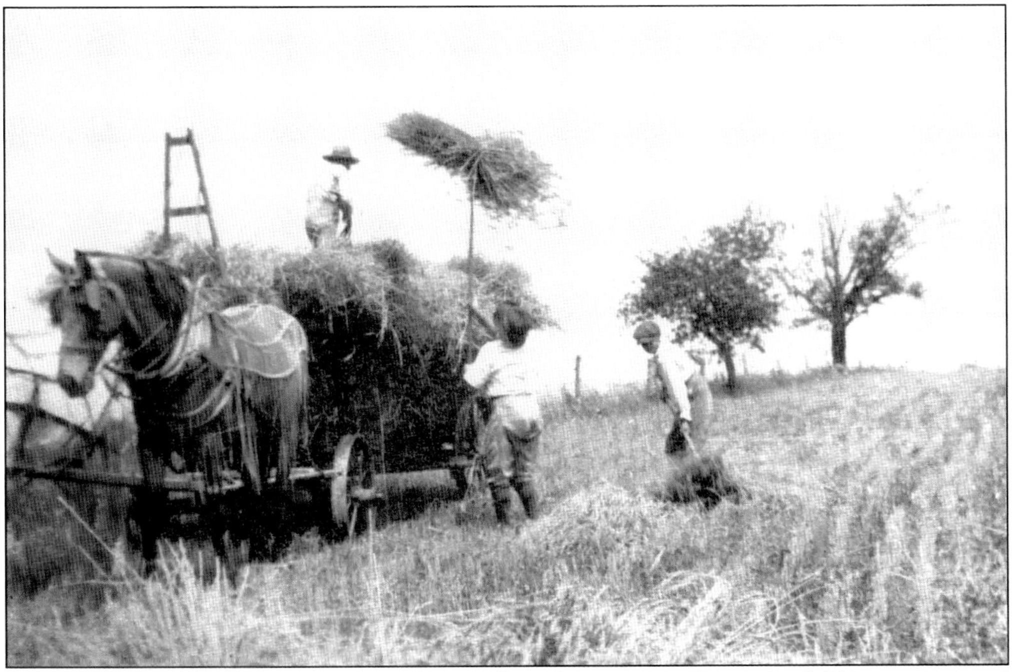

Sheaves then had to be stacked carefully to allow the grain to dry in the field, or, as pictured here, piled onto a wagon for transport back to the threshing area on the Weaver farm. The horse is draped with fly netting to help protect him from pesky horseflies. (EWB.)

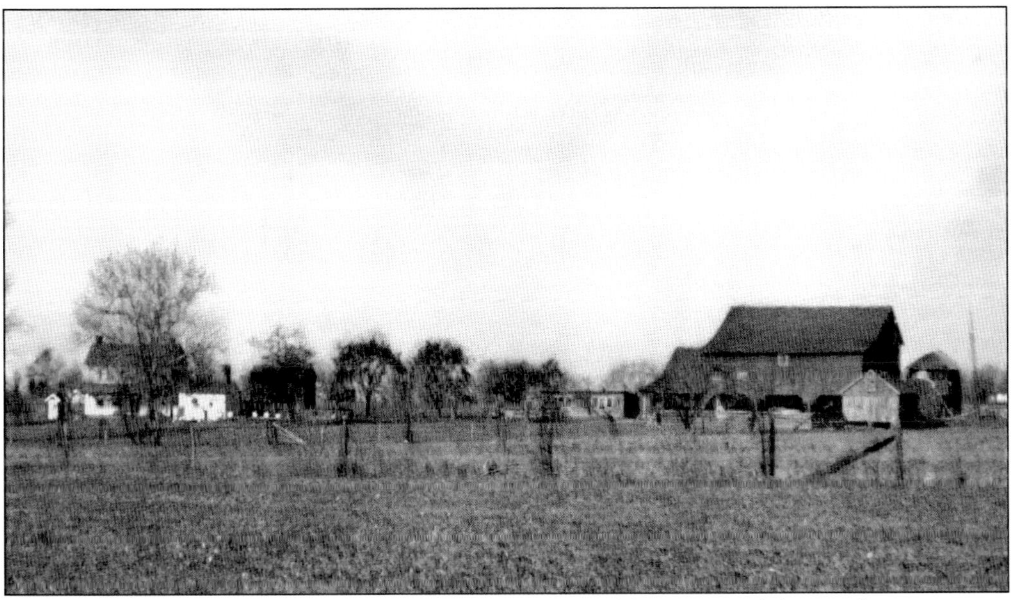

In 1949, the Haney farm had a typical array of farm buildings. From left to right are a privy, house, summer kitchen, wagon shed, chicken coop, and barn, with pigsty in front. Behind the barn, on the right, is a barrack, a device for storing wheat or rye for later threshing. Common in Holland, but rare in America, its movable roof could be raised or lowered to accommodate the size of the crop. (EWH.)

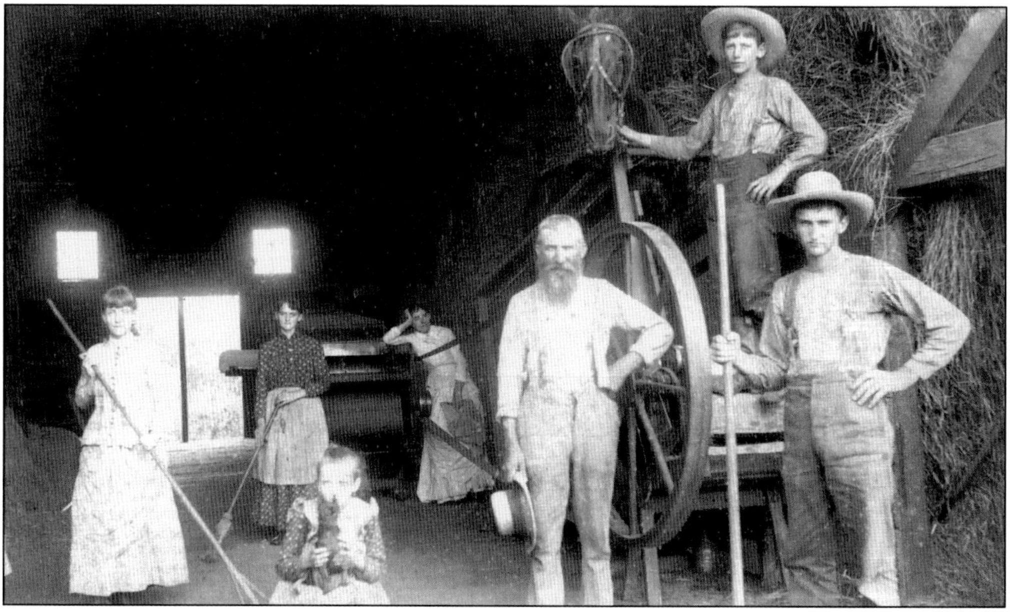

Workers pause during threshing in this 1885 photograph of Harold Steeley's family. On the far left is his grandmother Liveria Myers, while bearded great-grandfather Samuel Myers holds his hat. The horse on a treadmill powers the belts connected to the fanning mill in the background. The Steeleys continue to live on the 68-acre Bedminster Road farm, which has been in their family since 1813 and is permanently protected from development. (HST.)

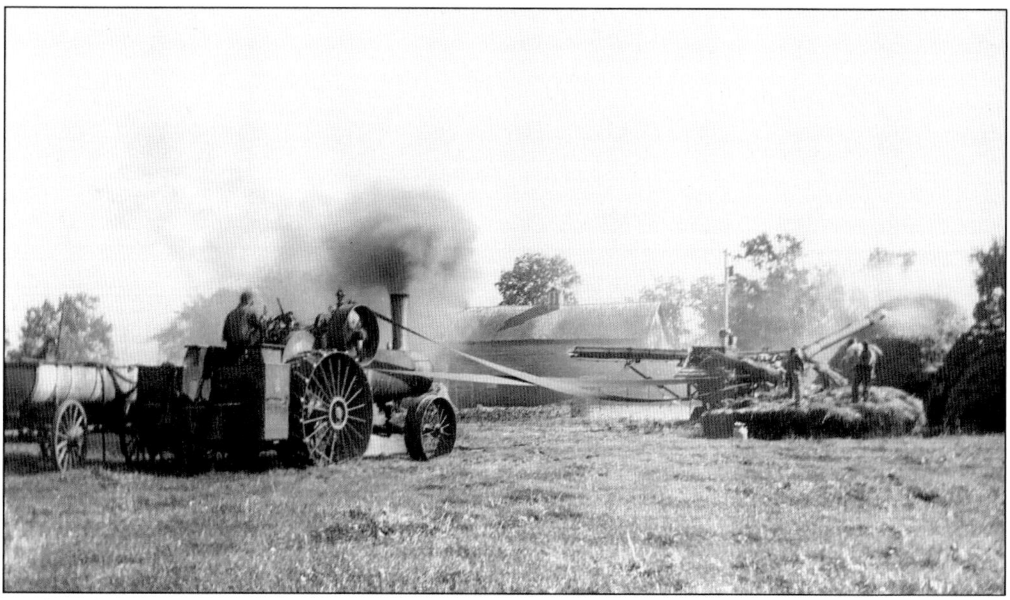

In this threshing operation on the Stover farm near Erwinna, around 1907, a smoke-belching steam tractor powers the belts that drive the grain separator. There a crew bags the grain flowing down the bagging spout, while the straw is blown onto a pile. Ed Lewis, owner of this machinery, was hired to harvest area fields. The 151-acre former Lewis farm, later a quarry, is now Giving Pond State Park. (TCA.)

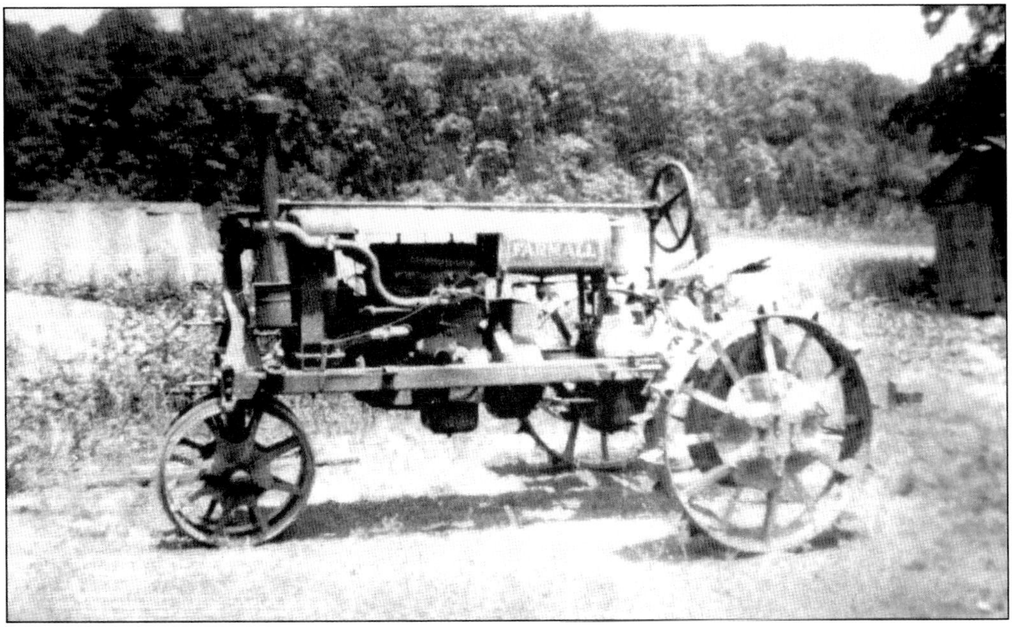

Farmall produced this general purpose row-crop tractor design from 1924 to 1939. It was still used on the Bickel farm in 1946. Before it could be driven onto the threshing floor of the barn, planks had to be laid down to prevent damage from the lugged wheels. The 90-acre former Bickel farm is permanently protected from development and is part of the Ridge Valley Rural Historic District on the National Register of Historic Places. (BBK.)

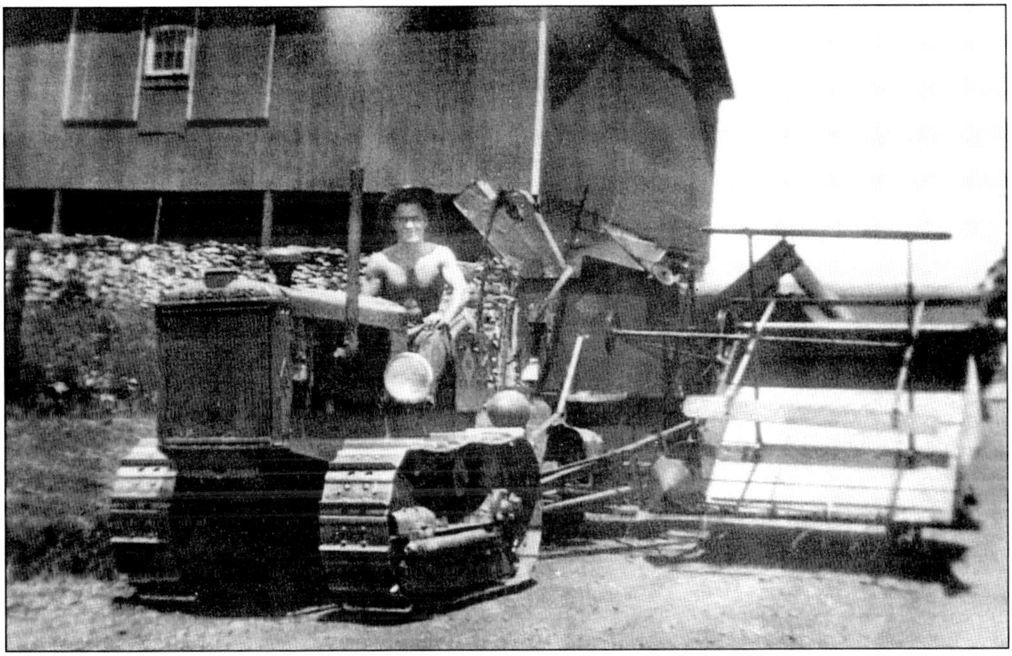

Pete Schaefer hauls his combine with an Allis-Chalmers Model M tractor past his barn on Headquarters Road near Erwinna, around 1940. The crawler design provided better traction than wheels. The barn survives, near the intersection of Headquarters and Tinicum Creek Roads. (LSG.)

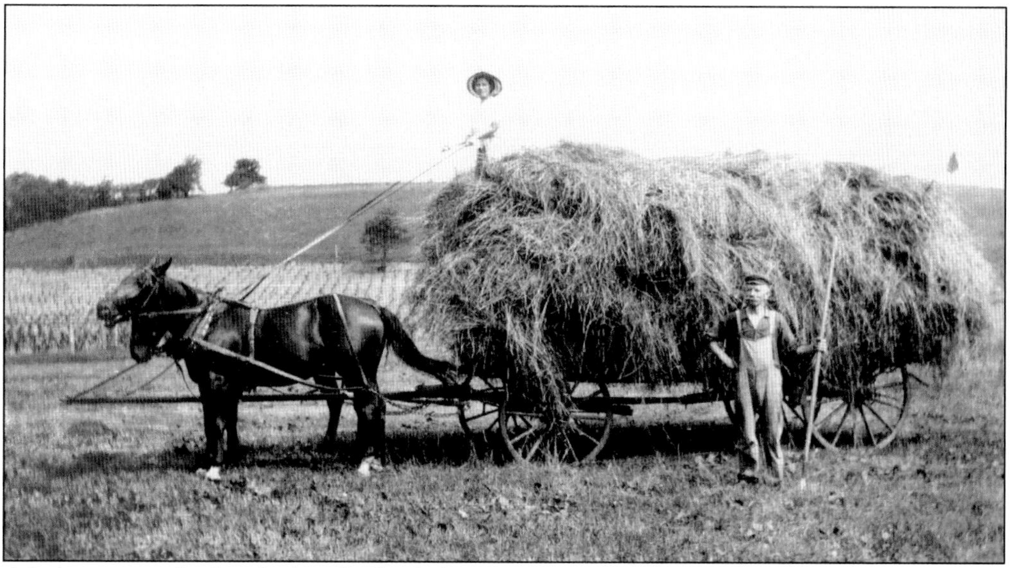

After mowing, the hay had to be loaded onto a wagon, carried back to the barn, and then unloaded into the haymow on either side of the threshing floor of the barn. In 1916, Ernst Schultz loads the wagon while his daughter, Bertha, manages the team. The load had to be arranged carefully, or the entire pile might slide off the wagon en route. (LSH.)

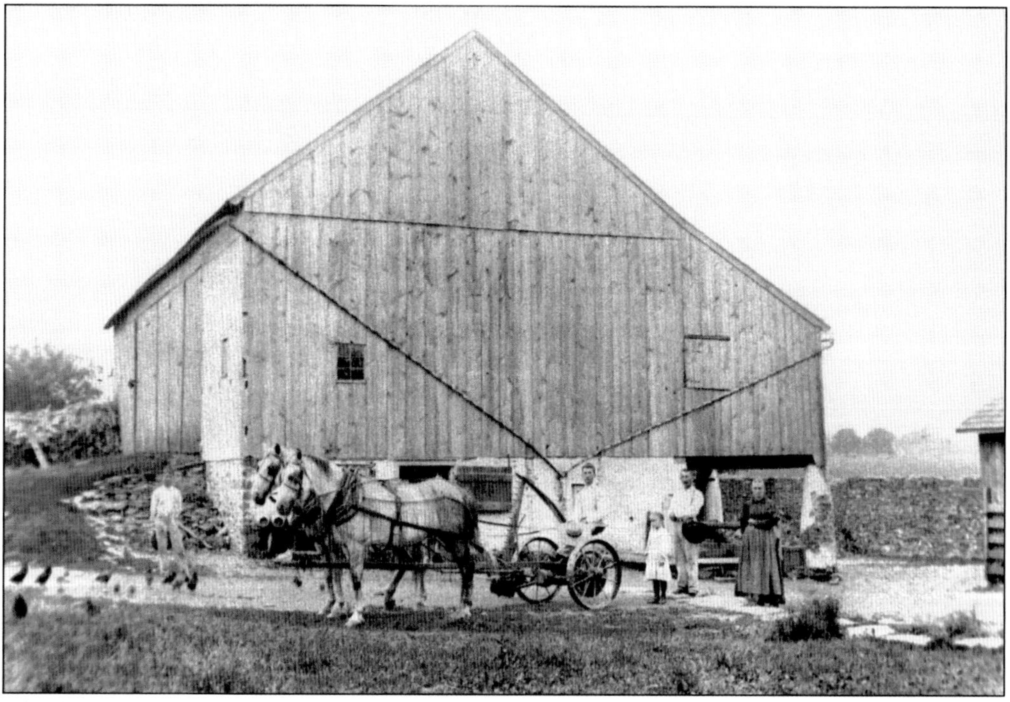

This large frame barn near Wormansville, with stone stabling on the ground floor, has a ramp to the threshing floor, with a typical pinwheel ventilation cutout beneath the peak of the roof. Unusual stone piers, instead of wooden posts, support the forebay. Michael Worman bought the original 200-acre farm in 1768. Both the barn, built around 1835, and brick house survive on the remaining 61 acres, which are permanently protected from development. (HNL.)

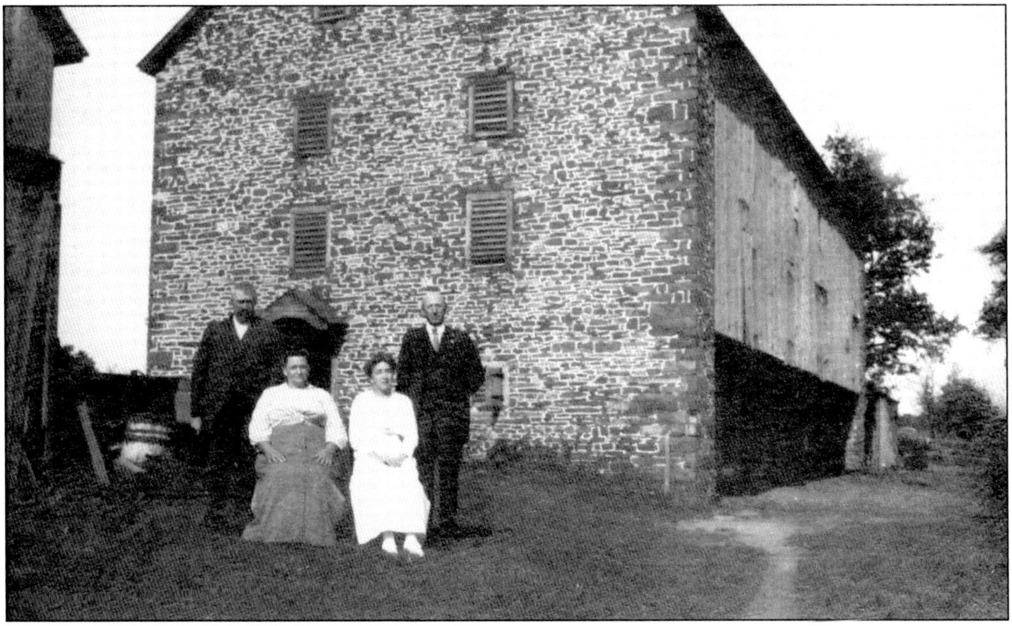

More durable than the frame barns are those built with stone ends. In front of this "stone ender" are, from left to right, William Bryan and his wife, Ella Reigle Bryan, and Mary Alice Reigle, and her husband, Samuel "Daddy" Reigle, son of Reuben Reigle. Basketball hoops were sometimes mounted on the wall beside the threshing floor of these barns, or on the inside wall of a covered bridge. (WMS.)

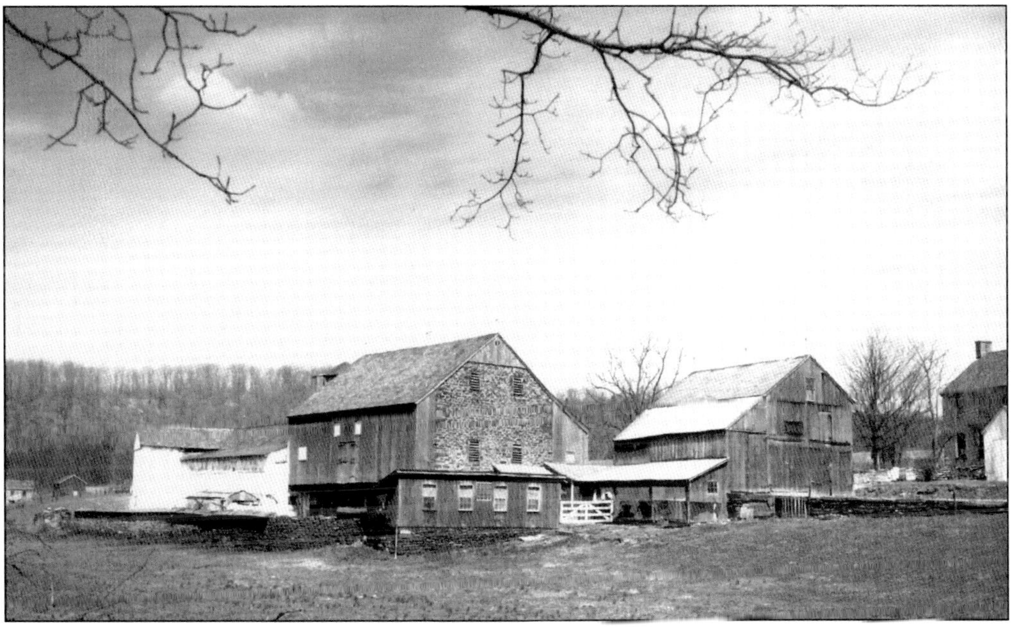

The handsome cluster of barns, both frame and stone enders, on the former McEntee farm at the intersection of Hollow Horn and Headquarters Roads is a familiar sight to passing motorists. This 1958 view from below the barns shows the opposite side, with chicken coops and a stone wall enclosing the barnyard. Violet Gruver recalled that bluebells, or grape hyacinths, sometimes covered fields in spring, "a sight to behold." (LNX.)

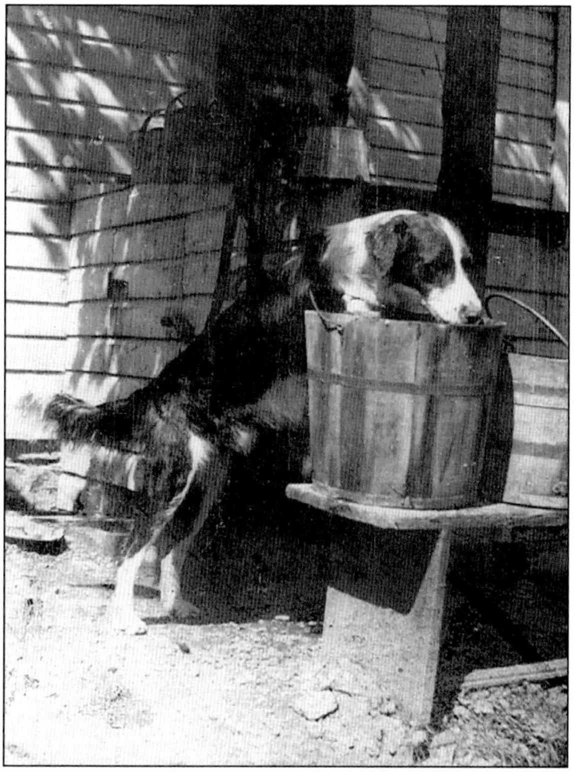

Threshing is hot, dusty work. A dog quenches his thirst at the water bucket on the wash bench beside the kitchen door before the noon dinner bell calls workers from the fields. (KLB.)

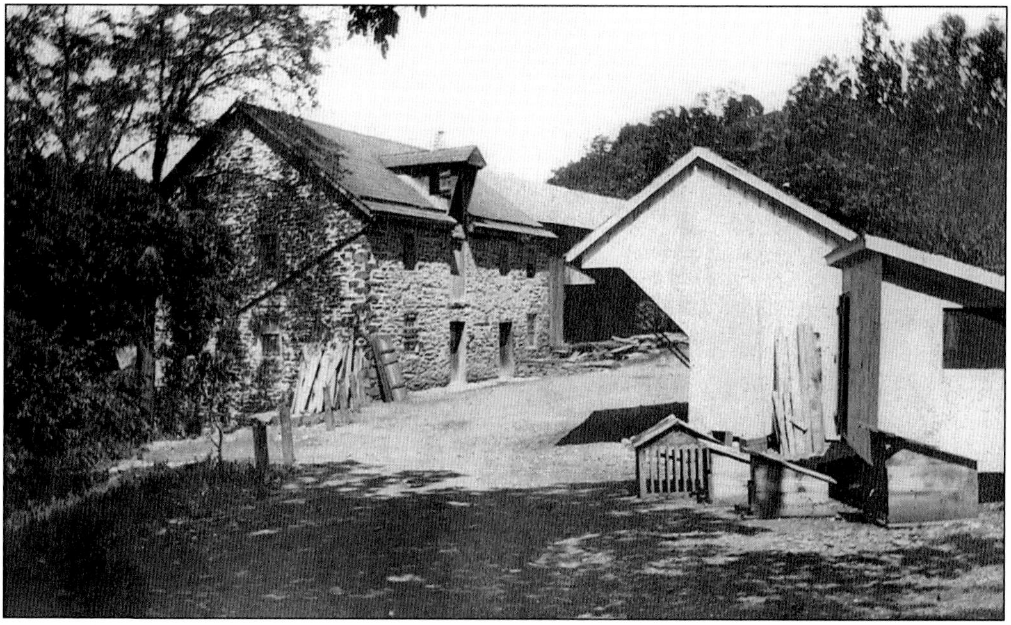

Bags of threshed grain had to be taken to the mill to be ground. The Ralph Stover Mill, located on Tohickon Creek at Point Pleasant, was one of several Stover mills in the region, each placed wherever waterpower existed. Many small streams originally capable of powering a mill dried up when their protective canopy of trees was cut down for making charcoal or farm fields. This mill survives as a private residence. (KLB.)

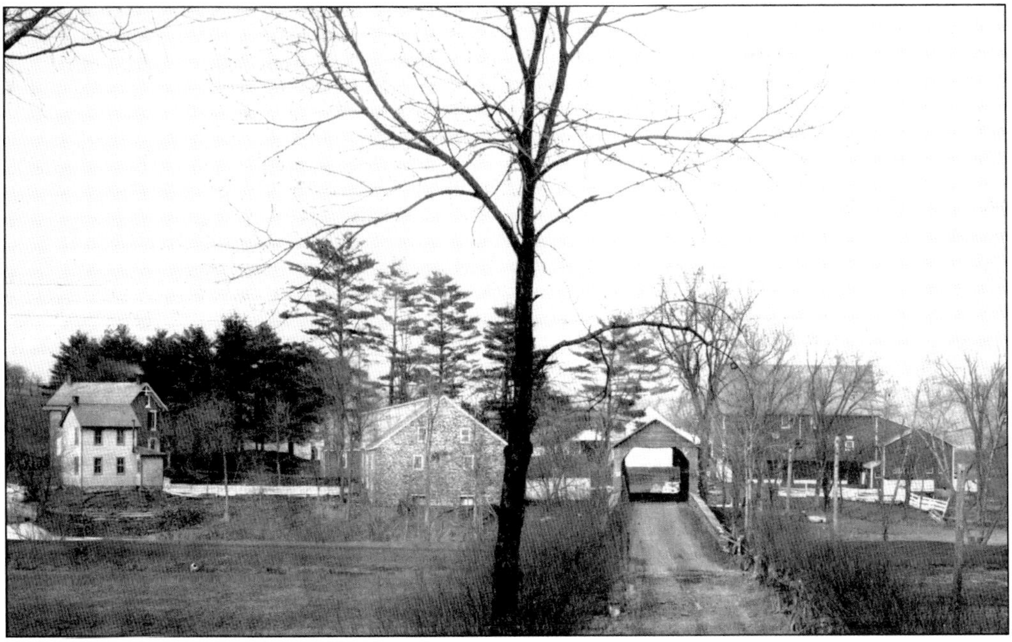

Except for the covered bridge, all the buildings surrounding the stone Randt's Mill in this 1908 picture survive at the intersection of Gruver and Randts Mill Roads. Violet Gruver recalled stopping at the mill after school to warm fingers over the miller's potbelly stove. Crossing the fields beyond the mill in warmer seasons "many four- or five-leaf clovers were discovered. . . . We must have been tired and moved slowly in order to spot them." (BNK.)

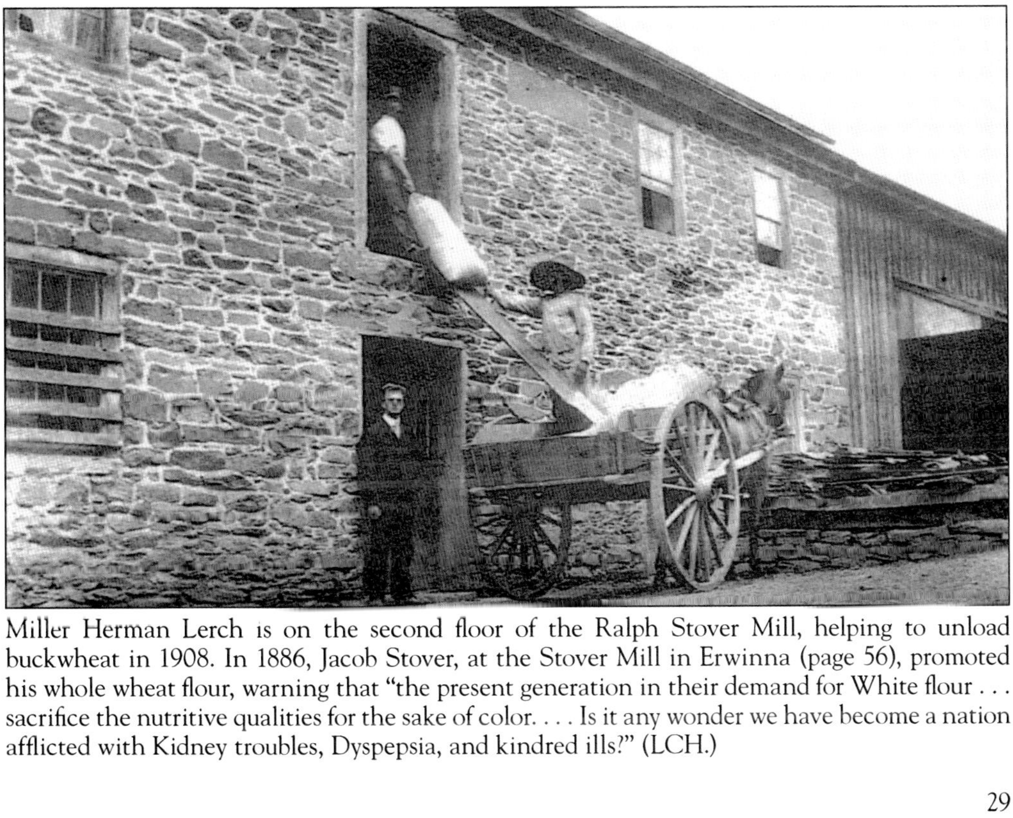

Miller Herman Lerch is on the second floor of the Ralph Stover Mill, helping to unload buckwheat in 1908. In 1886, Jacob Stover, at the Stover Mill in Erwinna (page 56), promoted his whole wheat flour, warning that "the present generation in their demand for White flour . . . sacrifice the nutritive qualities for the sake of color. . . . Is it any wonder we have become a nation afflicted with Kidney troubles, Dyspepsia, and kindred ills?" (LCH.)

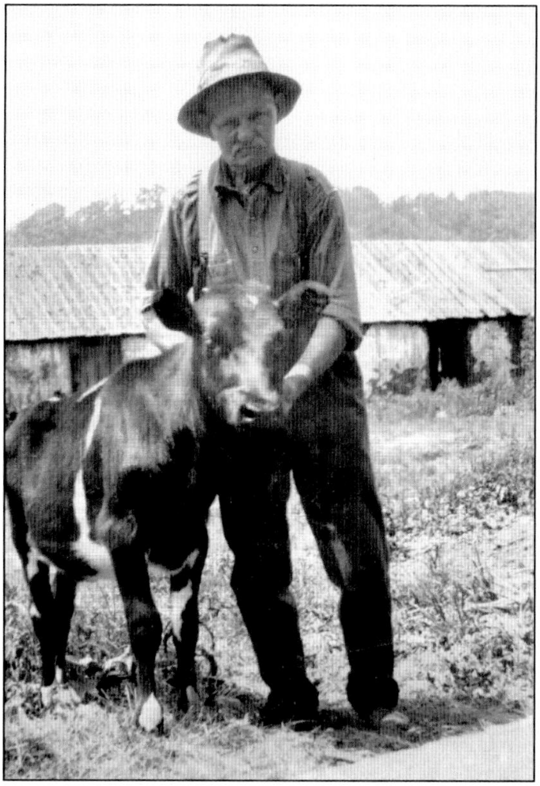

Both beef and dairy cattle grazed in Tinicum pastures and, to a lesser extent, continue to do so today. Phillip Hoffman stands with a young steer from his herd in 1924. His home was on Headquarters Road east of Sundale, but his beef cattle were pastured on Upper Tinicum Church Road. His wife, Alada Fox, was from a longtime Tinicum family. (FTZ.)

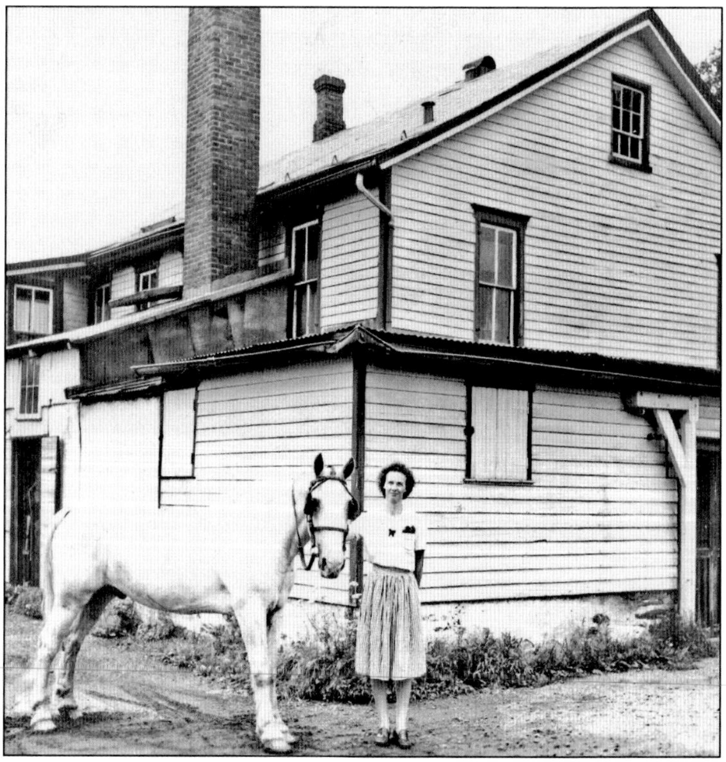

Members of the Ottsville Creamery, formed in 1913, included the names of Eichlin, Esser, Flagler, Foellner, Frankenfield, Ketterer, Kimenhour, Mood, Overpeck, Sassaman, Schaefer, Seifert, Snyder, Steeley, Wehrung, Wierbach, Williams, Wittig, and Yost. High-quality Ottsville butter sold for 10¢ higher per pound than the average in Philadelphia markets. In 1946, Eleanor Wittig stands beside the creamery, now gone, which closed after 50 years, partly due to competition from the introduction of margarine. (DWG.)

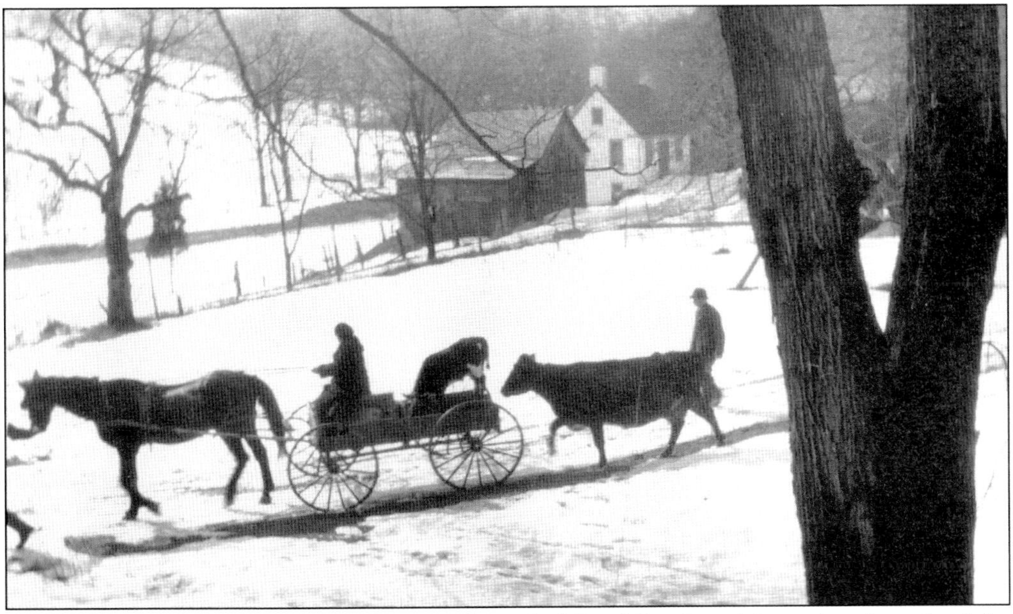

Nitro Schultz's 1917 note on this photograph reads, "Good Bye Lizzy." It implies the sale of the cow, following her calf in the wagon, when it is time for the cow to be bred again. In late winter, should feed be running low, less productive animals might be sent to slaughter. The Erwinna Creamery on Geigel Hill Road, visible in the distance, is a private residence today. (LSH.)

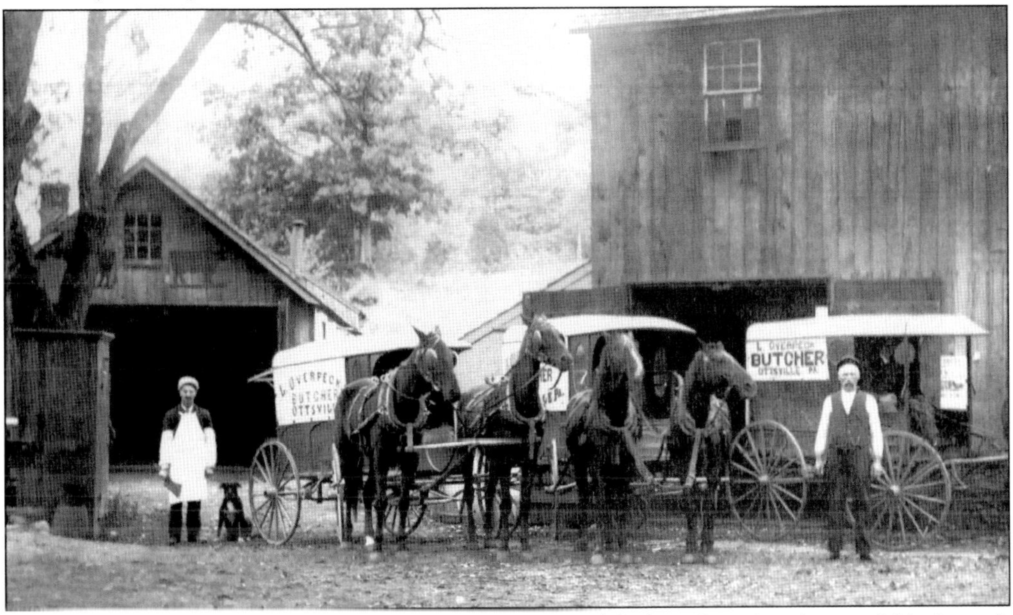

Cleveland Overpeck, left, and his father, Lewis, stand before their butcher and blacksmith complex on the bank of Tinicum Creek, at the Geigel Hill Road crossing near Ottsville, around 1904. The Overpecks served area residents into the 1950s with horse-drawn butcher wagons and, later, trucks. Unfortunately, butcher shop discharge sometimes affected downstream swimming. The complex survives today in the Ridge Valley Rural Historic District. The Overpeck family roots had been planted in Tinicum a century earlier and now appear on the family trees of many Tinicum residents. (OVP.)

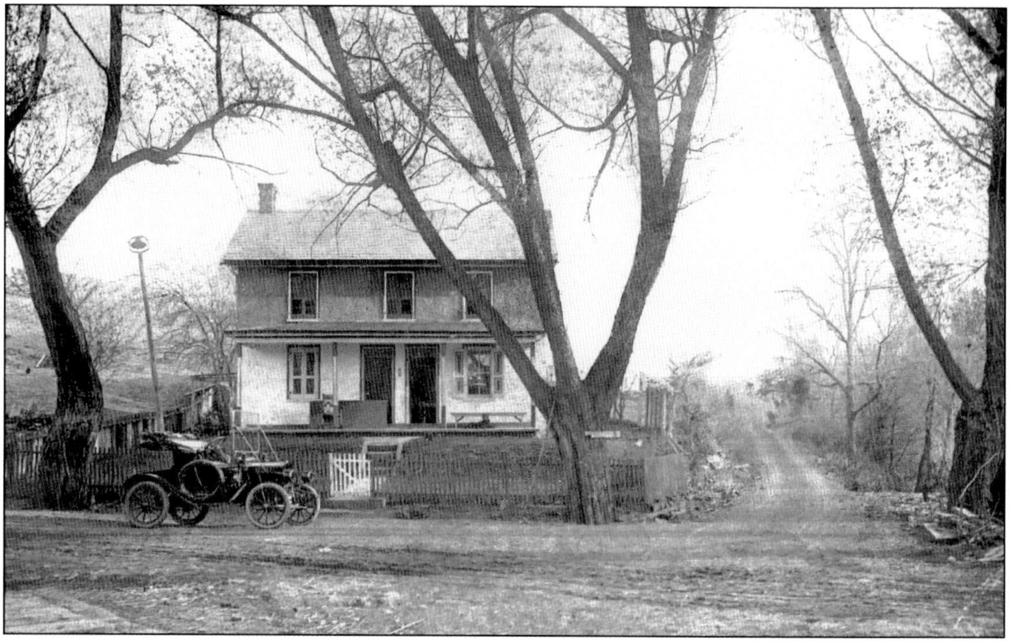

Twin front doors on the German-style Overpeck house, which also survives, do not indicate a two-family house. If a house had only one front door, it entered the kitchen, where a corresponding back door allowed cross ventilation. Contrary to oft-repeated myth, their purpose was not to permit a horse to drag firewood into the kitchen and exit without having to turn around. If budget permitted, a second front door entered the parlor. (BWG.)

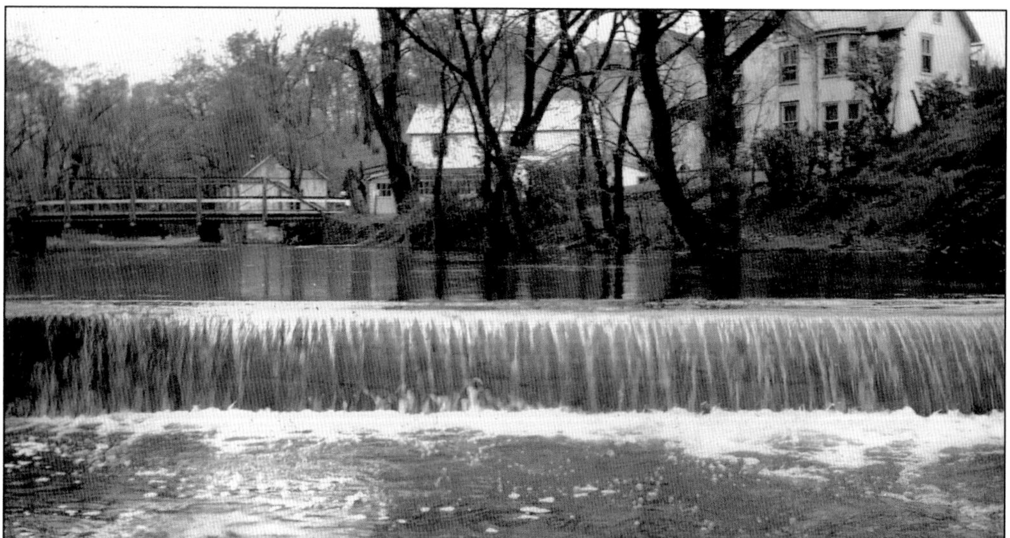

A dam in Tinicum Creek, below Overpeck's shop and the Geigel Hill Road Bridge, formed an ice pond. Blocks of ice, surrounded by insulating layers of sawdust, were stored in a barn, and neighbors were welcome to share the refrigeration facility throughout the year. (OVP.)

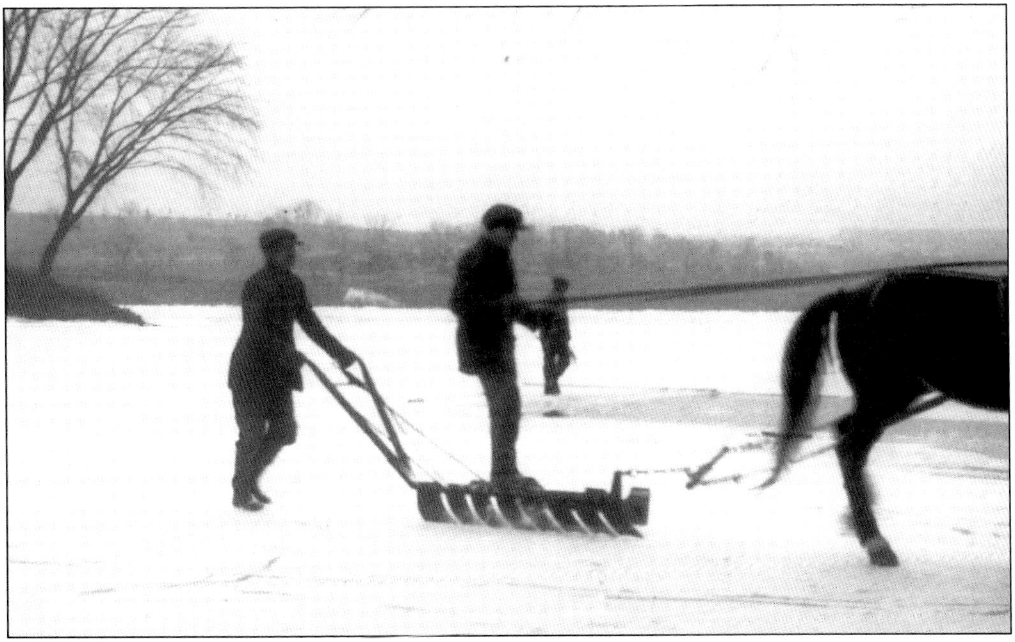

When thick ice formed in the coves of the Delaware River, a horse-drawn cutter sectioned blocks to be stored with sawdust insulation for summer refrigeration. In this undated photograph, ice is being cut for the Stovers' Riverside Farm in Erwinna. Studded overshoes helped to protect horses from slipping on icy surfaces. (TCA.)

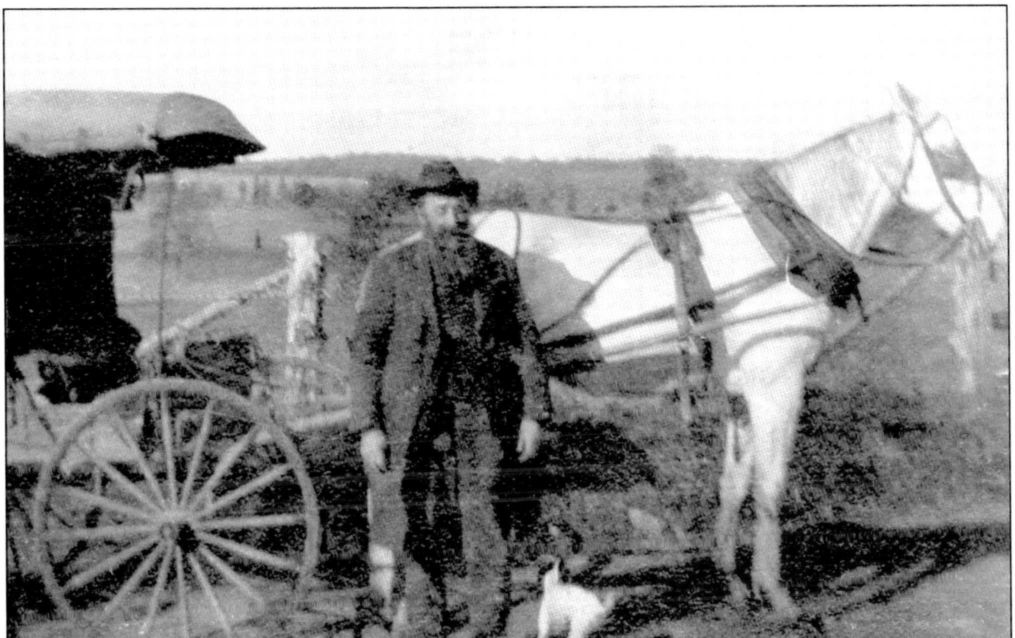

When rural mail delivery began early in the 20th century, it reduced the number of trips farmers had to make to the village stores, where post offices were located. Reuben Reigle's horse and wagon covered a mail route in the northern part of the township around 1910. (WMS.)

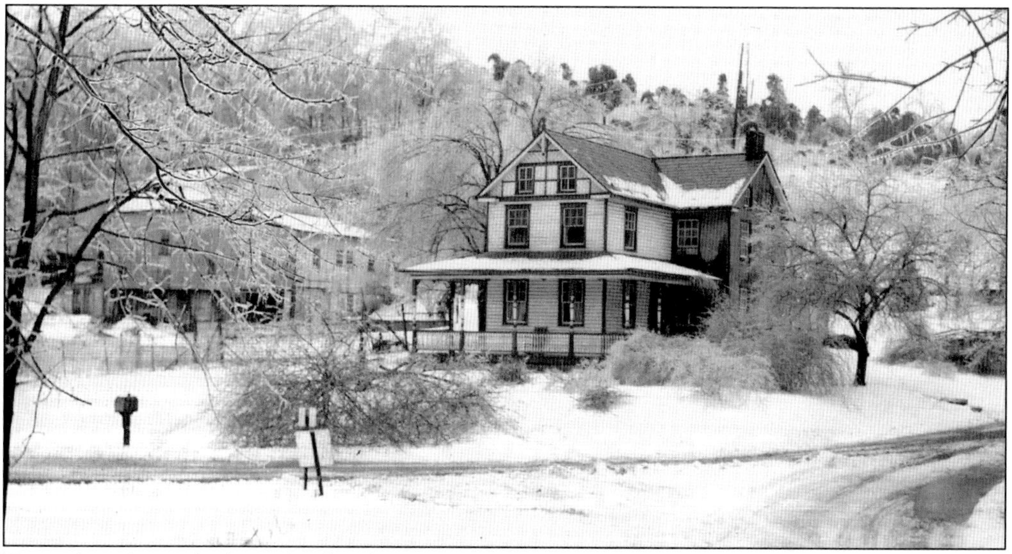

Every farm kept chickens for family consumption, but poultry farms were sometimes a better source of income than crop farming because of Tinicum's limited agricultural soils. Alex Wittig raised chickens on this farm, viewed in 1947, near the intersection of Geigel Hill and Sheephole Roads. The house and barn survive on 14 acres, permanently protected by a conservation easement, and are part of the Ridge Valley Rural Historic District. (OVP.)

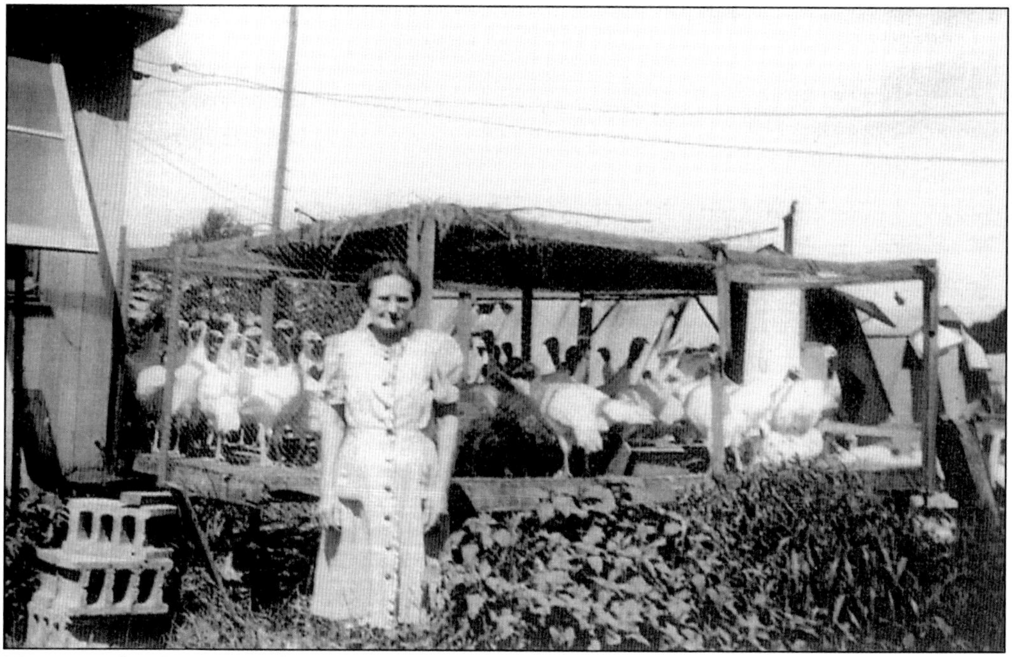

Verone Pathe, Romanian born, tended the family chicken and turkey farm on Union School Road while her German-born husband, Otto, worked at the Frenchtown Porcelain Company, a spark plug manufacturer that employed many Tinicum residents. During the 1903 flood, chickens came in one family's house, hopping up the stairs to safety. Collecting eggs required caution, with the risk of a sharp peck on the arm when reaching under a laying hen. (LSG.)

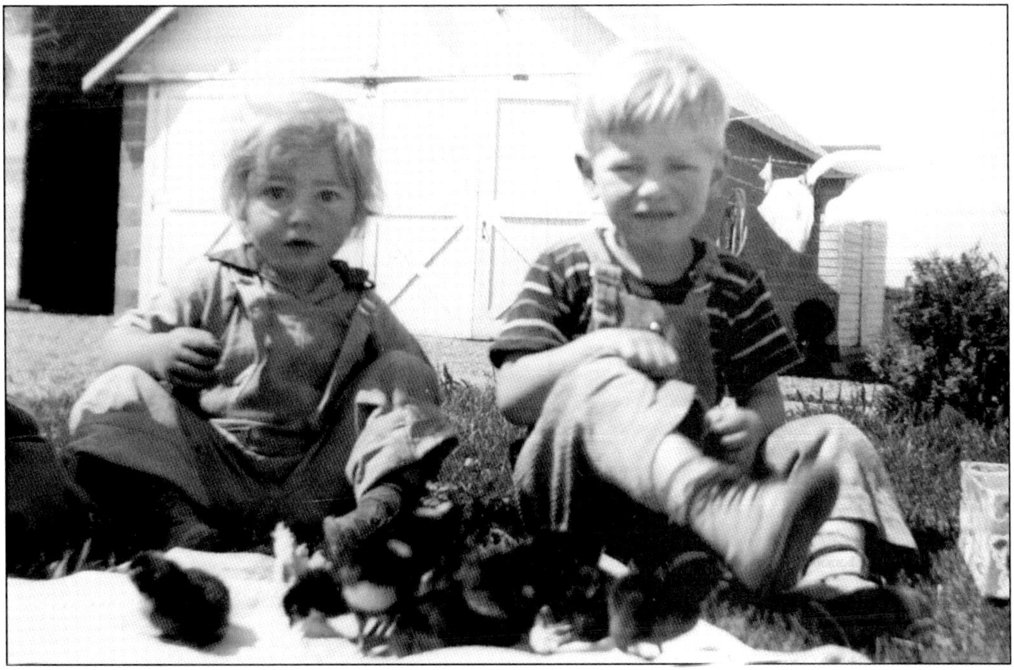

Billie and Arleen Bickel play with baby chicks in 1941. Violet Gruver remembered, "Fuzzy, yellow baby chicks arrived from the hatchery in late spring. . . . Each box contained about one hundred chirping little chicks . . . [which] had not yet learned to drink. Each one needed to have its little beak dipped into a bowl of water until it swallowed." This procedure, remembered by several sources, has since been declared unnecessary by others. (BBK.)

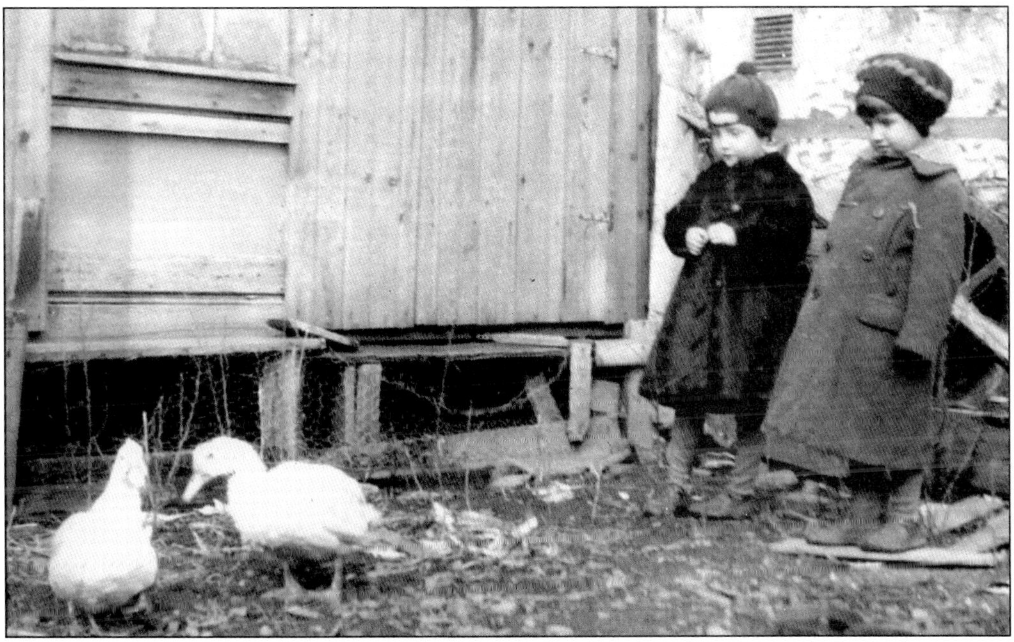

Although geese are more aggressive, twin sisters Elsie (left) and Evelyn Whitlock also ponder these ducks with caution in 1934. Their mother made most of their clothes, having learned her skills from her father, Paul Krebs, a professional upholsterer. (EWH.)

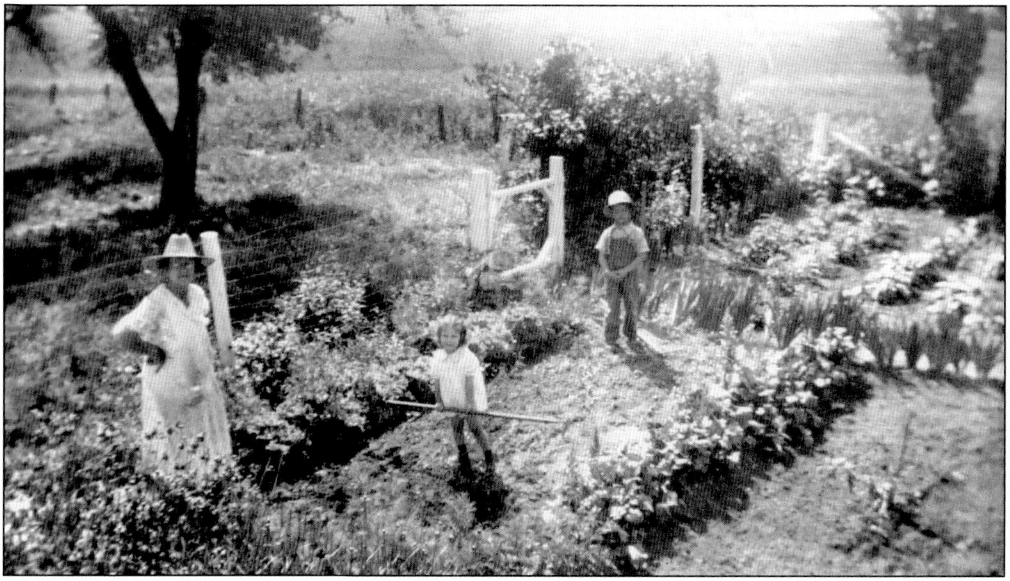

Farms were as self-sustaining as possible. Besides the essential chickens, a vegetable garden and fruit trees kept the women busy making apple butter and jams and canning or drying their produce. Lizzie Weaver Quinby tends her garden in 1939 with the assistance of grandchildren Erma Jean Quinby and Arthur Paul Quinby. The 198-acre Quinby farm on Upper Tinicum Church Road is permanently protected by a conservation easement. (QBY.)

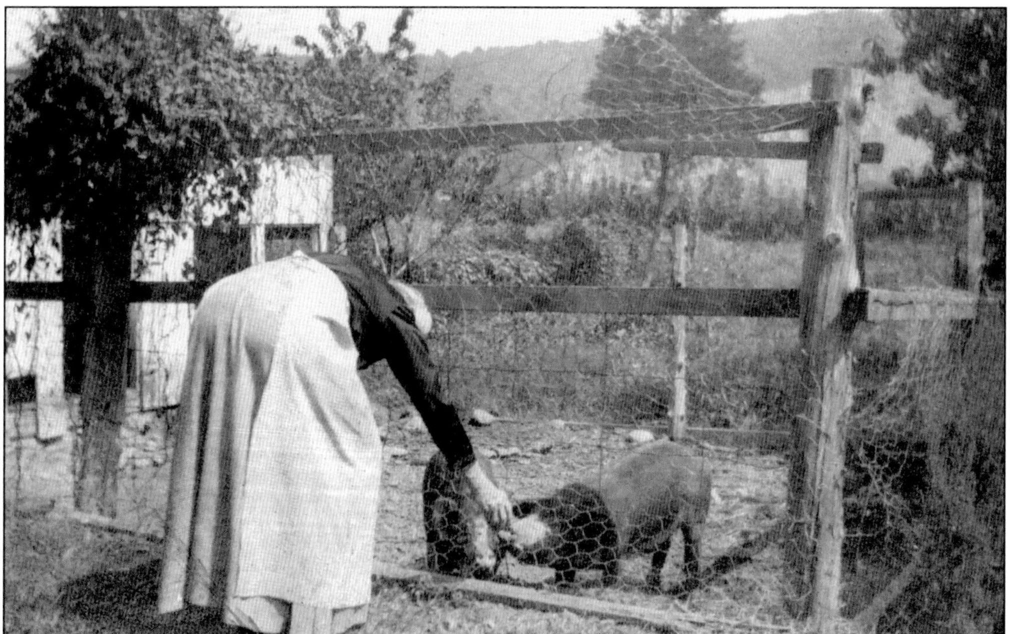

Farm families also kept at least a few pigs to be butchered in the fall for the family table. Susannah Walter tends the pigs at the Point Pleasant home of her son, J. Willis Walter, M.D., in 1918. (WLT.)

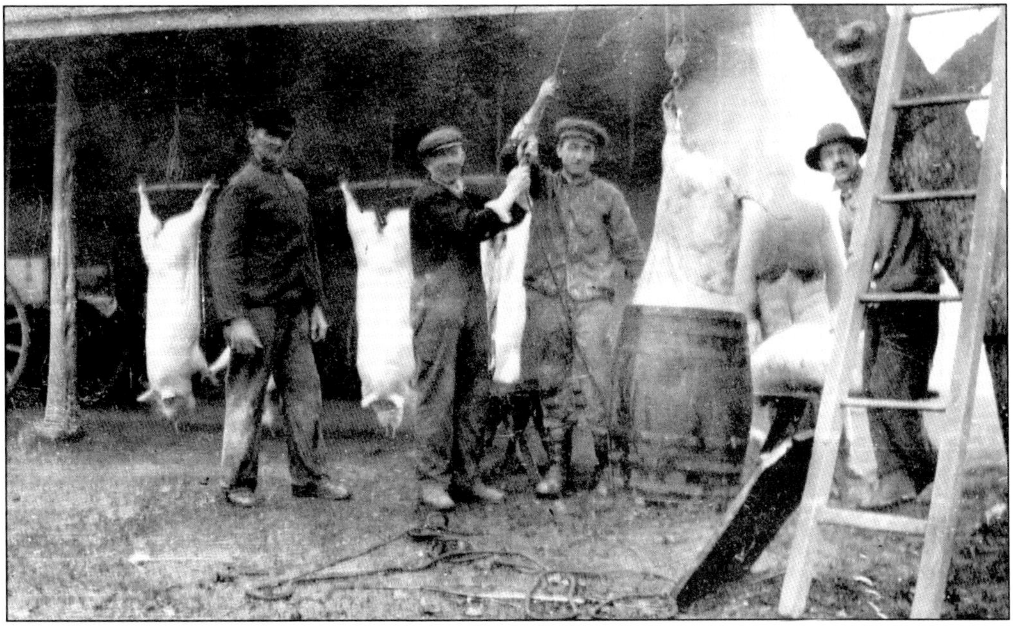

Hog butchering on the Schultz farm in 1916 shows the barrel of steaming water in which carcasses were scalded to clean the hide and loosen the bristles, which were then scraped off and sold to brush manufacturers. Pork was eaten fresh, canned, cooked and stored in lard, salted, or smoked. Soap was made from lard. The cleaned intestines were stuffed with sausage, and leftover scraps became scrapple, a breakfast delicacy. (LSH.)

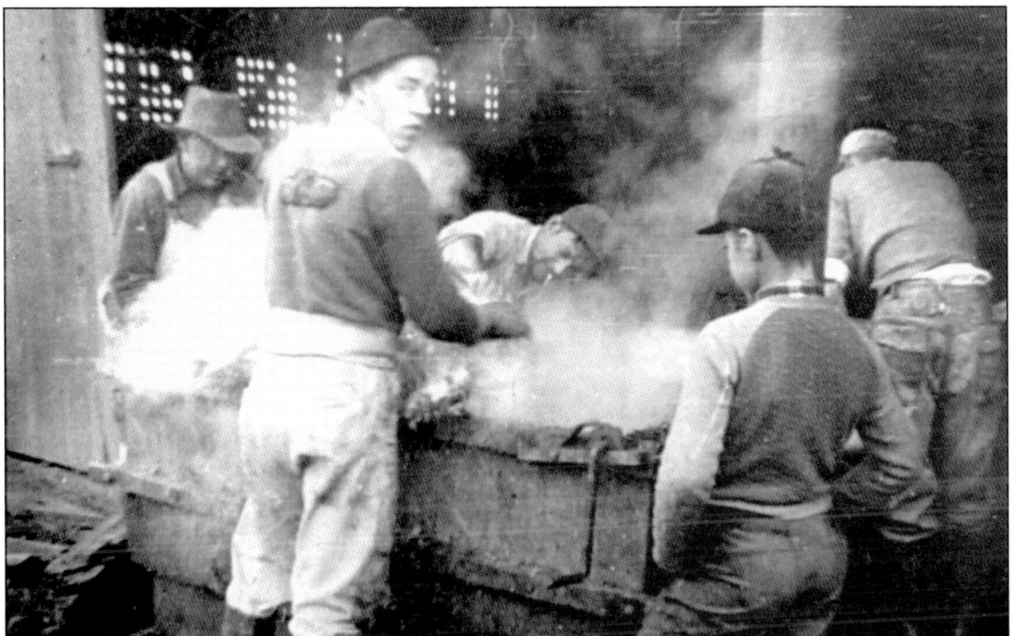

On the Bickel farm, in 1946, a butchering crew surrounds a steaming trough to lift the heavy carcass. From left to right are Sam Bickel Sr., in brimmed hat; his son, Sam "Junior" Bickel, eyeing the photographer; Sam Senkow; young Bill Bickel; and, with his back to the camera, Floyd Templeton. (BBK.)

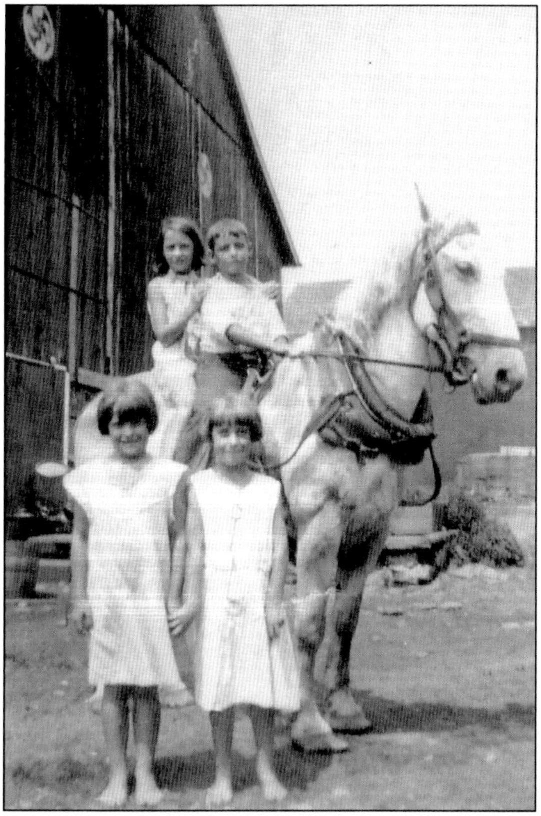

One blind draft horse named Dick provided all the horsepower on the Timochenko farm near Ottsville. Around 1933, Florence and John Timochenko are atop the horse, while Rose (left) and Viola Timochenko stand. Hex designs on Pennsylvania German barns varied from county to county. The swirling swastika designs seen here, and the six-petaled rosette designs on this same barn, pictured on page 126, were typical in upper Bucks County. (HUF.)

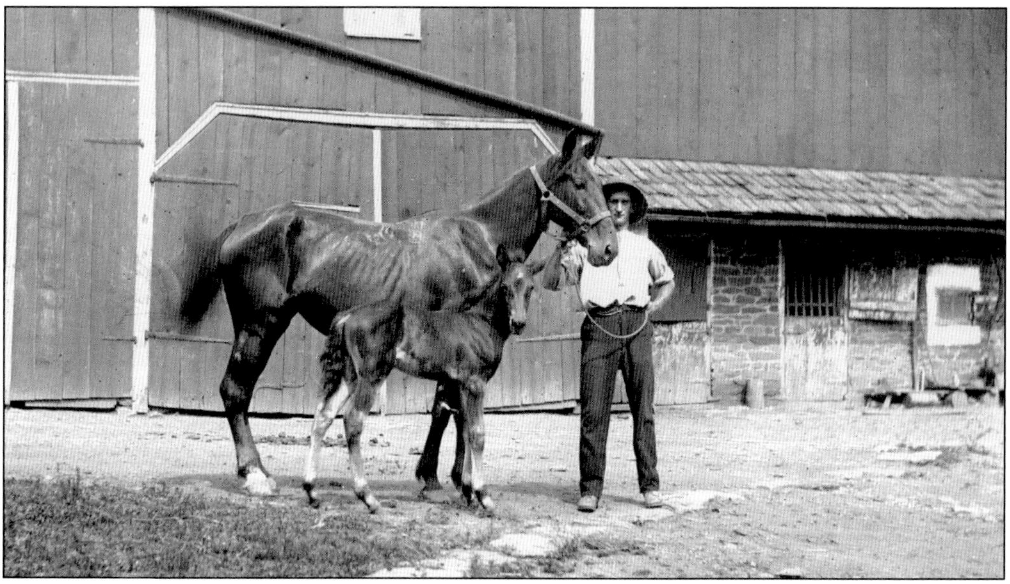

Quintus Lerch stands with his mare and her foal on his Dark Hollow Road farm, around 1915. Such an all-purpose horse was useful for pulling a passenger vehicle or as part of a team for heavier farm equipment. A respected member of the community, Lerch served in many capacities, including justice of the peace. He was known for his Solomon-like wisdom when solving neighborly disputes. The restored farm today specializes in organically grown products. (LCH.)

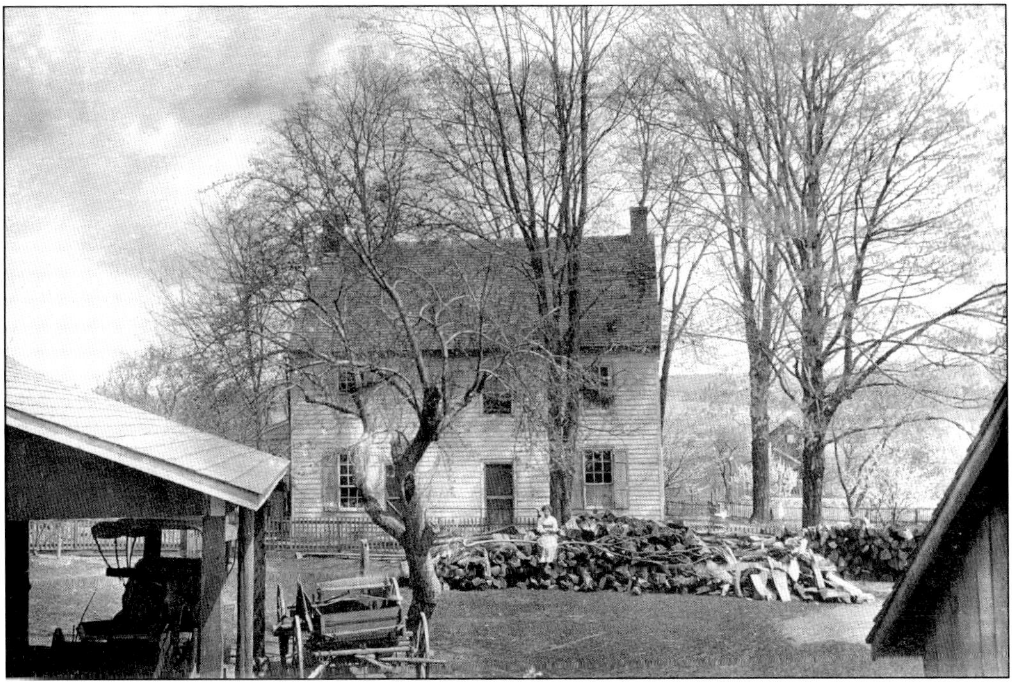

An ample supply of firewood, seen here at the Schultz farm near Erwinna in 1916, was essential for both cooking and winter heat. Nitro Schultz noted that his "old 1904 Cadillac" is parked beneath the shed in the left foreground. (LSH.)

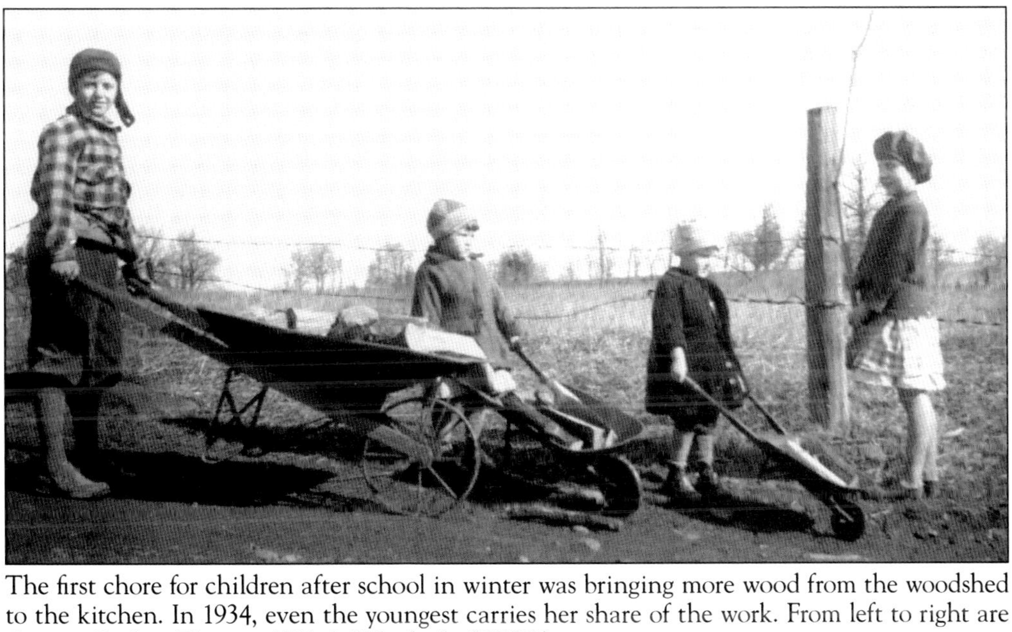

The first chore for children after school in winter was bringing more wood from the woodshed to the kitchen. In 1934, even the youngest carries her share of the work. From left to right are George, Evelyn, Elsie, and Edith Whitlock. (EWH.)

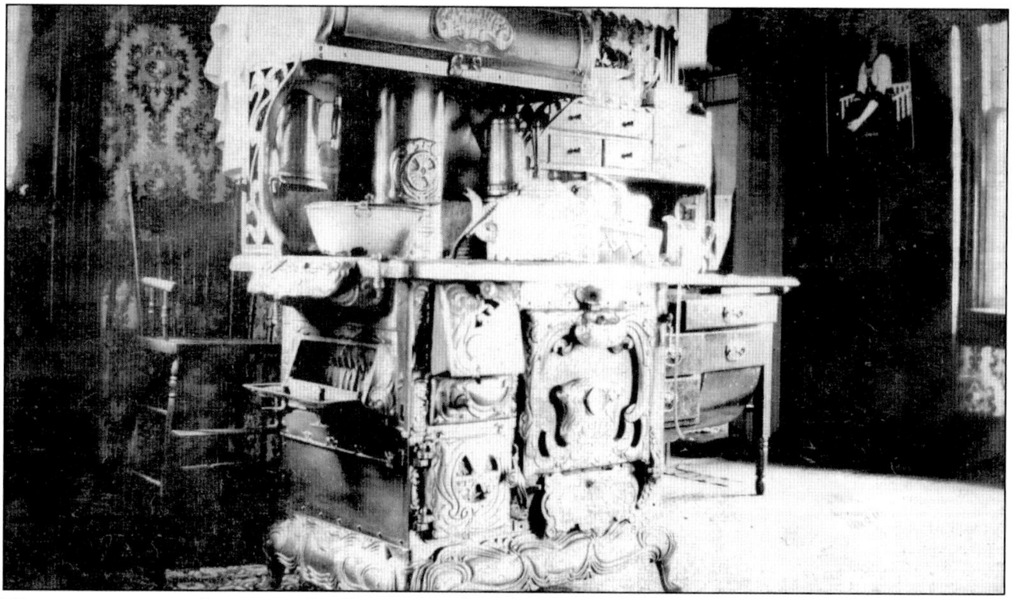

This massive woodstove in the Jonas Sigafoos kitchen served the family from rising time to bedtime. Children dashed from chilly bedrooms to dress by the stove, and evening baths were also conducted here. Meals were stored in the warming closet, denoted by the ornate sign above the cook surface. A Hoosier cabinet stands to the right of the stove, containing ingredients and a work surface for food preparation. (SIG.)

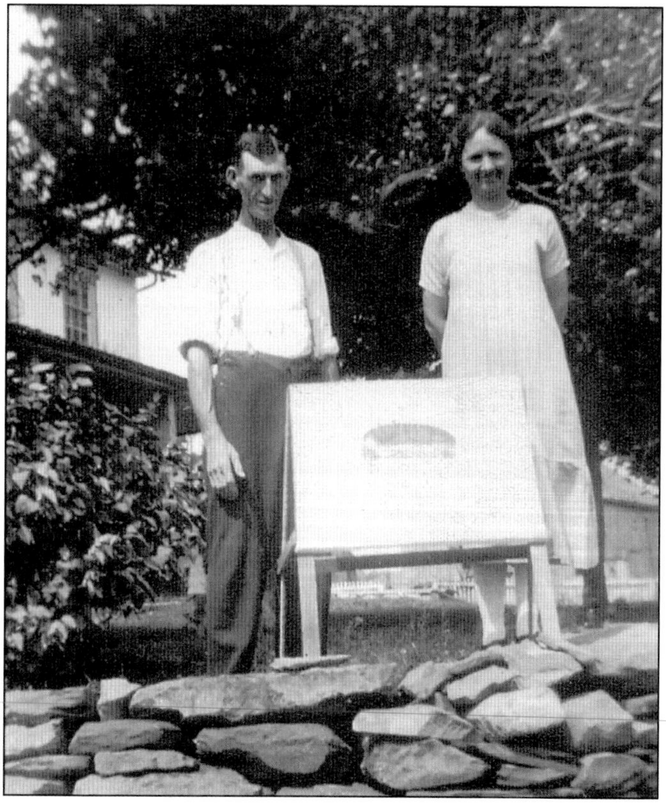

Walter Lowry and his wife, Ann, baked bread in a similar big stove during the Depression and sold it in front of their Cafferty Road home. In addition to baked goods, farm wives earned extra income by selling eggs, or stitching the covers on baseballs. Some sold Pitkins' oils and seasonings, while others left their children in the care of grandparents so they could work in the pants factory in nearby Pipersville. (DBM.)

When Marian Hobson posed for her school photograph in 1949, the dark stains on her neatly folded hands showed that she, like many other children in the fall, had recently been husking black walnuts, a tasty ingredient of baked goods. It has also been recalled that children sometimes deliberately stained their hands to confound their teacher in her daily inspection for clean hands and fingernails. (QBY.)

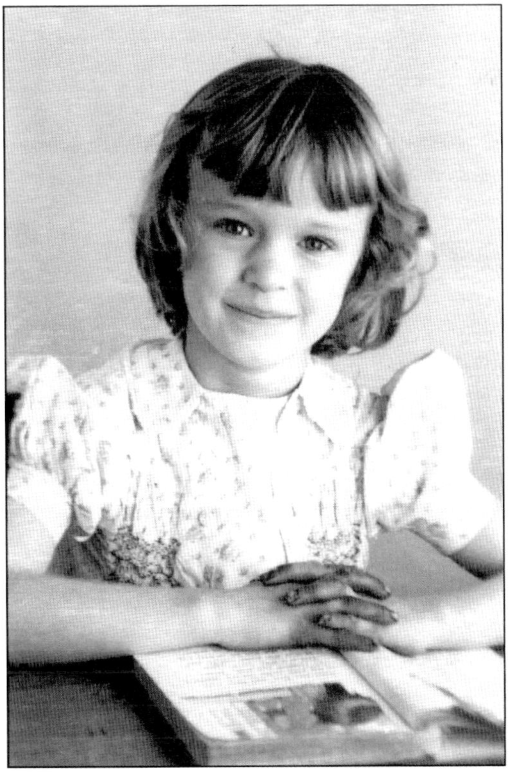

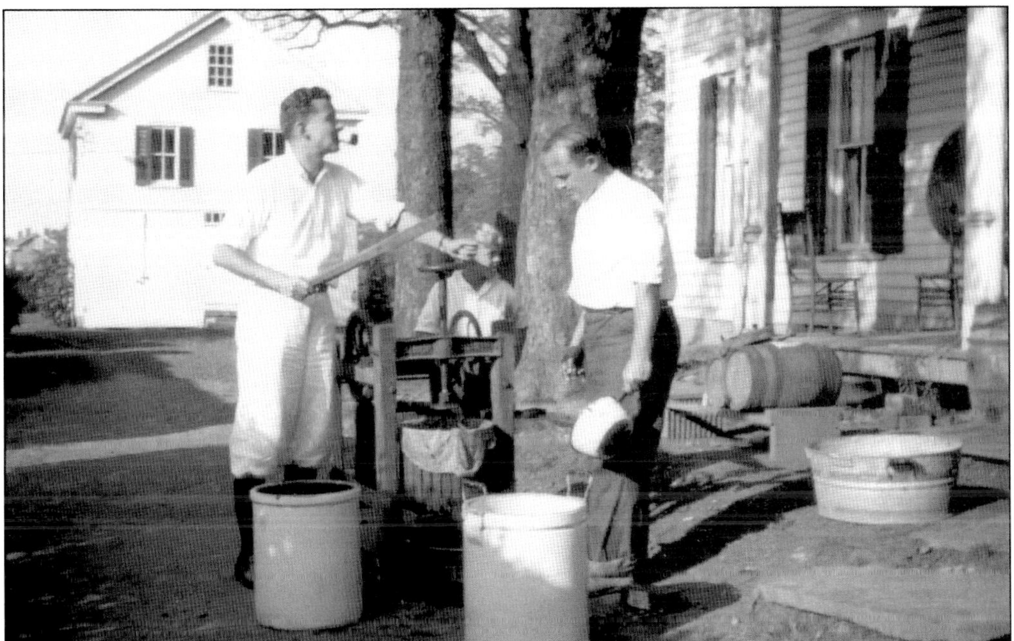

Edward Stover (left) supervises grape pressing for his homemade wine, which was popular with guests at Riverside Farm, the Stover home on River Road near Erwinna. He reportedly spiked the wine barrels with 90-proof alcohol. A family member remembered that many pitchers of Uncle Wardie's cocktails were served on the porch while dinner was slowly overcooked. (TCA.)

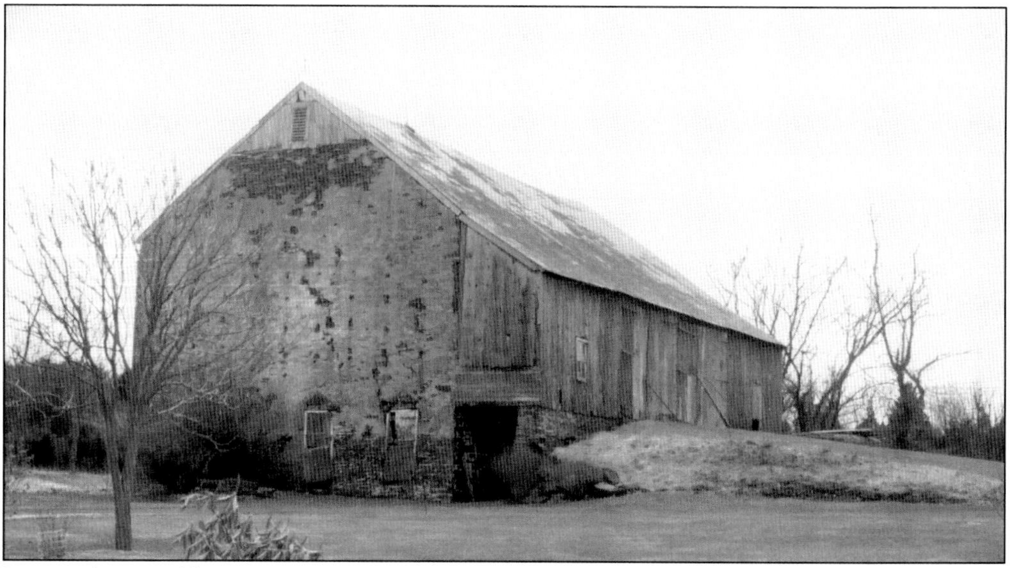

Less evident rural businesses were the moonshiners' stills known to have operated at clandestine sites throughout the township. Tinicum was reportedly well supplied with spirits during Prohibition. Thirsty men carrying empty jugs, who hiked up Jugtown Hill Road from the canal at Uhlerstown, were later observed staggering back down the hill, their thirst adequately quenched. In 1950, when this Hollow Horn Road barn was no longer needed for farming, it was rented to men from Philadelphia for an unspecified use. The farmer feigned complete ignorance when federal agents discovered a large-scale distillery in operation. Capable of producing 1,614 gallons of whiskey a day, the operation had 11,500 pounds of black market sugar stored near the 18-foot-high still. The barn survives, but under Tinicum's ordinance permitting adaptive reuse of historic buildings, a distillery would not qualify as a new use. (Above, TTP; below, BCHS, INT.)

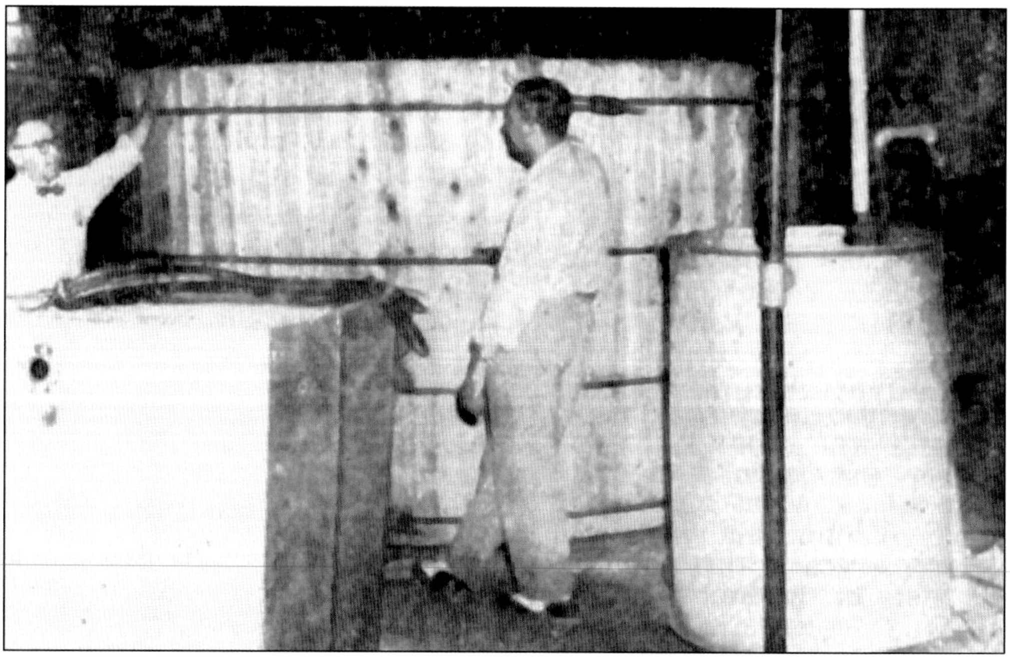

Three

Life in the Villages

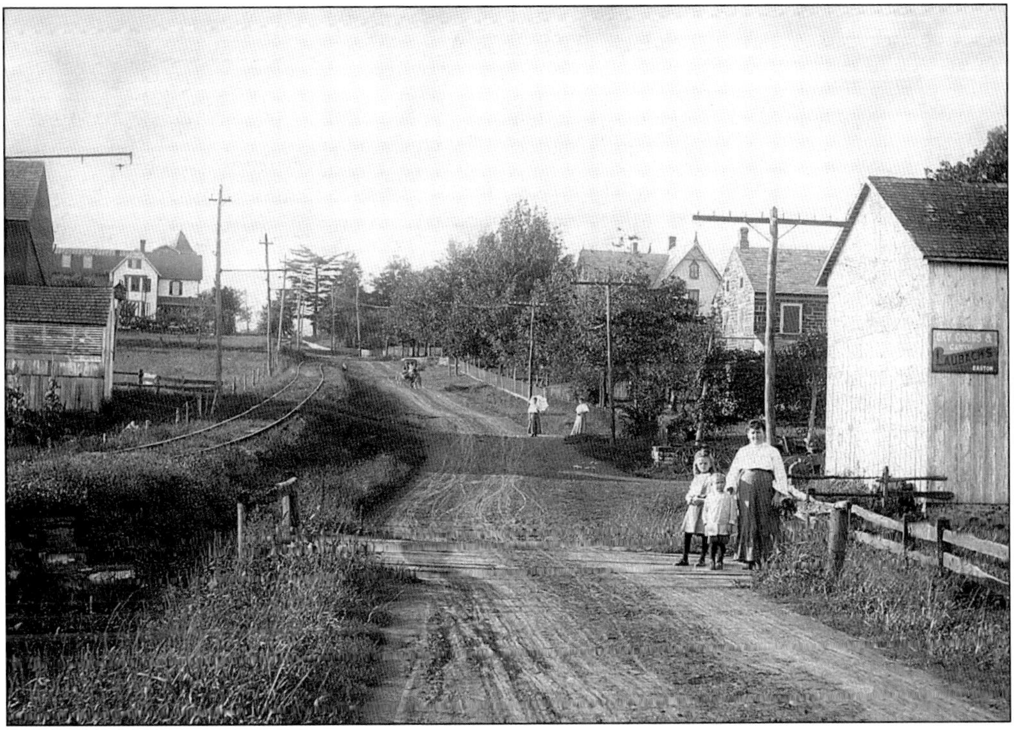

Scotch-Irish first settled east of present-day Ottsville in 1735, then gradually moved to Red Hill along the Durham Road trade route from Philadelphia. The name Red Hill was later changed to Ottsville when Michael Ott became the first postmaster. In this 1908 view, Durham Road meanders north toward the center of Ottsville. Christian Wehrung's home and blacksmith shop are in the right foreground. Trolley tracks (left) lead up past the home of Jacob S. Snyder. (BWG.)

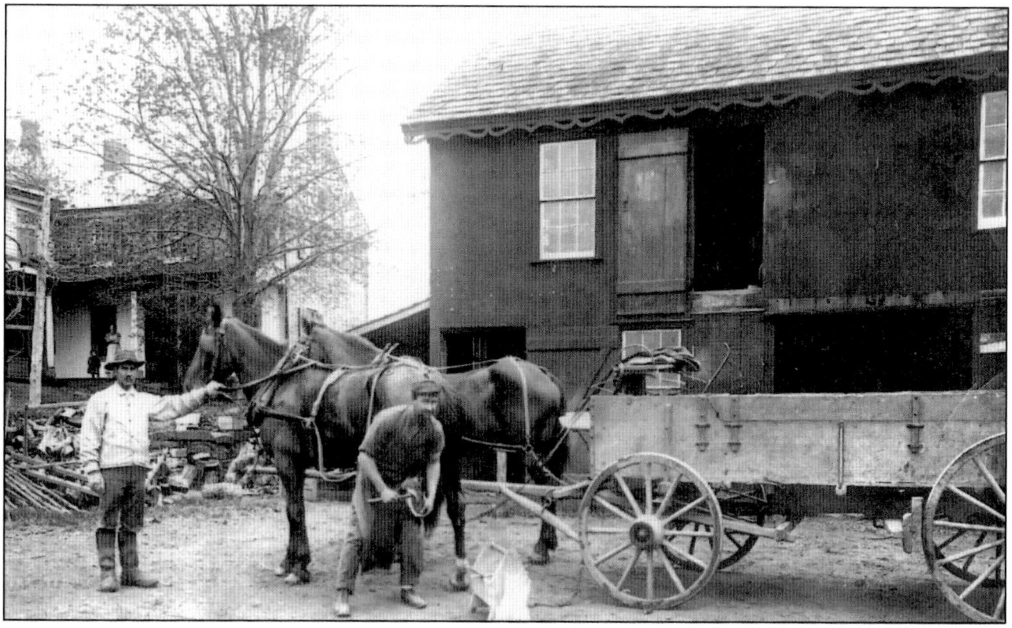

Christian Wehrung's blacksmith and wheelwright shop employed several workers, pictured here in 1915. In addition to shoeing horses, Wehrung made new iron rims and spokes for wagon wheels. A pond beside the Modern Concrete office now occupies the site of the shop. Another building in the smithy complex, which Wehrung purchased from Michael Haney, who had preceded him as village blacksmith, later housed the New Holland farm engine dealership. (BWG.)

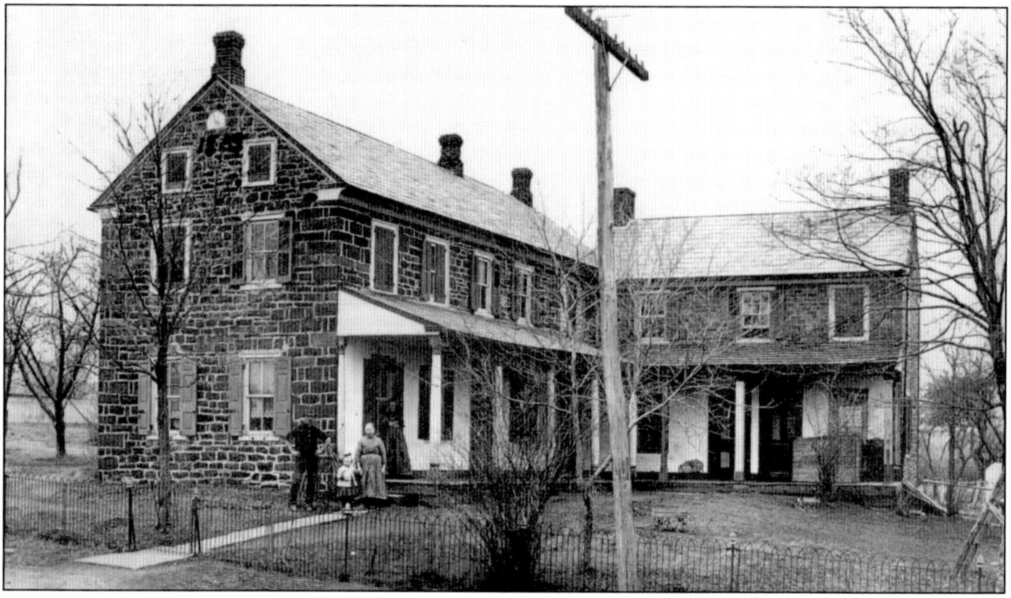

The surviving Wehrung stone house illustrates several architectural features. Solid light-colored shutters on lower windows reflected lamplight when closed at night. Darker louvered blinds ventilated upstairs bedrooms. Stone walls beneath the porch roof were plastered to reflect light. The larger section was added in 1839 to the original 1776 section. Pictured in 1910 are, from left to right, Christian Wehrung with his daughter, Caroline; his mother, Caroline; and, on the porch, his wife, Hannah. (BWG.)

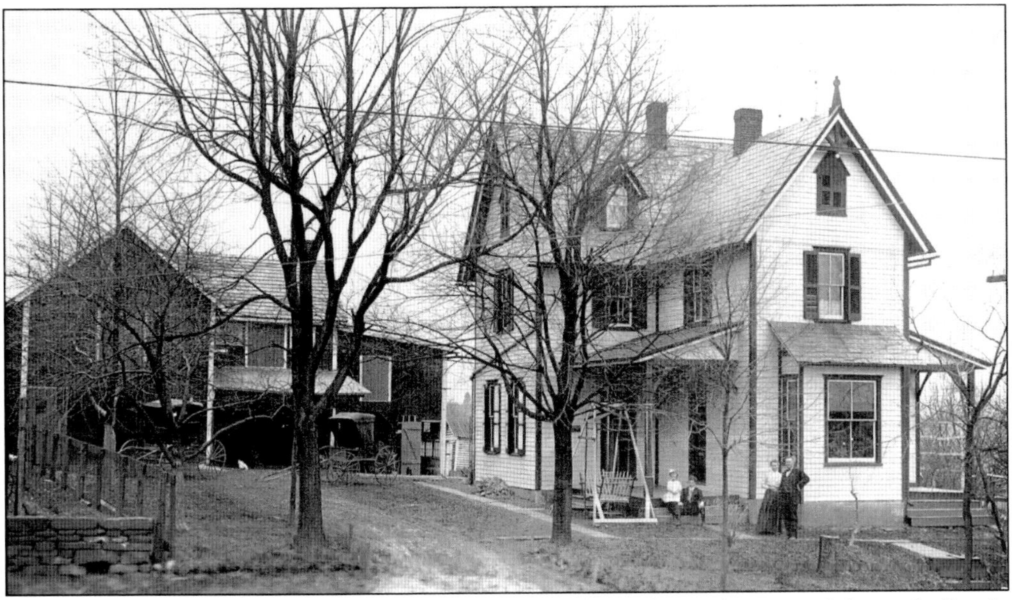

In 1910, Dr. George Grim stands at his home, next to the Wehrung home, with his wife, Sarah, and children. Grim also served as school board secretary for many years. Later Dr. Edward E. Koonce, in the house beside Grim's, also served as village doctor. Both houses survive. Residents also used a number of home remedies for health problems. In 1906, George Lower of Ottsville manufactured his Camphor Ointment "for Man or Beast." (EWH.)

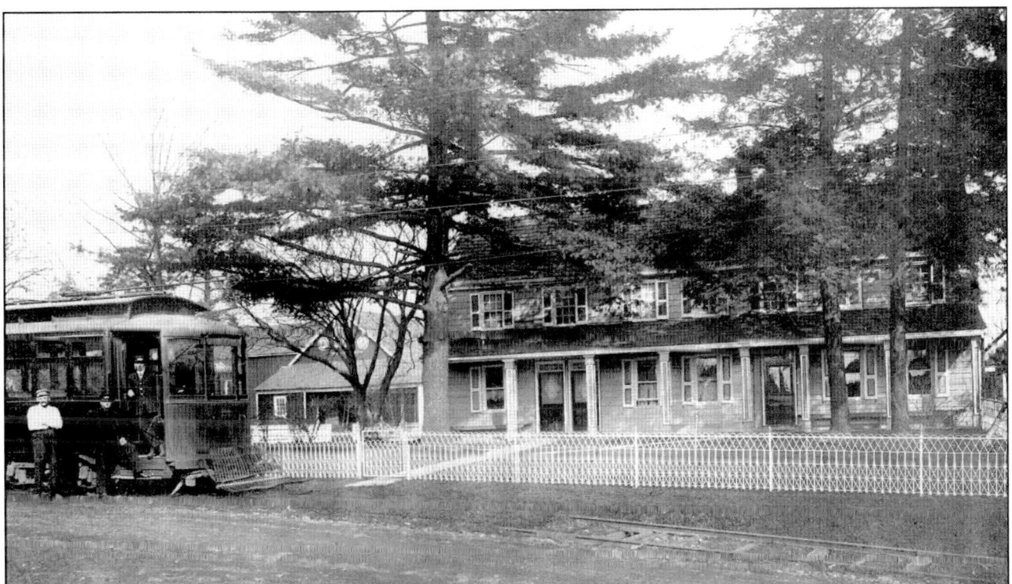

The trolley stop was strategically located across from the Ottsville Inn. The rise of automobile transportation and improving roads lead to the demise of the trolley in 1926, when it was replaced by bus service. The house pictured here survives, but Lotsgazell's Pine Tree Inn, a popular ice-cream parlor into the 1960s, which is visible behind the trolley, has been lost. (GBK.)

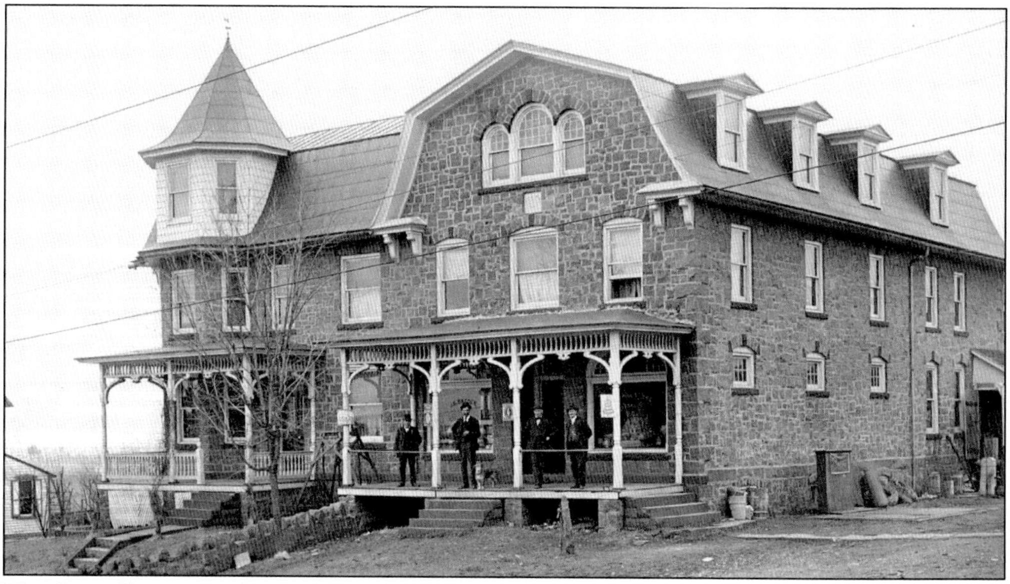

The Ottsville store and post office was run by Jacob S. Snyder in 1908. Since the early 1870s, the store had provided dry goods, groceries, building materials, and tools. Ed Wolfinger, who ran the store beginning in the 1930s, boasted that if he did not have something, he would get it. After several years of other uses, the building now houses Brig O'Doon, an organic foods and coffee shop. (EWH.)

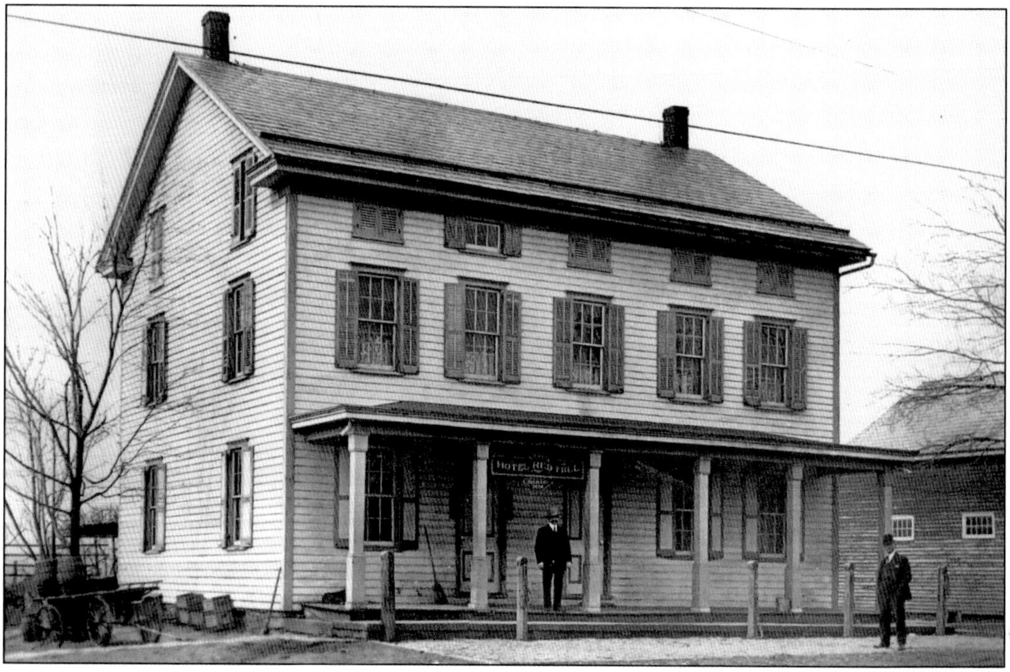

The Ottsville Inn, still a local landmark, was established in 1871 by Thomas Harpel. Beneath the Hotel Red Hill sign, around 1910, is manager Steve Dillon. The hotel was a major trolley stop where passengers and others could procure meals, drinks, or a room for the night. The building features narrow "eyebrow" windows on the third floor, and the remaining windows have the early six-over-six arrangement of glass panes. (GBK.)

On election day, November 5, 1912, Christian Wehrung celebrates with friends the victory of Pres. Woodrow Wilson and the birth of his son, Woodrow Wilson Wehrung. Gathered at the Ottsville Inn are, from left to right, manager and bartender Steve Dillon, unidentified, shoemaker Warren Bean, auctioneer Ed Mathias, Henry Wehrung, Christian Wehrung, John Meyers, and Asa Hochman. "Woody" Wehrung grew up to found the Modern Concrete Company in 1951. (DWG.)

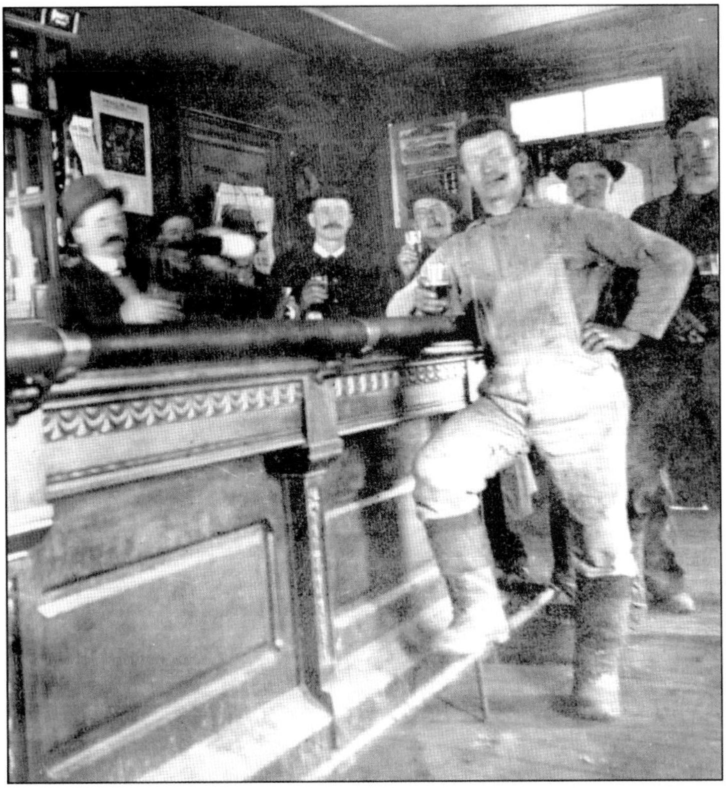

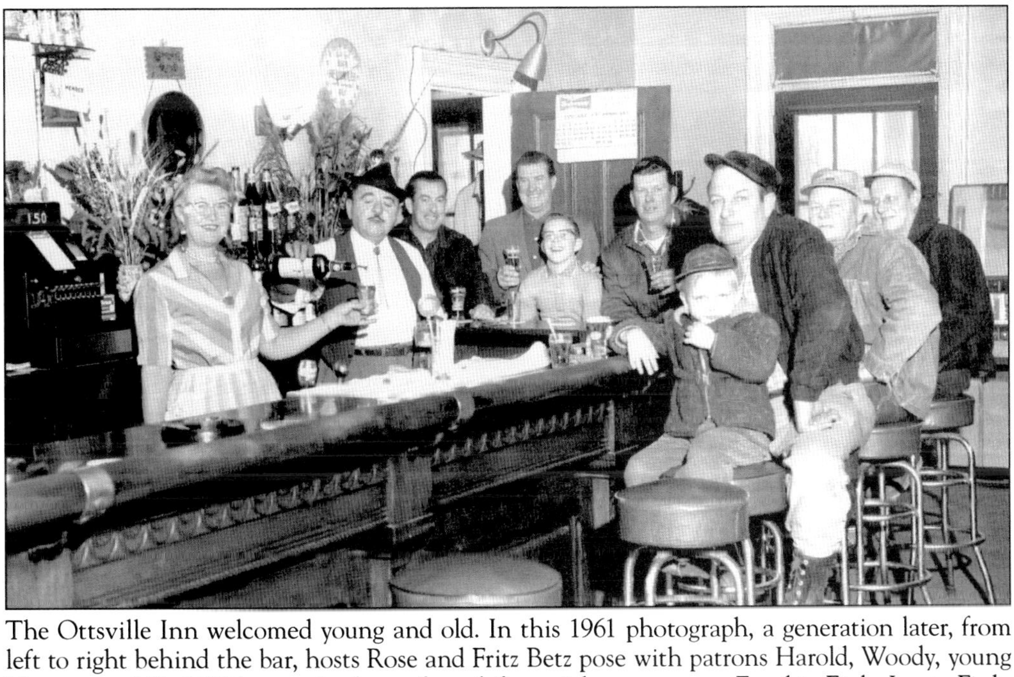

The Ottsville Inn welcomed young and old. In this 1961 photograph, a generation later, from left to right behind the bar, hosts Rose and Fritz Betz pose with patrons Harold, Woody, young Vernon, and Earl Wehrung. In front, from left to right, are young Frankie Fink, Louie Fink, John McIntyre, and Joseph Curry. Fritz appears to be creating a boilermaker by adding a shot of Seagram's 7 to Rose's beer. (GBK.)

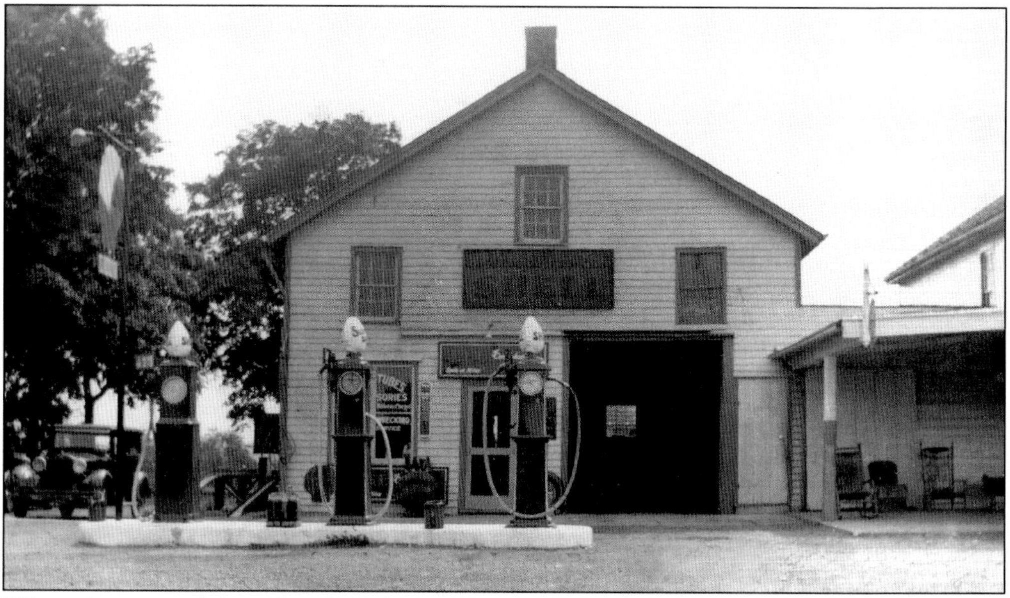

When the automobile replaced the horse as a mode of transportation, it became necessary to have the support of a local mechanic, tire salesman, and gas station attendant. While other businesses were selling only gas, the Ottsville Shell station, along with Good Brothers Ford, provided full service, including battery charging, Lee tires, and wrecking service. The site is now the home of the Ottsville Volunteer Fire Company. (GBK.)

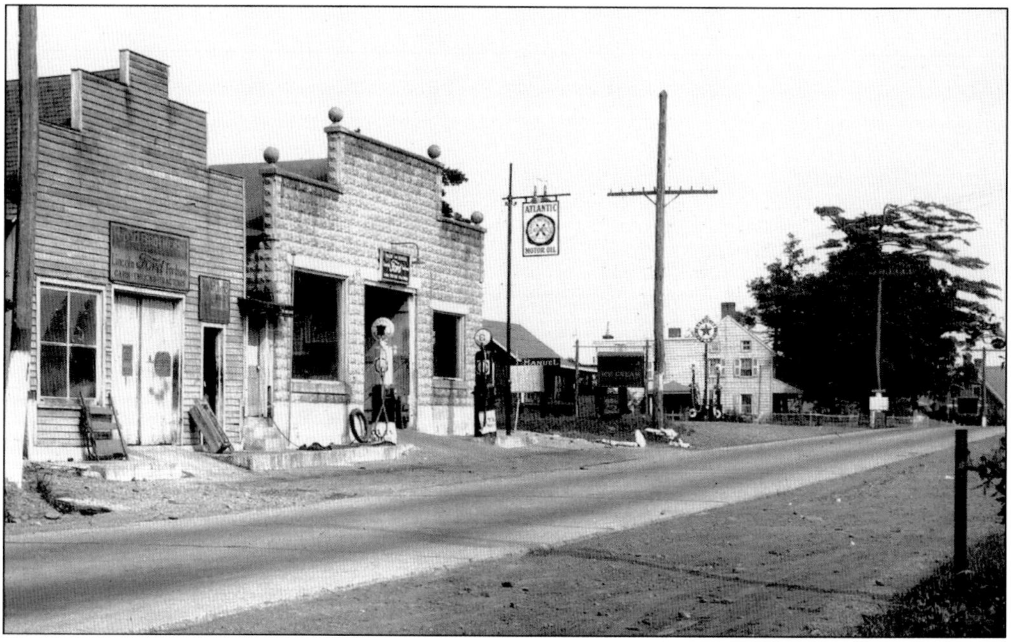

Howard and George Good opened a Ford agency when mass-produced automobiles first came on the market. Selling Model Ts, then Model As and the V-8, Good Brothers also sold Fordson tractors and the first fire trucks to the Delaware Valley and Ottsville fire companies. A cabinetmaker currently occupies the former Good building. The ice-cream parlor and Texaco gas station on the right are now gone. (OVP.)

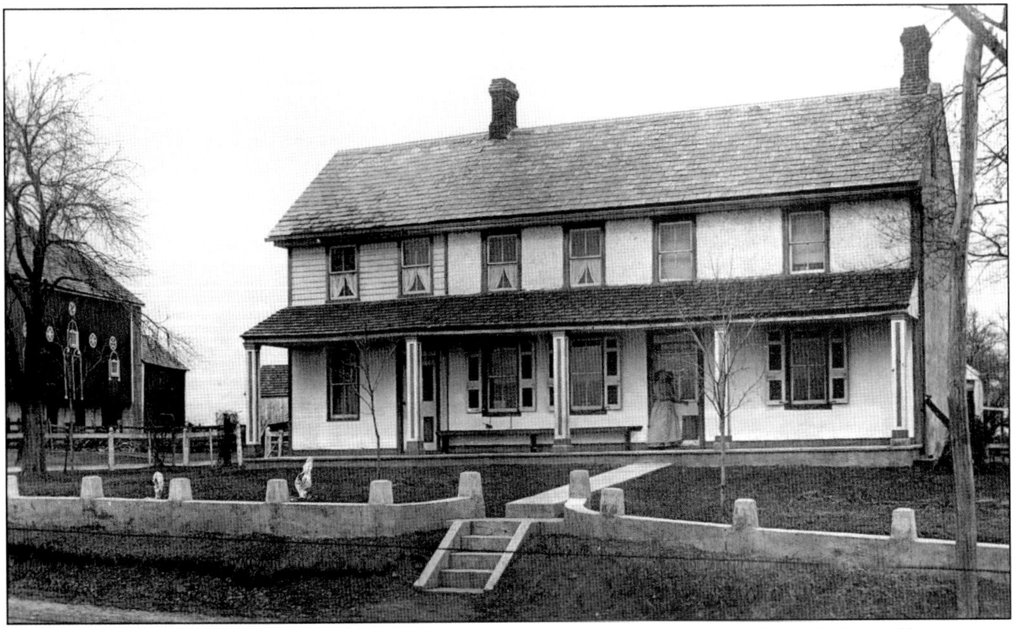

The Maple Leaf Dairy Farm was a large operation on the southern edge of Ottsville next to the Red Hill Church. The hex signs on the barn are a combination of the three most common designs in Bucks County: the six-petaled rosette, the five-pointed star, and the swirling swastika. As larger panes of glass became available around 1875, windows were built with the two-over-two design seen on this house. All these buildings survive. (GBK.)

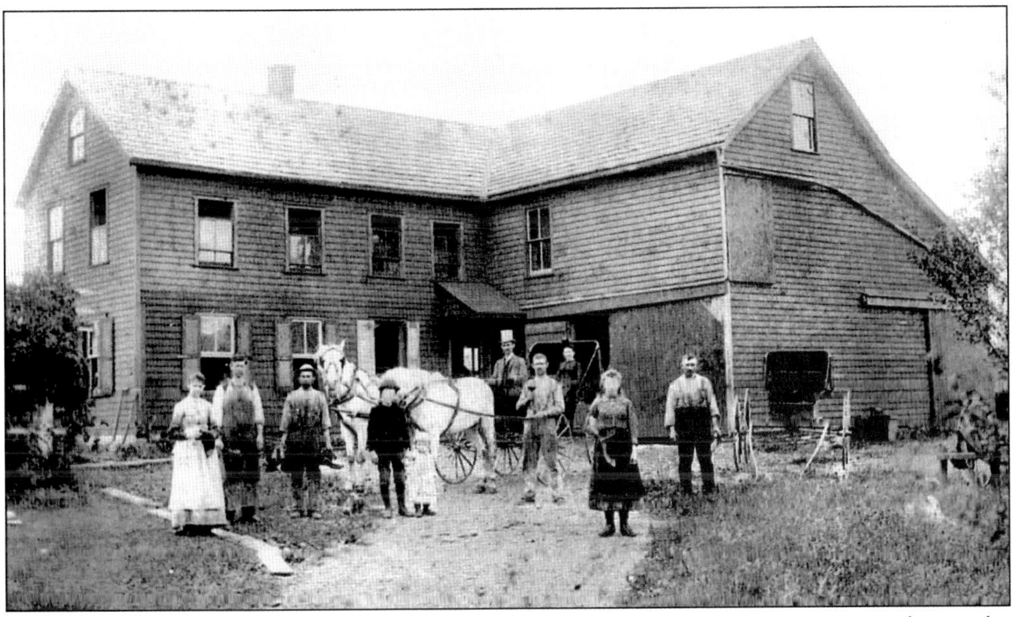

In 1920, Andrew J. Bean's shoe factory, which manufactured shoes for miners, stood near the corner of Durham and Geigel Hill Roads. In later years, Andrew and his son, Warren, ran a shoe repair business here. Although the factory is gone, the handsome brick Bean home survives on the corner of Geigel Hill Road. Its steeply pitched roof is typical of late-Victorian Queen Anne–style architecture. (LSG.)

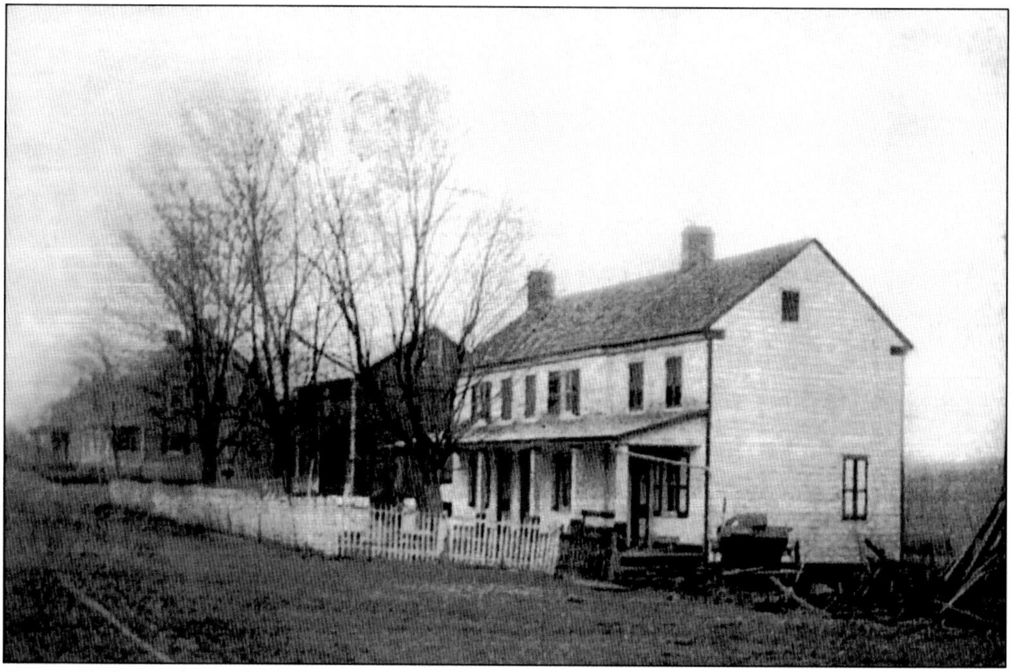

Centrally located Sundale, previously known as Headquarters, was a small cluster of homes, a school, a blacksmith and wheelwright shop, a post office and general store, and a hotel. Horace Fabian, son of the blacksmith, recalled that nothing ever happened in Sundale. "There were so few people that you couldn't even make mischief on Halloween because everyone would know who did it." The Fabian home and barn, along with the hotel, in this 1915 view remain intact. (LSG.)

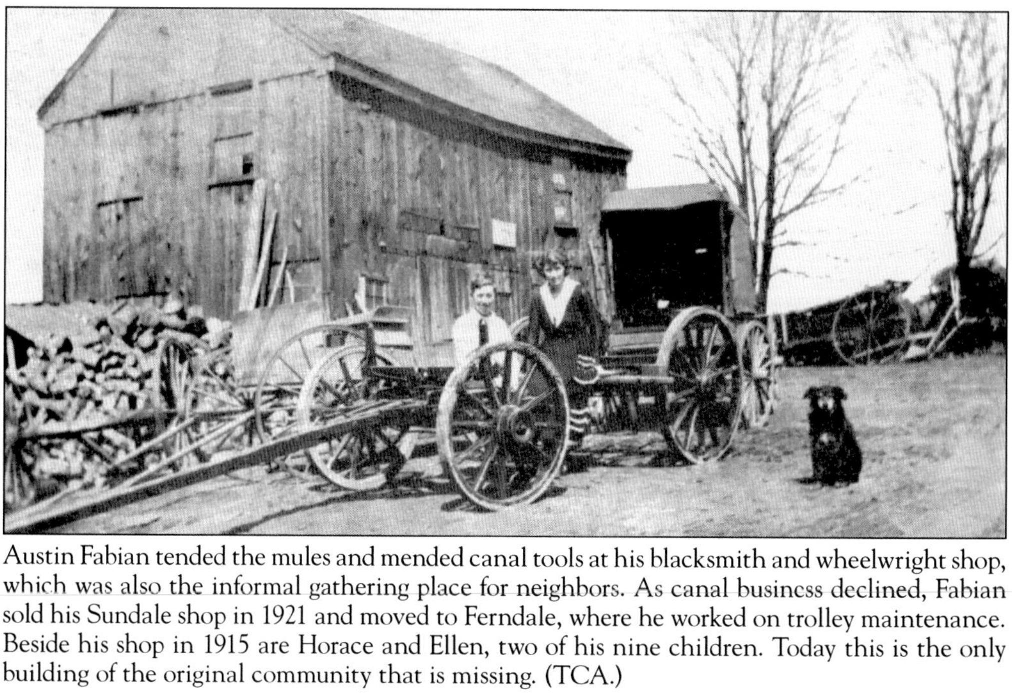

Austin Fabian tended the mules and mended canal tools at his blacksmith and wheelwright shop, which was also the informal gathering place for neighbors. As canal business declined, Fabian sold his Sundale shop in 1921 and moved to Ferndale, where he worked on trolley maintenance. Beside his shop in 1915 are Horace and Ellen, two of his nine children. Today this is the only building of the original community that is missing. (TCA.)

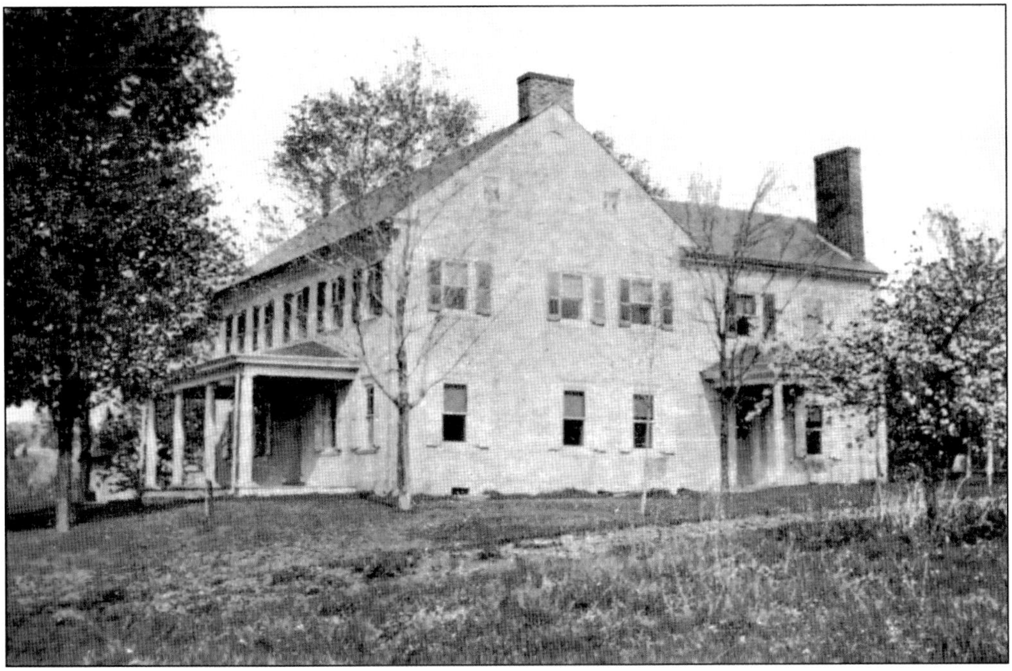

Members of the Frankenfield family lived in and around Headquarters for over a century, leaving their name on the nearby covered bridge. This stately Frankenfield home, identical in appearance today, welcomed boarders early in the 20th century. John Van Sant bought the farm in 1951 and established the Erwinna Airport on its lofty fields in 1954. He attracted aficionados of vintage aircraft, including biplanes, which continue to perform aerobatics over Tinicum today. (DBM.)

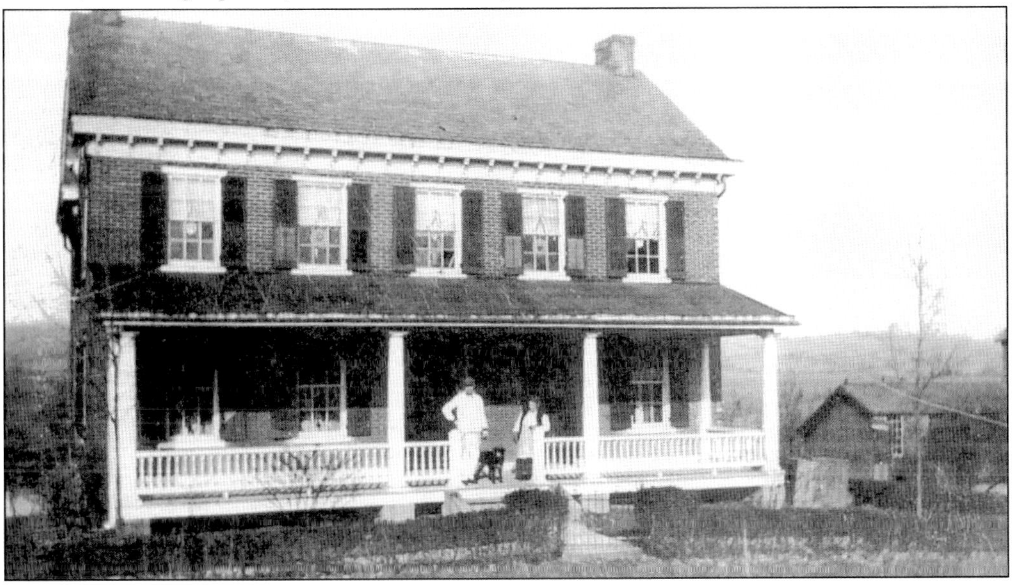

As the unofficial township headquarters, where public meetings and elections were held, the Sundale Hotel, formerly the Spread Eagle Tavern, offered rooms, refreshments, and occasional dances, which attracted a rowdy crowd. Several of the signatures scratched by guests into the brick walls of the hotel have survived. As Ottsville grew with the arrival of the trolley, Sundale declined and lost its post office. The hotel and general store are now private residences. (LSG.)

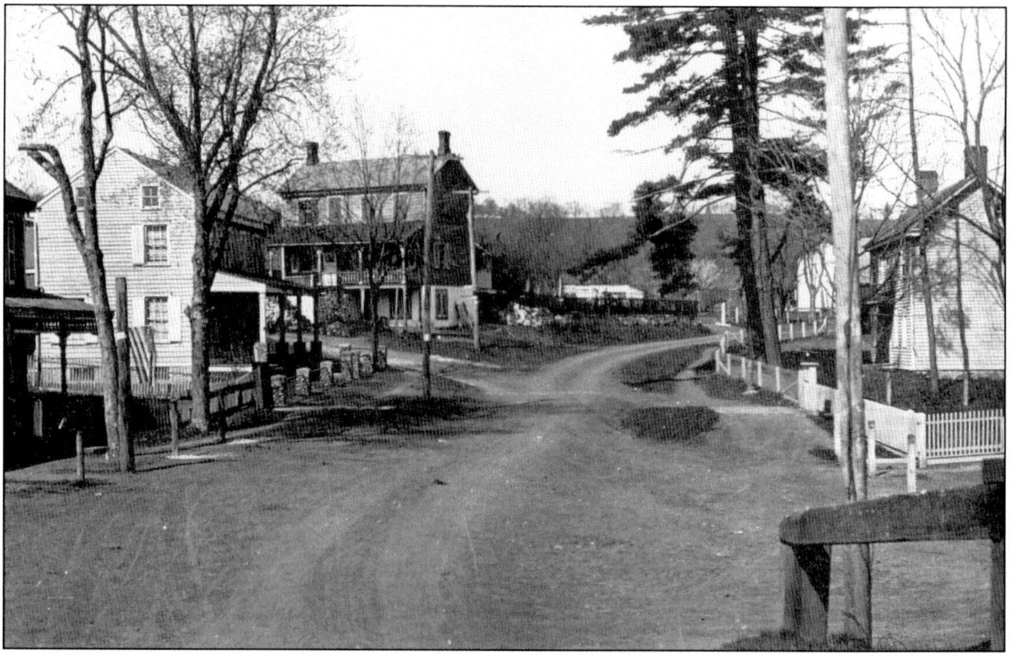

The historic district of Erwinna, a large rural area rich with surviving buildings, has been declared eligible for the National Register of Historic Places. In the village, viewed here in 1920 from the canal bridge, Geigel Hill Road curves right, while Headquarters Road turns left before the three-story building on the corner. One of several boardinghouses along the canal owned by John Free, it survives, as do those on the right. (LSH.)

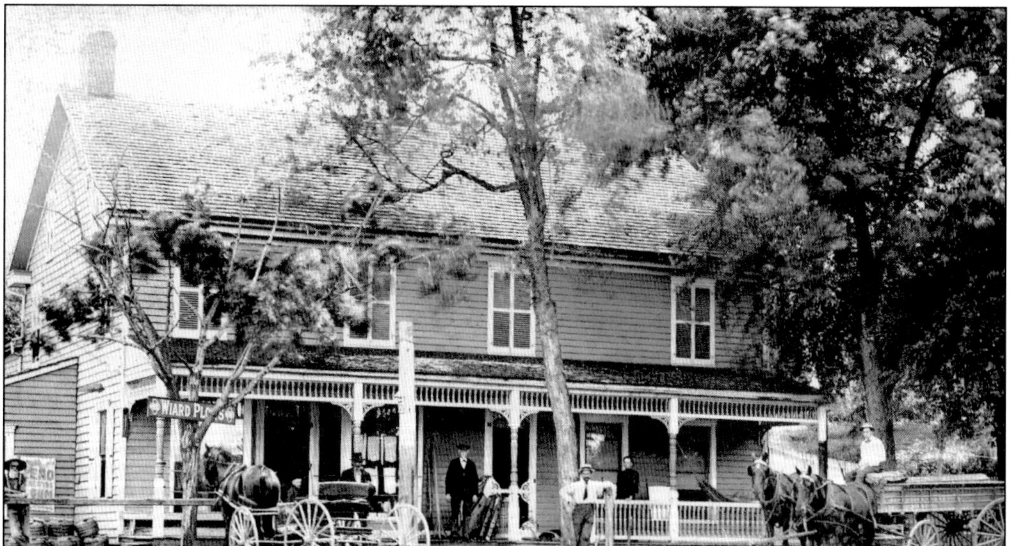

Pictured in 1910, Erwinna's combination general store, hotel, and bar was where neighbors gathered to share news or play pool over a glass of beer. Later owned by Frank Sispera, there was penny candy for children and Breyer's ice cream for all ages. The old Sispera building is gone. At Russell Gary's funeral parlor near the covered bridge, Esther Weaver remembered playing hide-and-seek among the caskets with the Gary children. (EWH.)

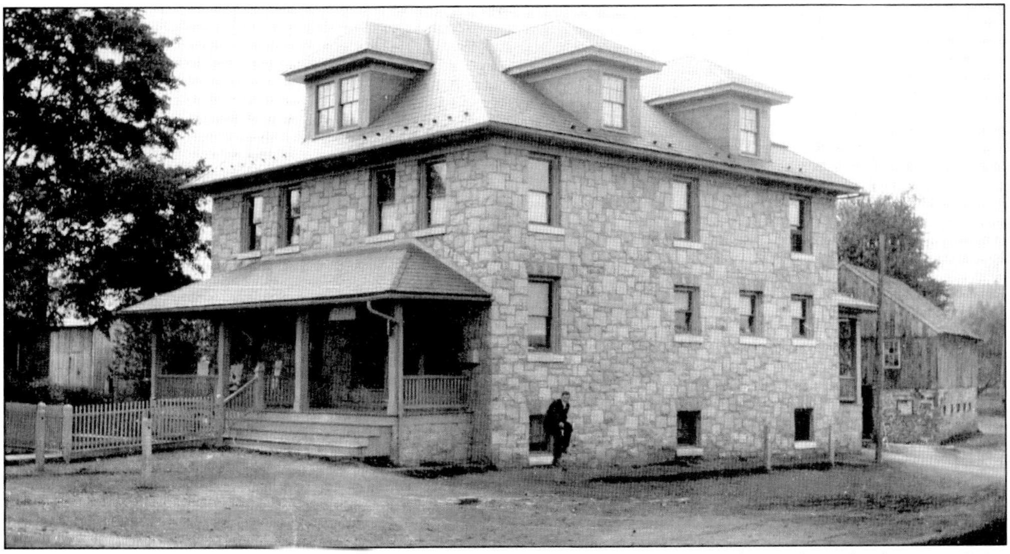

The Williams store, rebuilt after a 1900 fire, survives as a private residence beside the canal. In this 1915 view, young Art Williams sits atop a hitching post. He ran the store and post office here for four decades, selling ice cream, candy, cigarettes, and cans of Spam and corned beef, as well as coal, kerosene, and gasoline. His mule barn is visible behind the store. (JKN.)

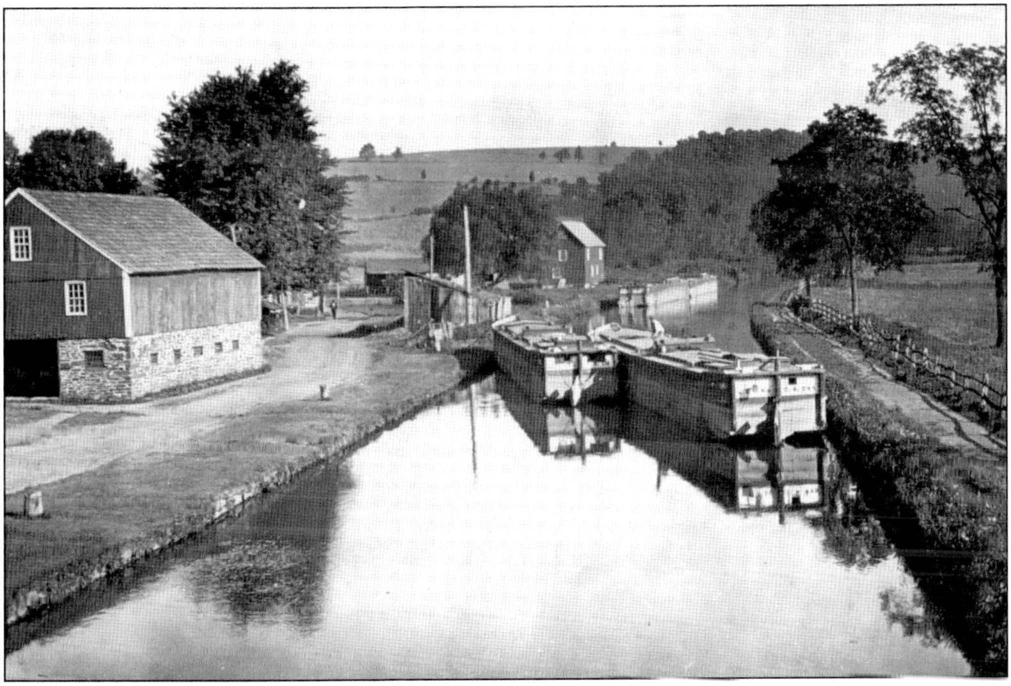

This tranquil 1920 photograph looks north from the Erwinna canal bridge. Williams's mule barn is on the left, where dusty Second Street follows the canal before turning west after the group of trees. The Erwinna boathouse is in the distance. Neither building survives, but the open fields on the hillside are part of the 123-acre Schultz farm, now permanently protected from development by a conservation easement. (LSH.)

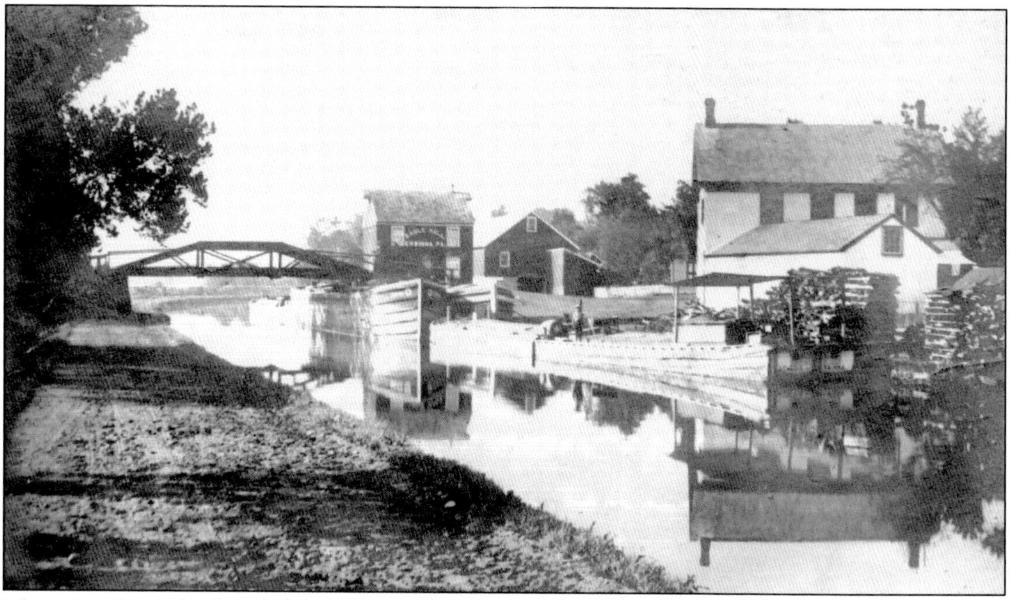

This view from the late 1890s looks south into Erwinna. Right of the canal bridge is the Eagle hall, a fraternal lodge and dance hall. It survives, but has been modified. The white building on the right is the old Williams store, which burned in 1900. The Williams family also ran the lumber and coal yard on the far right. (DBM.)

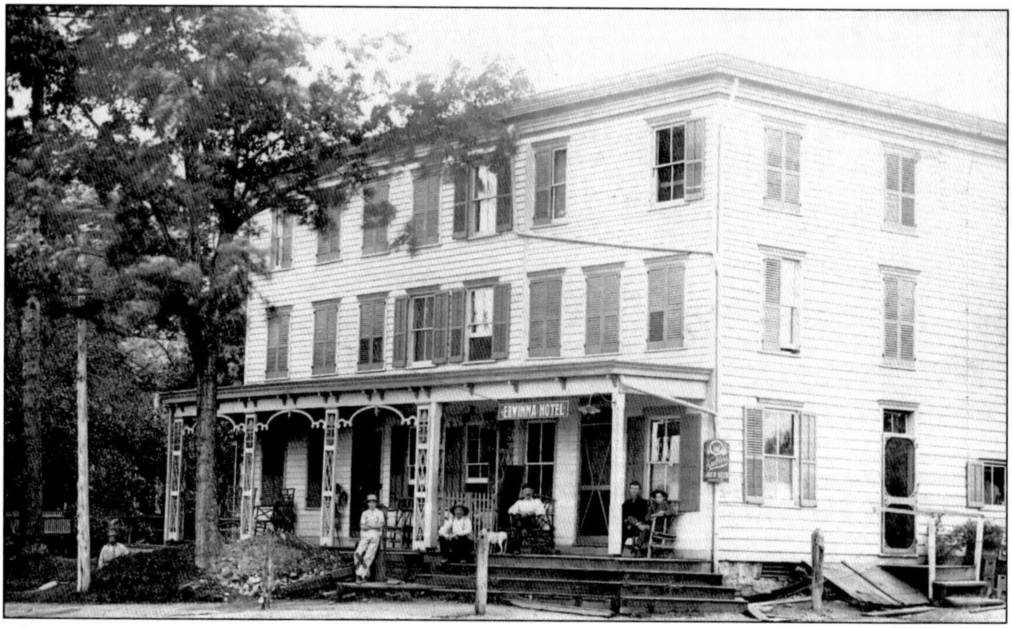

The Erwinna Hotel, located near the canal on Second Street, was managed by Jacob Kooker, seated in the light shirt beside the door. His son is on the far left. The bar served Kuebler's beer. Its two-over-two paned windows date its construction to late 19th century. The message on this postcard, mailed from Erwinna, refers to Saturday night musical entertainment here. The hotel burned in 1918 and was never rebuilt. (EWH.)

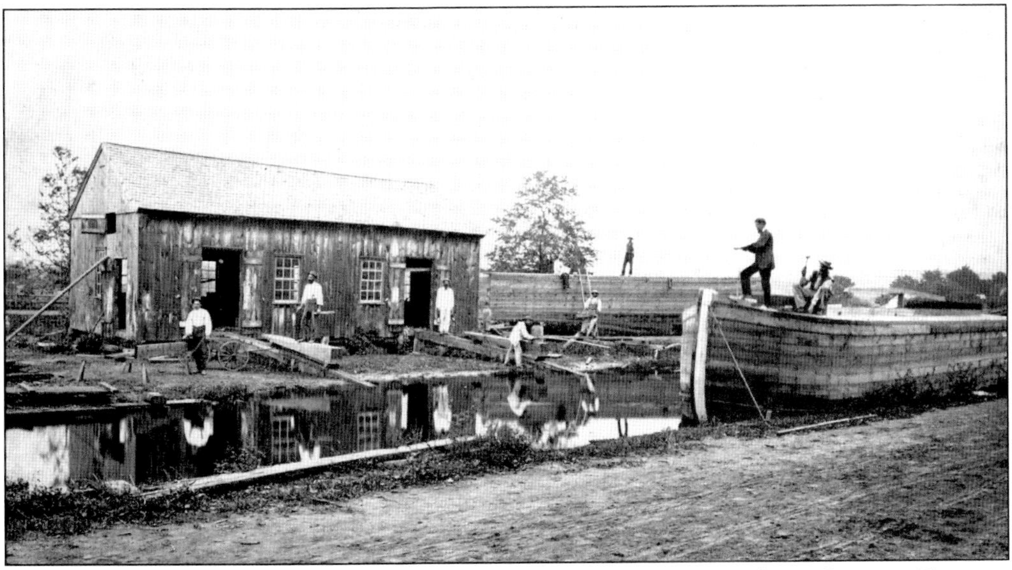

At Francis Rapp's Boatyard several boats are under construction in this 1871 view. Erwinna residents include Francis Rapp, in dark suit, standing with plans on the bow of a boat, Marshall Purcell, and Barzilla Williams. Located north of Erwinna, on a branch of the canal referred to as "wide waters," all that remains of this operation are portions of a stone foundation and a few rotting timbers of boats, engulfed by forest. (BCHS.)

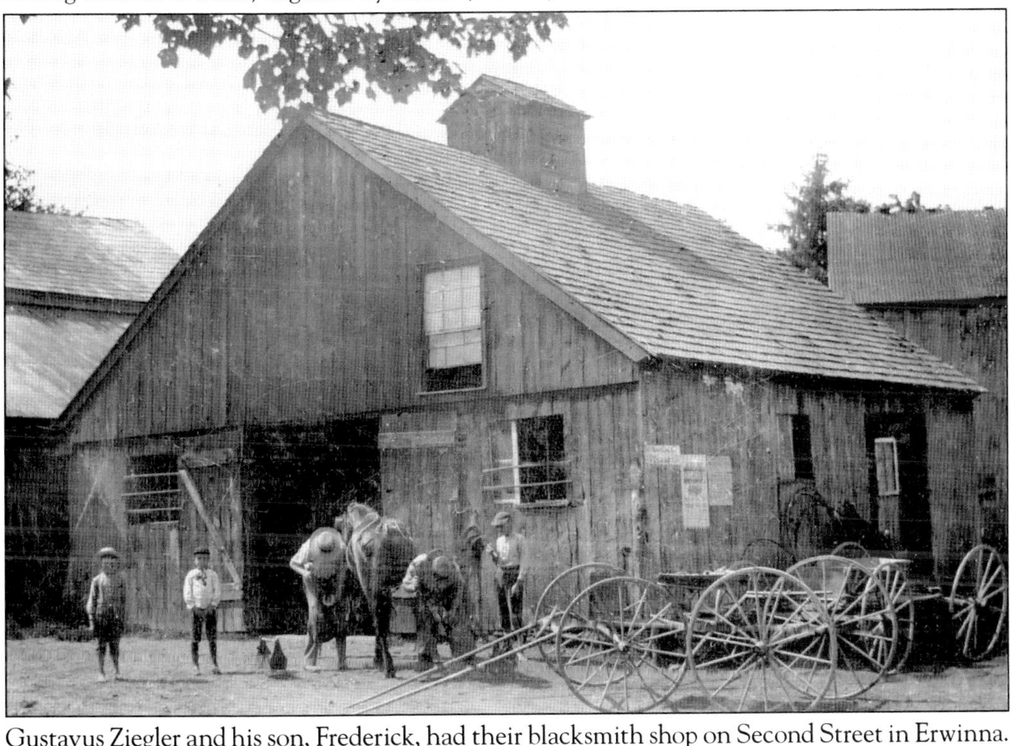

Gustavus Ziegler and his son, Frederick, had their blacksmith shop on Second Street in Erwinna. Seen here around 1908, the two blacksmiths appear to be shoeing the left fore and right hind legs simultaneously, a careful balancing act for the horse, which is still demonstrated as a stunt by modern farriers. The building is now only a distant memory. (BCHS.)

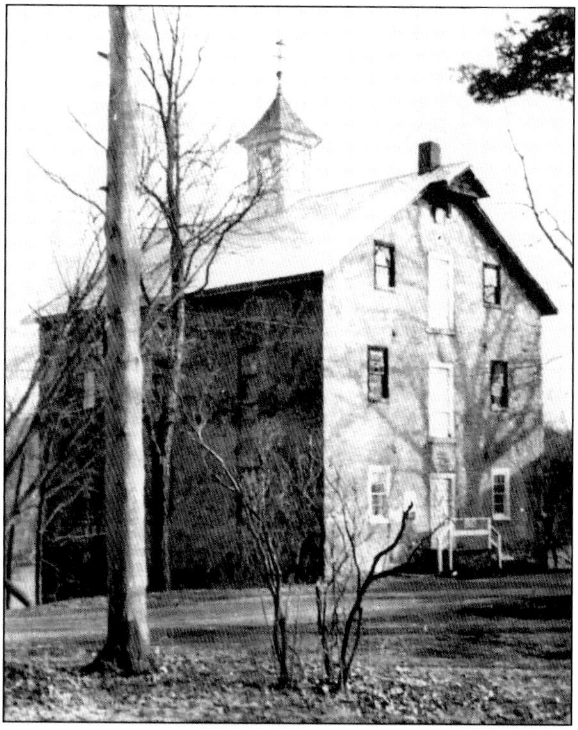

Stover Mill, built beside the Delaware River in 1832 by Henry S. Stover, was run by the Stover family until 1902. John J. Stover donated the mill in 1955 to the Tinicum Civic Association. The restored mill, with machinery intact, is on the National Register of Historic Places. The Tinicum Civic Association presents regular art shows and other programs here. (EWH.)

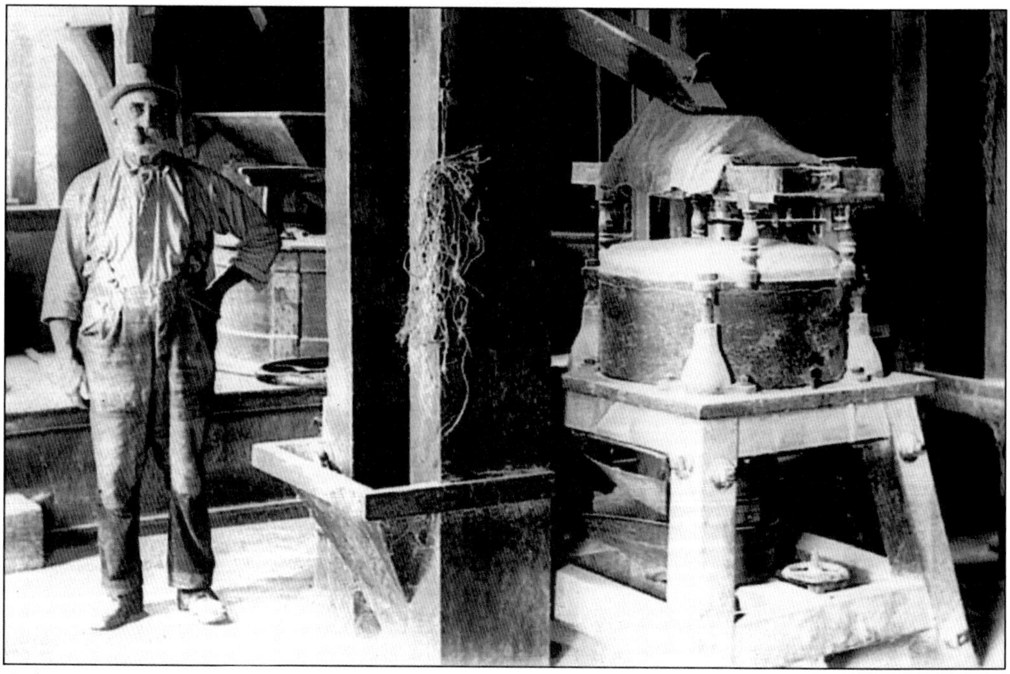

Calvin Bryan, seen here around 1915, and his son operated the mill from 1902 until it closed in 1922. After John J. Stover installed a dynamo to provide electricity to Erwinna, Bryan flickered the lights each evening at 9:30 to warn residents to light their kerosene lamps before he closed down for the night. The Stovers also installed the independent Stover Telephone Company, connected to Philadelphia, and managed the switchboard from their home. (HWV.)

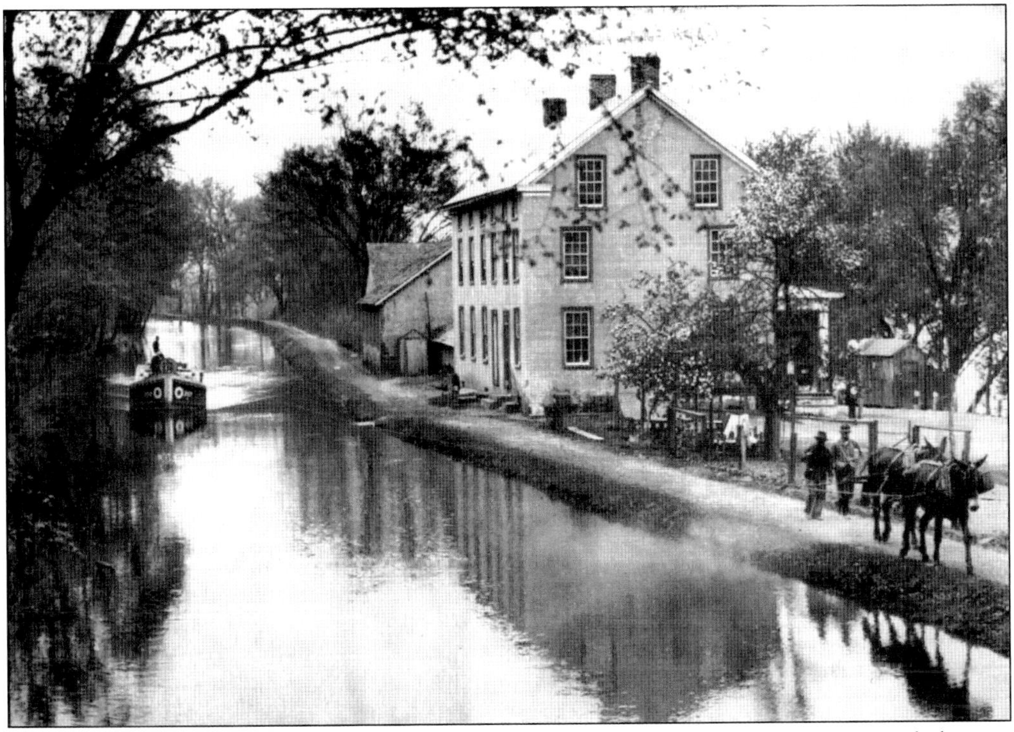

A team of mules pulls a canal boat past Jacob Oberacker's Delaware House, previously known as Keeler's Hotel, in 1914. Many spirited arguments and political debates occurred here, and combatants were often tossed into the canal. Located south of Erwinna, where River Road crosses the canal, it is now the Golden Pheasant Inn and serves a more orderly clientele. (FOC.)

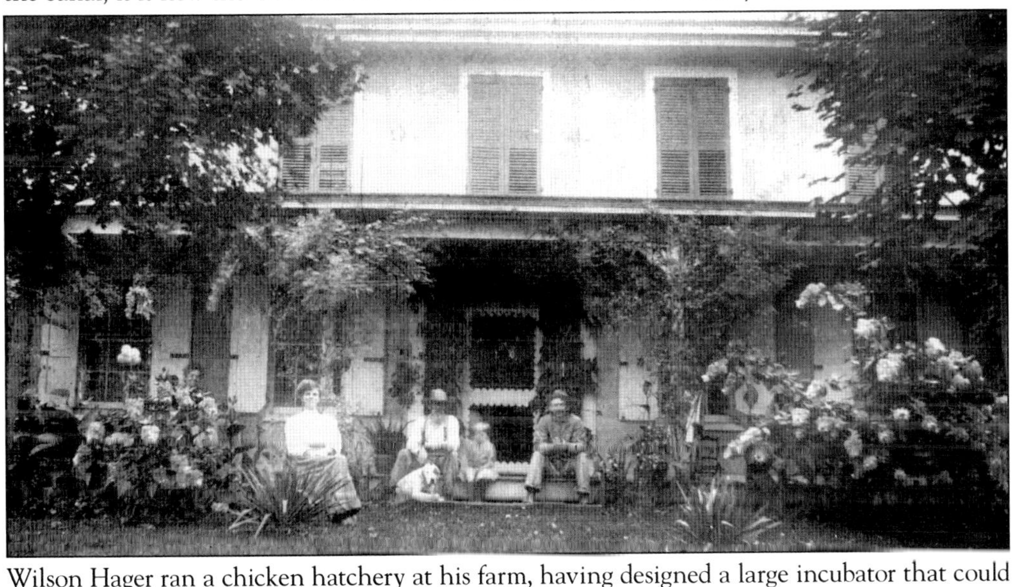

Wilson Hager ran a chicken hatchery at his farm, having designed a large incubator that could hatch many chicks at a time. Hager children washed and candled the eggs sold by the operation. Pictured on their porch in 1908 are, from left to right, unidentified, Bessie (Sigafoos) Hager, Enoch Tettemer, Victor Hager, and Wilson Hager. The house survives on Geigel Hill Road, overlooking the covered bridge, but only the stone foundation of the barn remains. (RPK.)

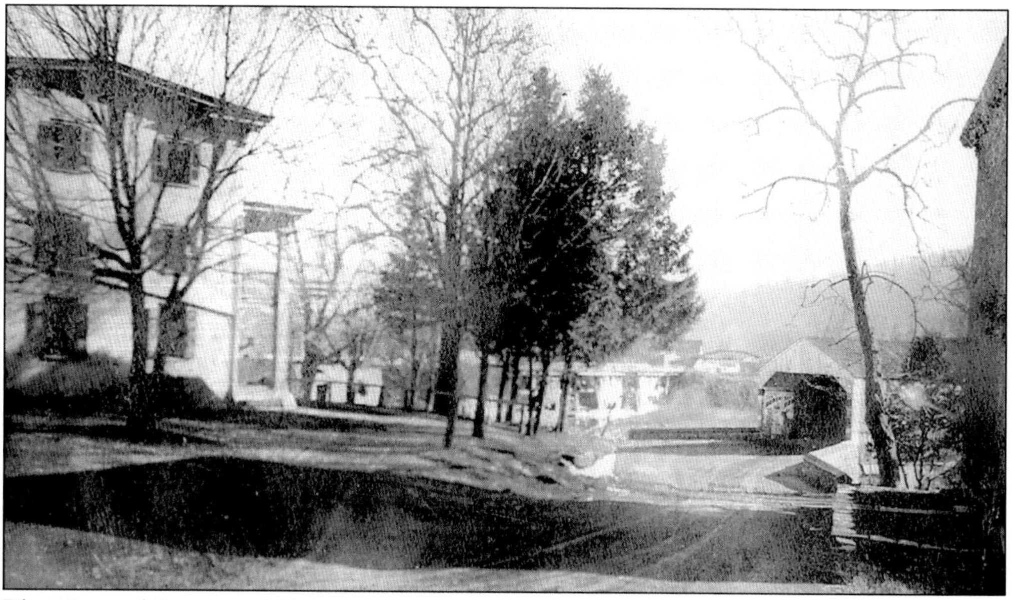

The National Register of Historic Places's Point Pleasant Historic District spans Tinicum and Plumstead Townships. Landmarks visible in this 1908 scene in Tinicum are, from left to right, the Point Pleasant Inn, the canal aqueduct over Tohickon Creek, a camel-back bridge, and the covered bridge over the creek. A Lenni-Lenape ford, and then Pearsons Ferry, crossed the Delaware River here until an 1855 covered bridge was built to connect with the railroad in Byram, New Jersey. (KLB.)

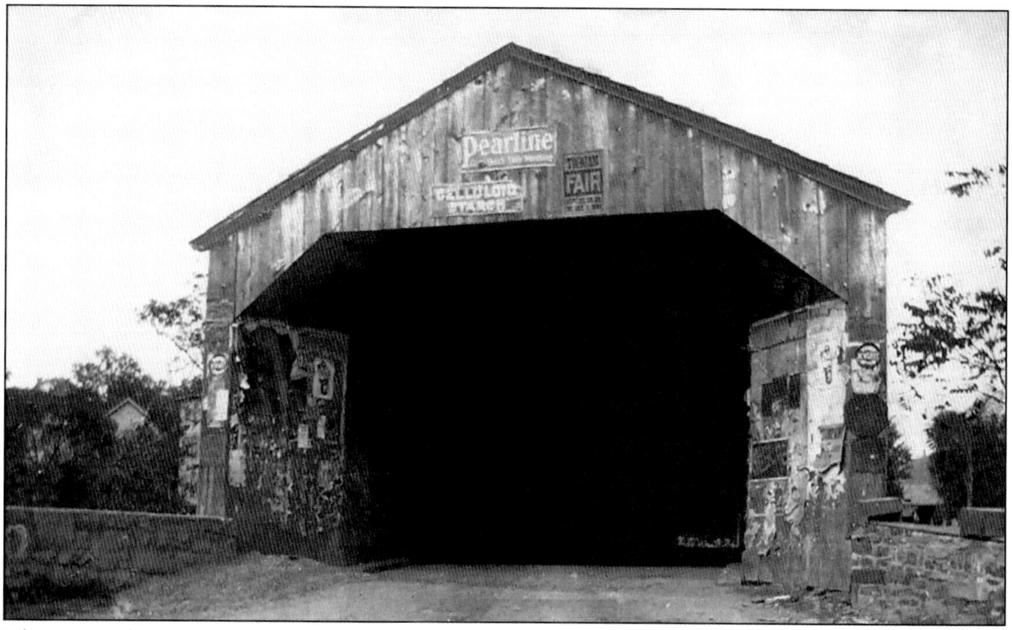

The covered bridge crossing Tohickon Creek in Point Pleasant served as the community bulletin board until it was replaced in 1922. Greeting travelers crossing into Tinicum, advertisements include Pearline Soap "for quick safe washing," Celluloid Starch, and the Trenton State Fair. Nearly obscured by all the advertisements is the official warning of severe fines for driving over the bridge at a pace faster than a walk. (KLB.)

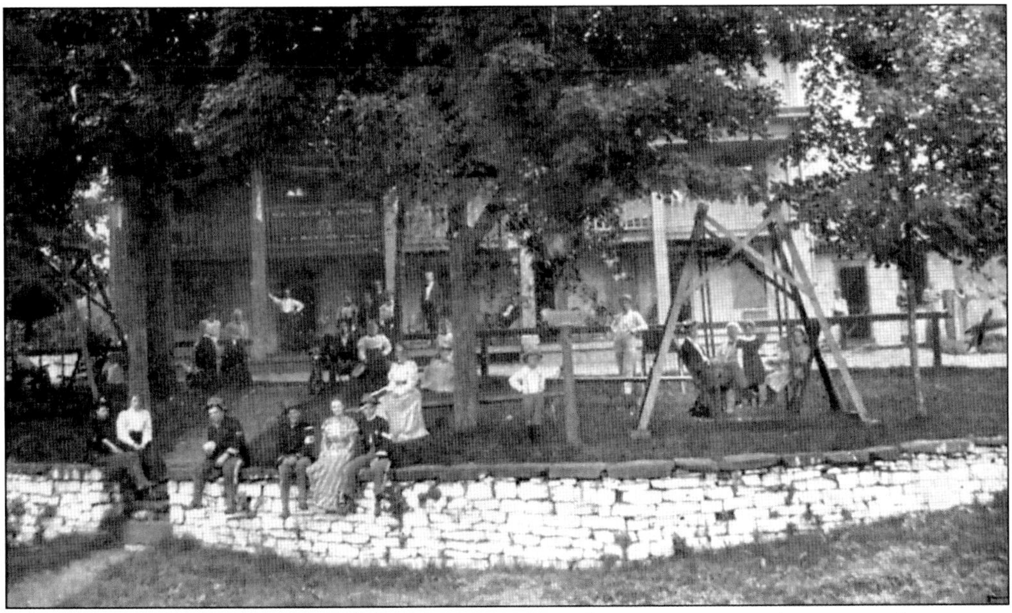

The Point Pleasant Inn, established in 1792, has been a stagecoach stop and vacation boardinghouse and is now F. P. Kolbe Company, offering decorative articles from around the world. Notable guests of the inn have included Pres. William McKinley and Pres. Grover Cleveland and members of the Wanamaker and Astor families. Army enlisted men with Red Cross armbands are sitting on the front wall, possibly dating this photograph to the Spanish-American War of 1898. (DBM.)

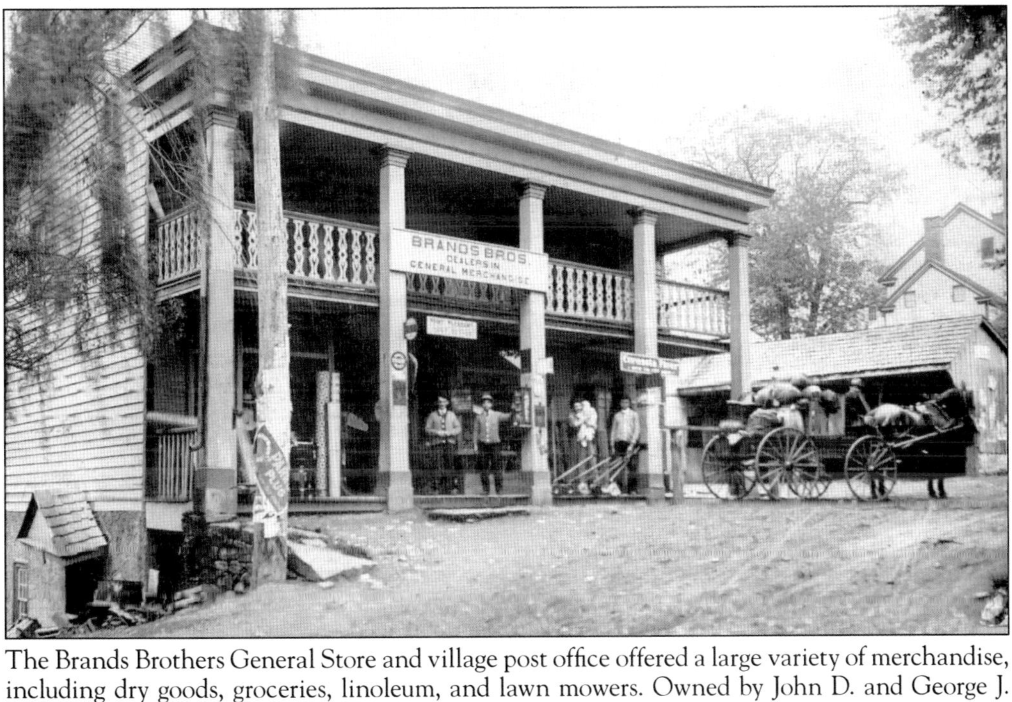

The Brands Brothers General Store and village post office offered a large variety of merchandise, including dry goods, groceries, linoleum, and lawn mowers. Owned by John D. and George J. Brands, it had previously been managed by John D. Walter and Andrew Shaddinger. The store burned and was rebuilt in 1924. Today it serves sandwiches and sells selected groceries. (DBM.)

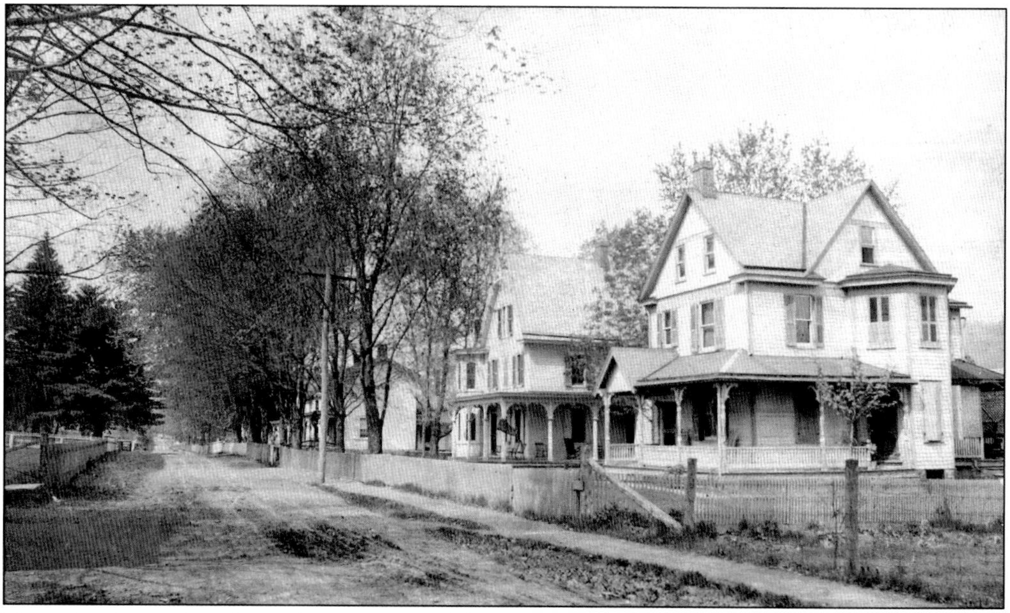

Victorian houses line River Road in Point Pleasant in this 1912 postcard. From left to right are the Point Pleasant Baptist parsonage, the Dr. J. Willis and Mary (Ingram) Walter home, and the Jordan and Ella (Walter) Schiveler home. Although River Road is now paved, this scene, partially obscured by trees, remains the same a century later. (DBM.)

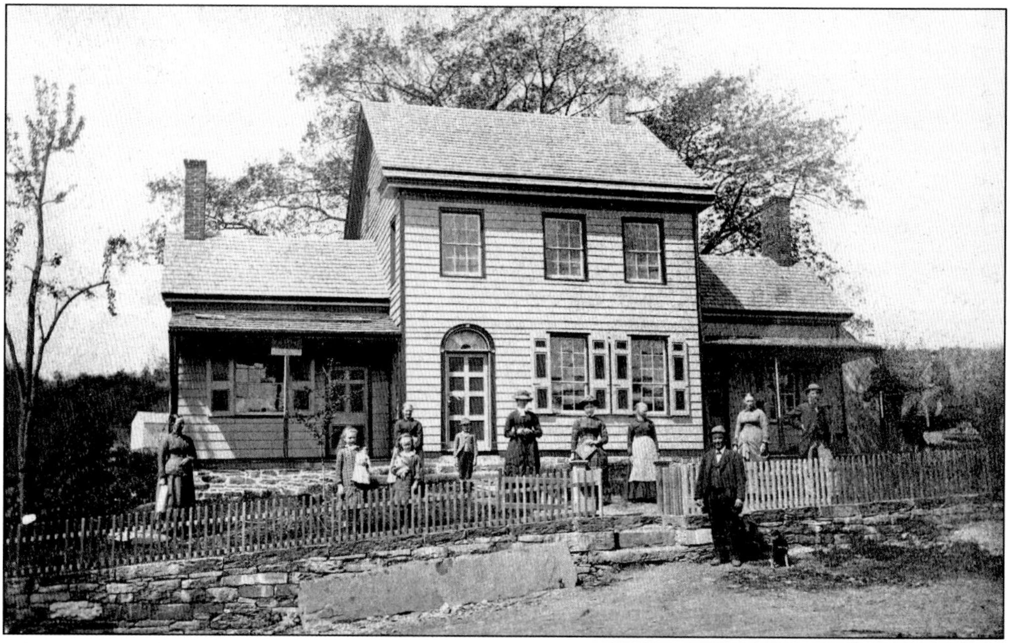

Clockmaker John Nicholas Solliday built this house on Cafferty Road in 1826, with typical nine-over-six paned windows downstairs and six-over-six panes upstairs. The Andrew Schaddinger family poses before their new home in 1880. Pictured are, from left to right, Hannah, Mary, and Adda Schaddinger, three unidentified individuals, Martha, Mary, and Andrew Schaddinger, Susannah (Schaddinger) Walter, John D. Walter, and an unknown horseman. This handsome home survives. (WLT.)

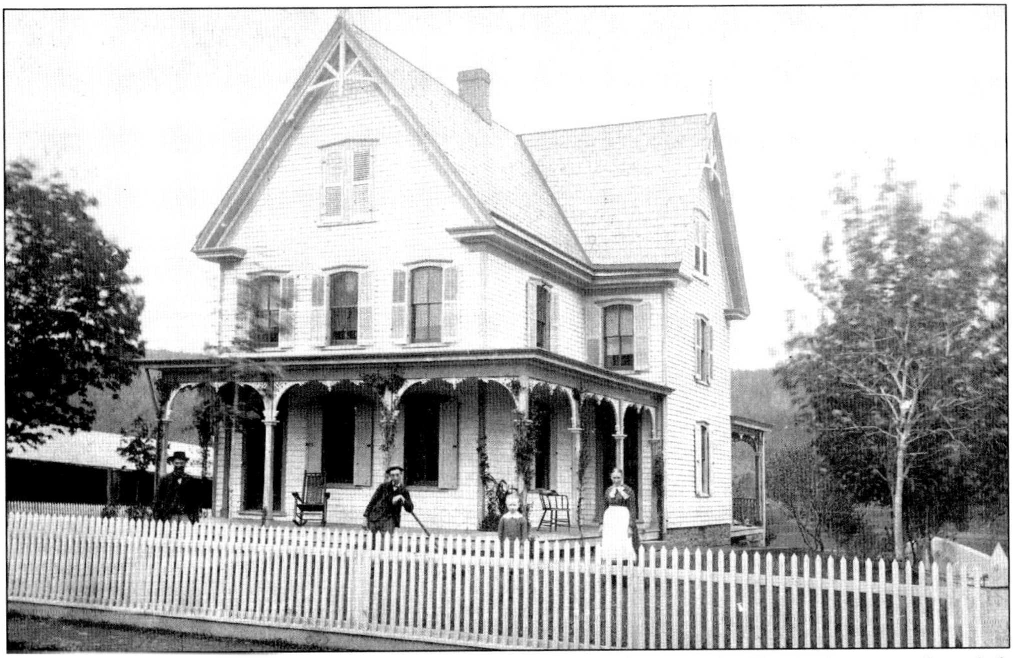

John D. Walter's home on River Road was new in this 1879 photograph. On the lawn are, from left to right, John D. Walter and his son, John Willis Walter, leaning on a lawn mower; his daughter, Ella; and his wife, Susannah. John D. Walter served in the Union army in the Civil War and was imprisoned in Libby Prison. The house is presently occupied by the great-great-grandson of the original owner. (WLT.)

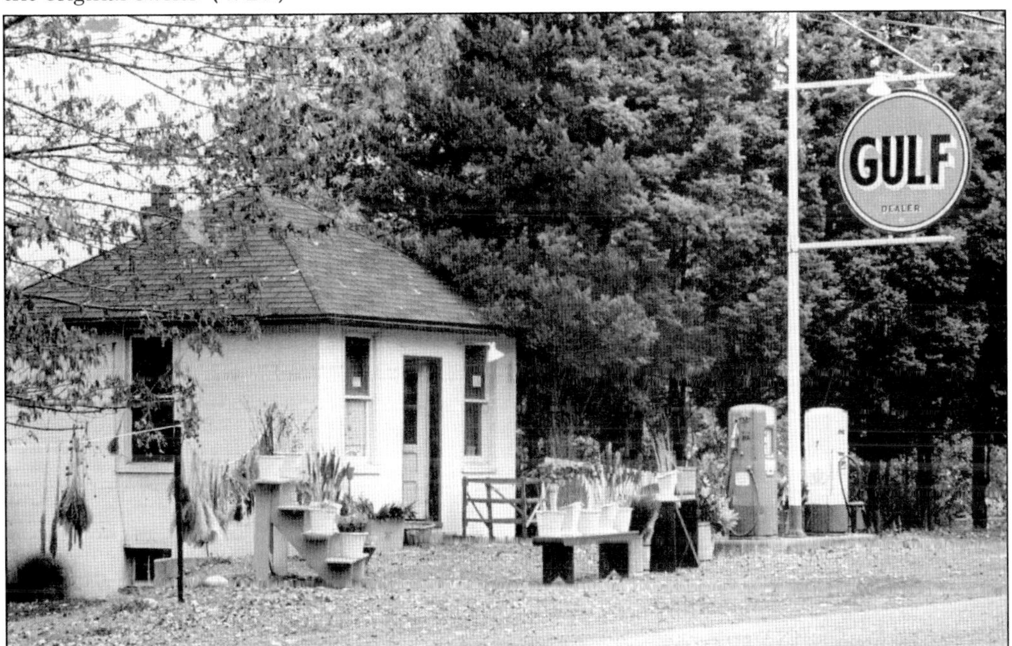

Oscar Wood and Sons operated this small hardware and paint store and Gulf gas station, in addition to its coal, fuel oil, and seed business, on River Road. During the 1940s and 1950s, Paul and Helen Wood sold dried plants, dyed in many colors, for use as decorations. (DBM.)

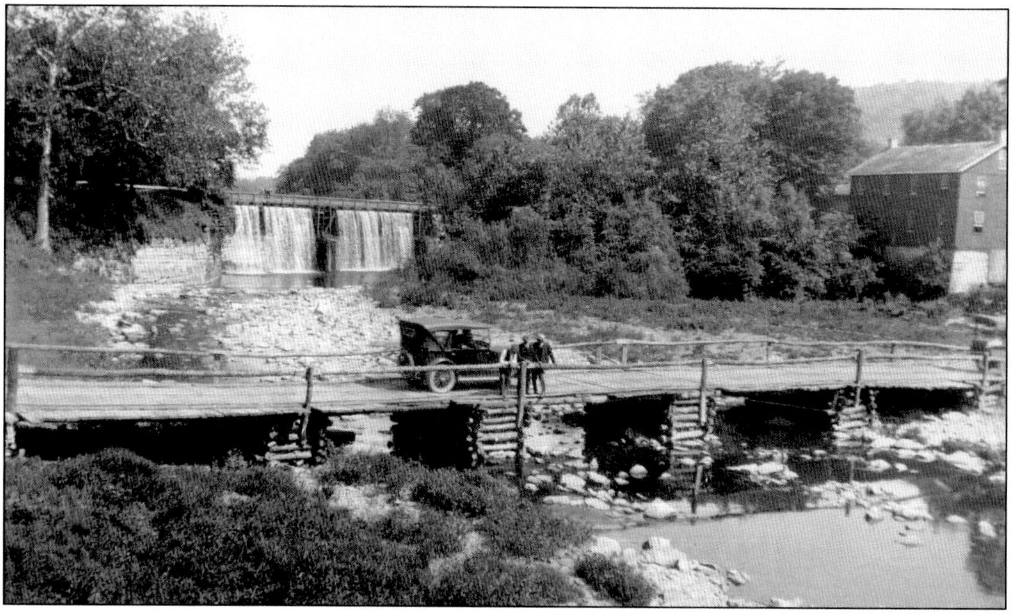

In 1922, while the new concrete bridge was being built over Tohickon Creek to replace the covered bridge, this temporary bridge on log piers was built to accommodate traffic along River Road. The apparent waterfall in the background is the leaking aqueduct that carried the canal over the creek. It leaked throughout its lifetime, creating a scenic frozen fall in winter. It was recently replaced with a historically accurate duplicate. (DBM.)

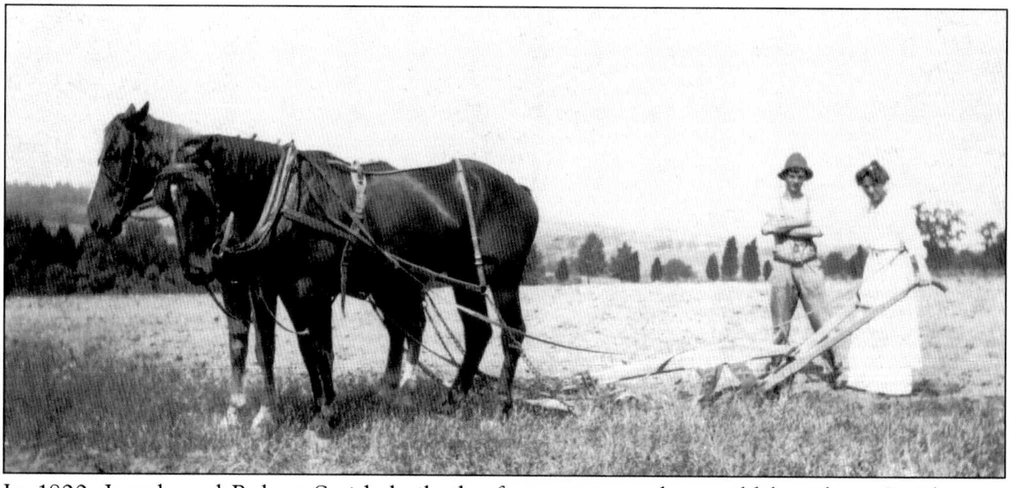

In 1800, Joseph and Robert Smith built the first cast-iron plow mold boards at Smithtown. When Thomas Jefferson ordered "your best plow," they replied, "All our plows are the best." The Smiths, who promoted adding lime to fields and planting clover, also improved the method of burning anthracite coal. Coal could now replace charcoal, the manufacture of which had been decimating forests. Smithtown, demolished during the building of the Delaware Canal, is represented by this 1917 photograph of Jake Wampfler and unidentified partner, who were among the many benefiting from the Smiths' inventions. (LSH.)

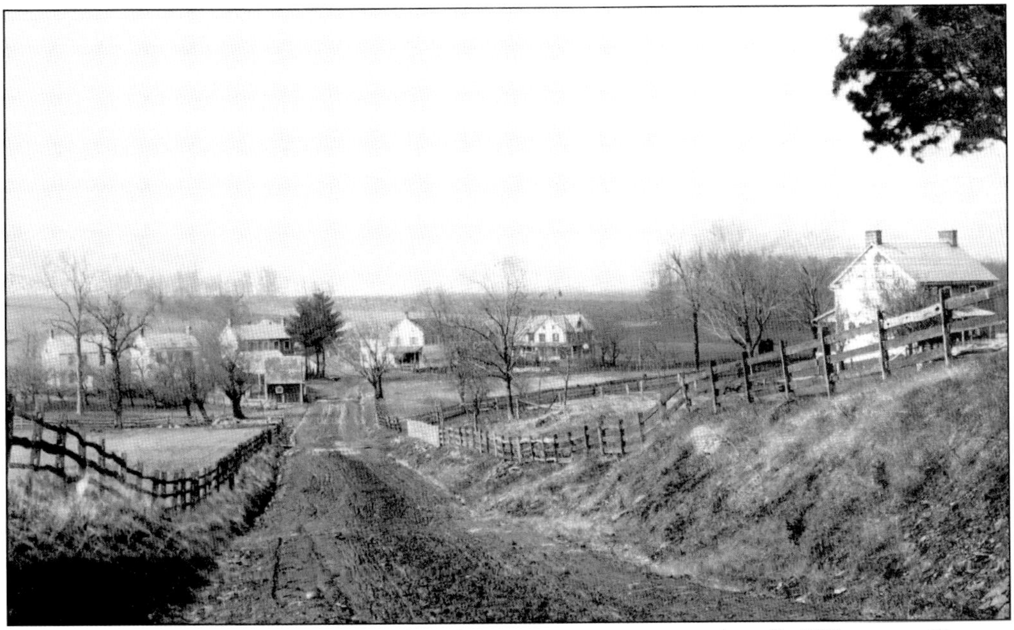

This 1906 panoramic view of the hamlet of Tinicum, more commonly called Wormansville, was taken from Dark Hollow Road, looking west. A century later, it remains virtually unchanged, except for the addition of Lower Tinicum Lutheran Church, now Christ Lutheran Church, which was built on the far right in 1908. The fields in the foreground are still farmed, but the open fields behind the village are now largely wooded. (BNK.)

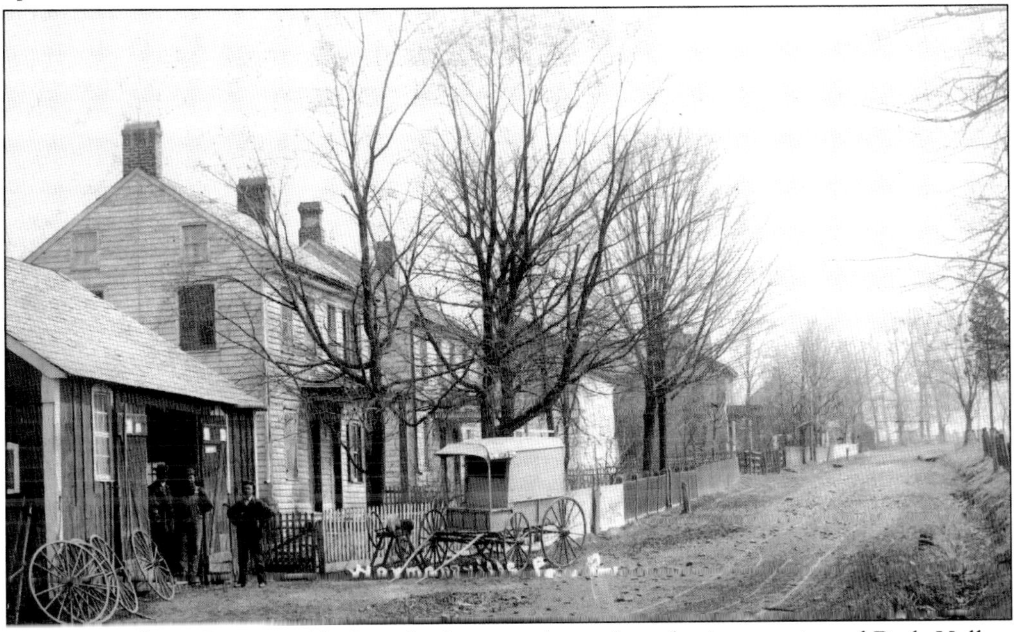

In 1912, William Deemer's blacksmith shop was located at the intersection of Dark Hollow and Smithtown Roads. The wagon in for repairs, or perhaps a friendly visit, belonged to W. H. Hockman, butcher. In this view looking east along Smithtown Road there are hitching posts outside the fence in front of each house. Except for the blacksmith shop, all these buildings survive. (BNK.)

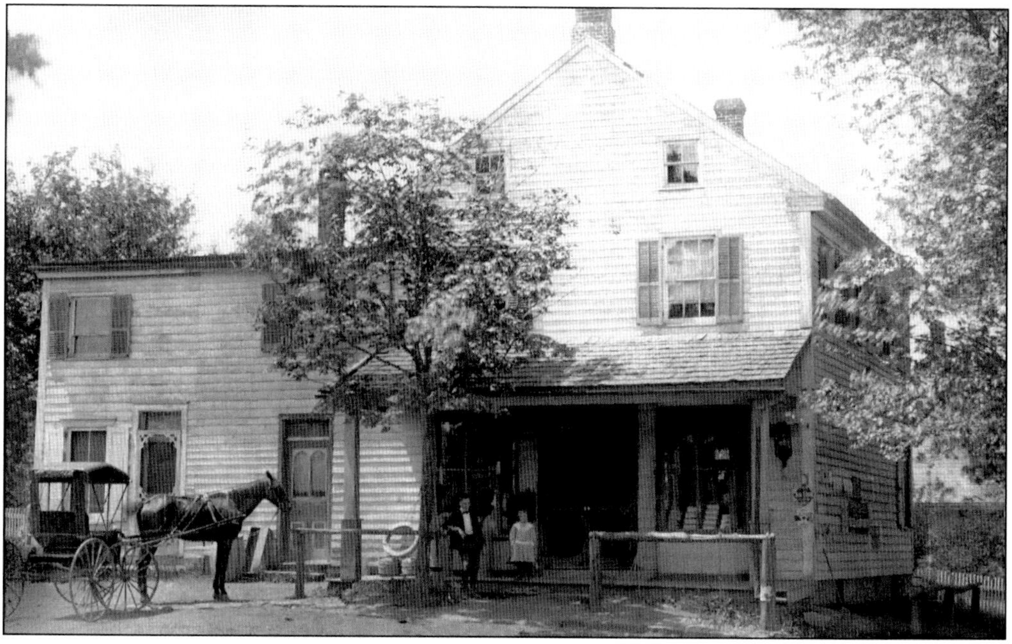

A potbelly stove in the center of the general store was flanked by a pair of benches polished by the pants seats of the elder statesmen of the neighborhood. Shelves reached to the ceiling, filled with everything from yard goods to nails, straw hats, lamps, and kerosene. Roy Haney also sold surplus produce—eggs, lard, and vegetables—from the surrounding farms, which he took in trade. The building is now Dark Hollow Apartments. (BNK.)

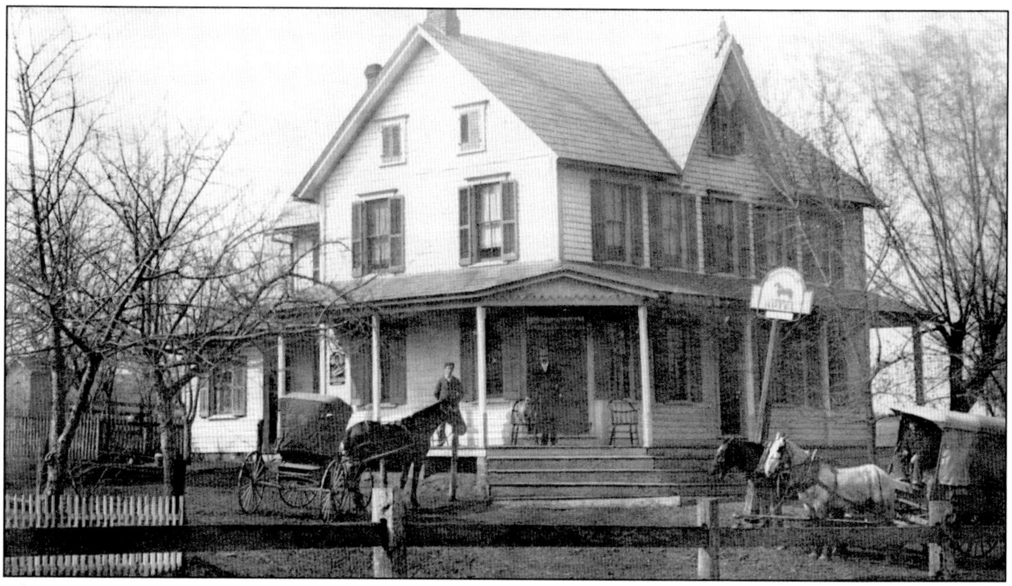

The Wormansville Hotel, seen here in 1914, offered lodging, a bar, and meals for guests. One discouraged hunter sent a postcard home with the brief message "Am well. Game scarce." Reflecting the dual names that persist today, mail sent from the post office in the store was postmarked Tinicum. Located near the corner of Dark Hollow and Iron Bridge Roads, the building has survived as a residence. (LCH.)

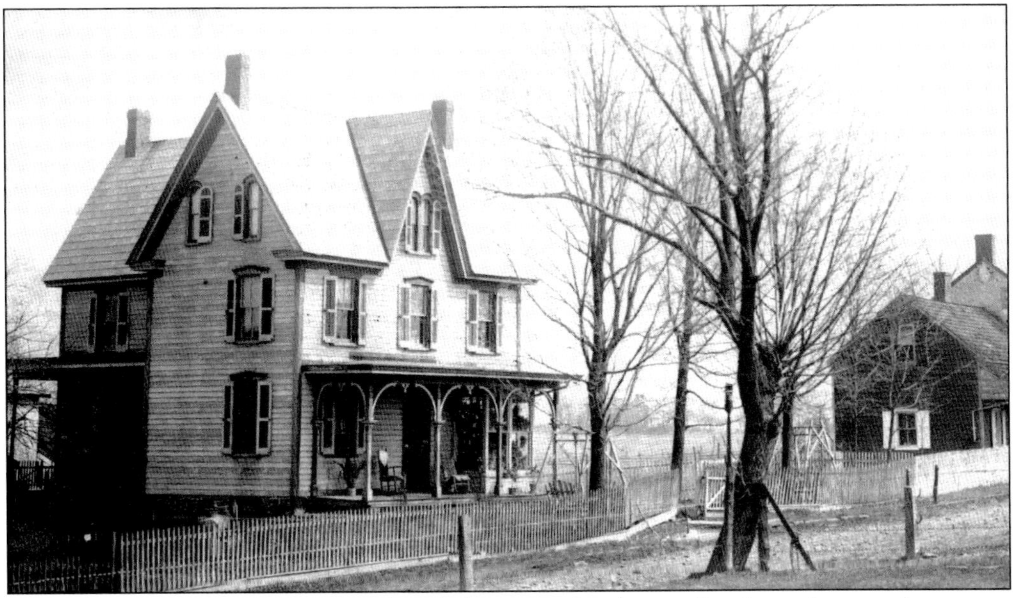

This imposing 1875 Gothic Revival–style home on Smithtown Road stands in stark contrast to the earlier vernacular style of its neighbors. The adjacent home, at the intersection of Wormansville Road, was the home and blacksmith shop of Mahlon Closson in 1814 and was owned by J. Worman in 1876. The plastered stone house has twin front doors (see page 32) and a frame addition. Both homes survive. (DBM.)

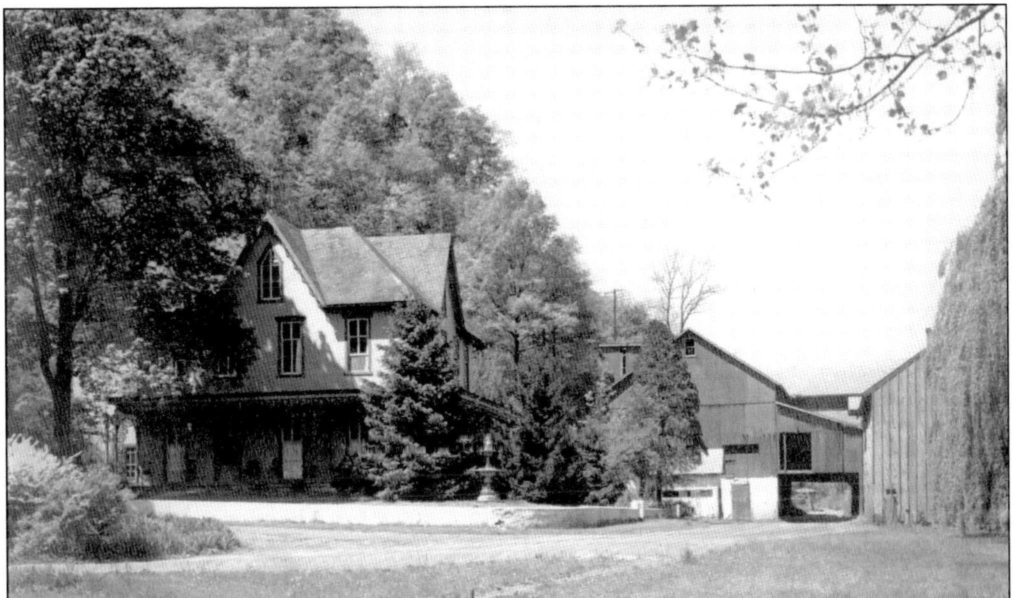

Uhlerstown, a National Register of Historic Places historic district, was the last of Tinicum's villages to be established. Its economy revolved around the Delaware Canal, which was completed in 1832. Michael Uhler built this mansion in 1854 and established a number of business operations, with over 100 employees by 1887. A Catholic church, St. Rose of Lima, served the area from 1873 to 1920. Today Uhlerstown includes 324 acres of permanently protected farms and parkland. (YGR.)

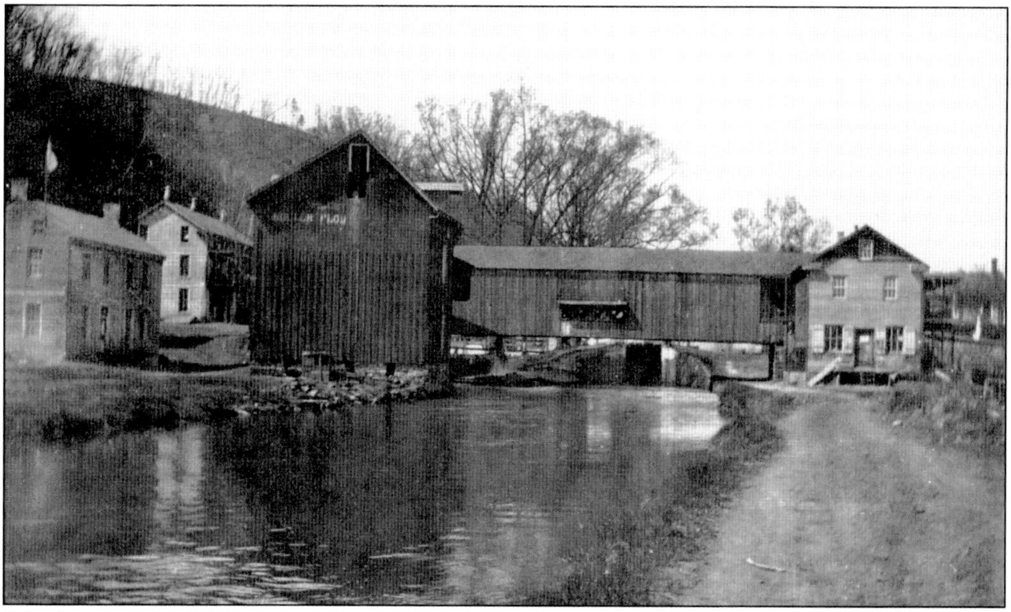

Windows in the Uhlerstown Covered Bridge, built in 1832, give the lock tender a view of approaching boats. The lock is visible behind the bridge. Surrounding buildings are, from left to right, a tenant house, the Uhlerstown Hotel, a mill, a bridge, a harness shop, and the Sigafoos store. In 1900, after Michael Uhler's death, the entire village was sold, including boatyard, coal yard, limekilns, and 14 acres of land. All but the tenant house and mill survive. (LSH.)

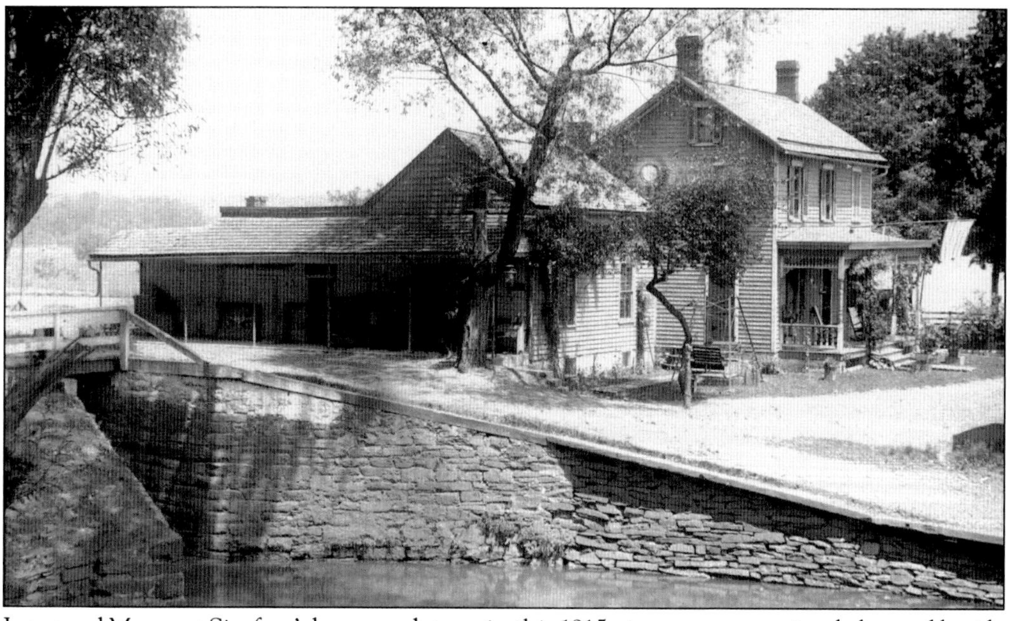

Jonas and Margaret Sigafoos's house and store, in this 1915 view, was conveniently located beside the lock at the covered bridge. Business was brisk as boatmen had to wait their turn while up to 50 barges a day passed through the lock. The store sold everything from tobacco and candy to flour, starch, and molasses by the barrel. The lock, in the left foreground, survives, and the store is now a private residence. (SIG.)

Jonas Sigafoos, who served for 50 years as Uhlerstown's postmaster, carries mailbags past his sleeping dog to his waiting horse and wagon around 1920. With the demise of canal business as the whole country sank into the Depression, people moved elsewhere in search of work, and business at the store dwindled. The post office was closed in 1935, by which time Sigafoos was 91 years of age. (SBL.)

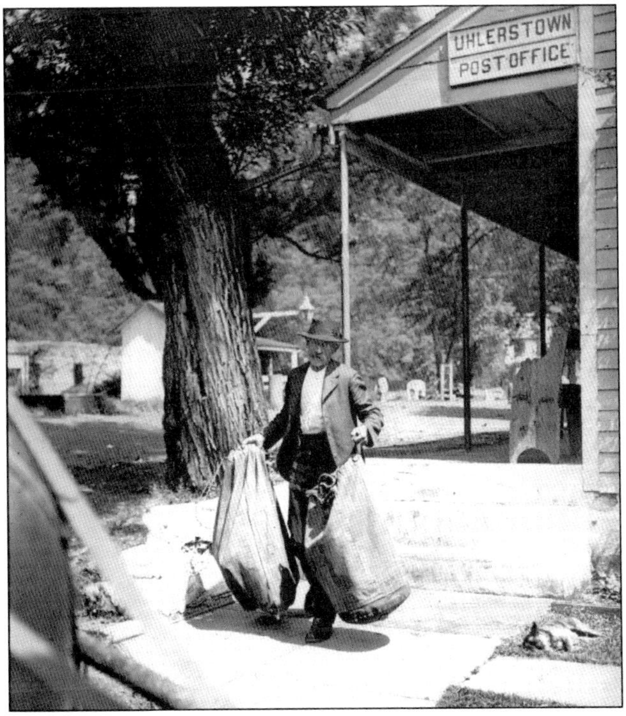

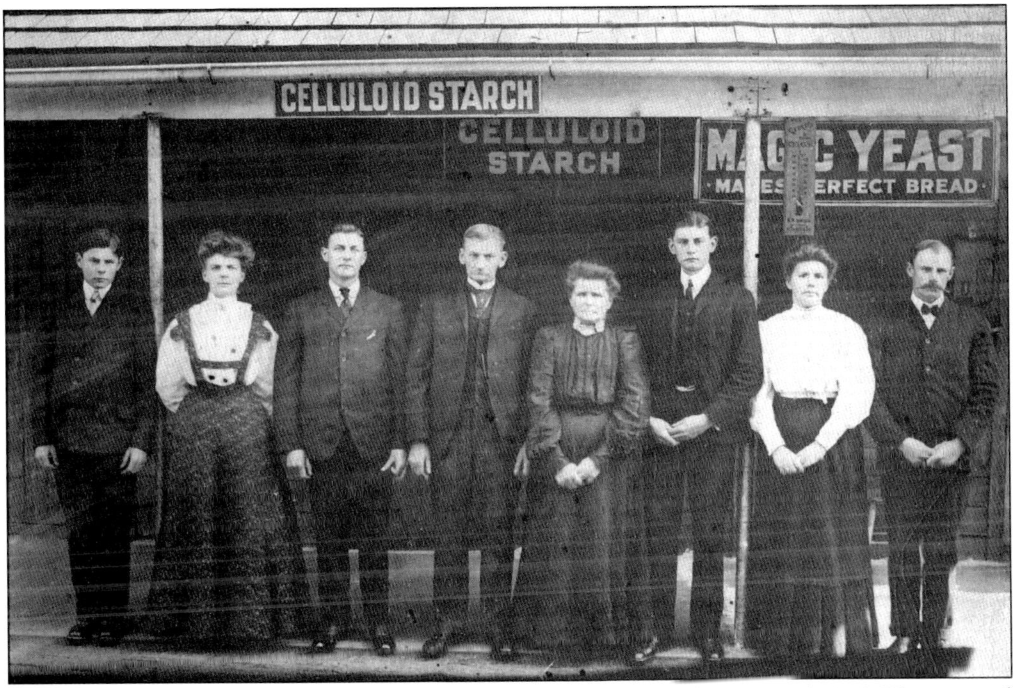

The Sigafoos family stands on the porch of their store and post office, around 1900. The original German spelling of their name was Ziegenfuss. From left to right are children Harry, Bessie, and Bert; parents Jonas and Margaret (Ruth) Sigafoos; and children William, Jennie, and Frank. Magic Yeast and Celluloid Starch were among the essential items for running a household. Margaret was the niece of Michael Uhler. (SIG.)

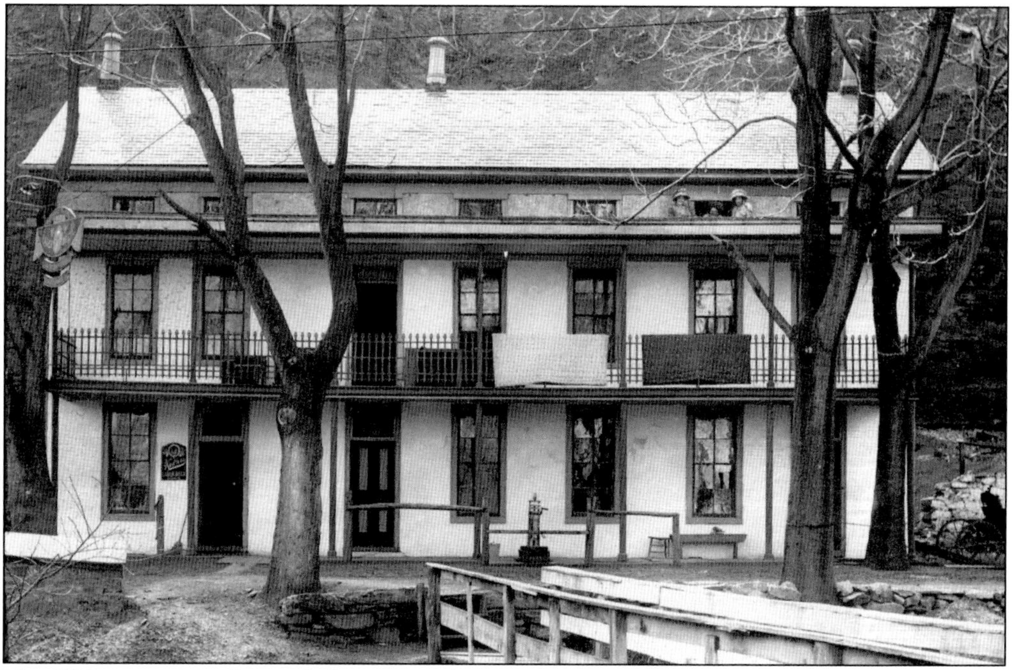

The Uhlerstown Hotel provided accommodations, meals, and drinks in 1912. While bedding airs on the railing outside the second-floor rooms, three attractively dressed ladies appear at the far right third-floor eyebrow window to greet the photographer. When the Gilt Edged Circus used Uhlerstown as winter quarters around 1886, animals, including elephants, boarded in area barns, while clowns, acrobats, and other circus folk kept fellow hotel boarders entertained. (SIG.)

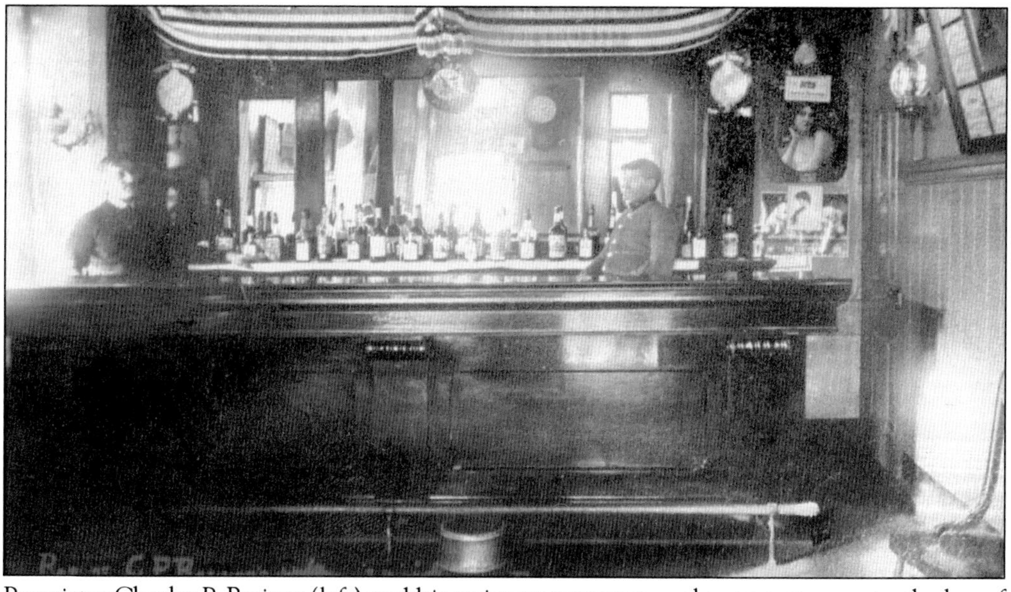

Proprietor Charles P. Breiner (left) and his assistant prepare to welcome customers to the bar of the Uhlerstown Hotel. Bunting over the bar stresses a patriotic theme, and a spittoon is centrally located on the floor. Kerosene lamps near the window and on the wall provide nighttime lighting, and entertaining posters of Gibson girls appear to be designed for the male customer of 1906. (YGR.)

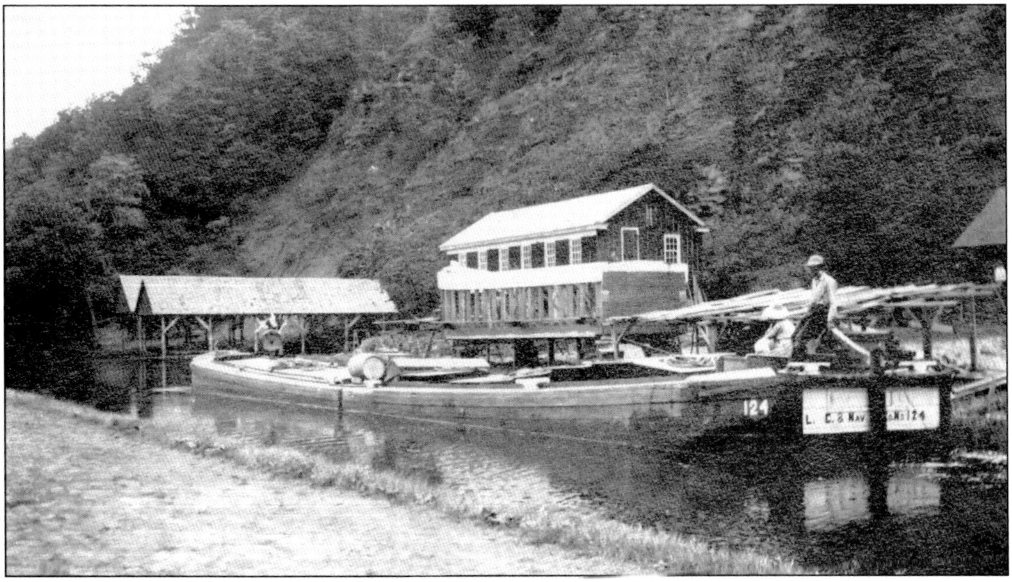

Uhler's boatyard, south of the village, produced several boats a year. Lumber drying on racks and the frame of a boat under construction appear behind the passing canal boat with operator at the tiller in this 1912 scene. Uhler also operated a fleet of canal boats known as the Michael Uhler Line. Nothing of this once-thriving operation has survived. (WMS.)

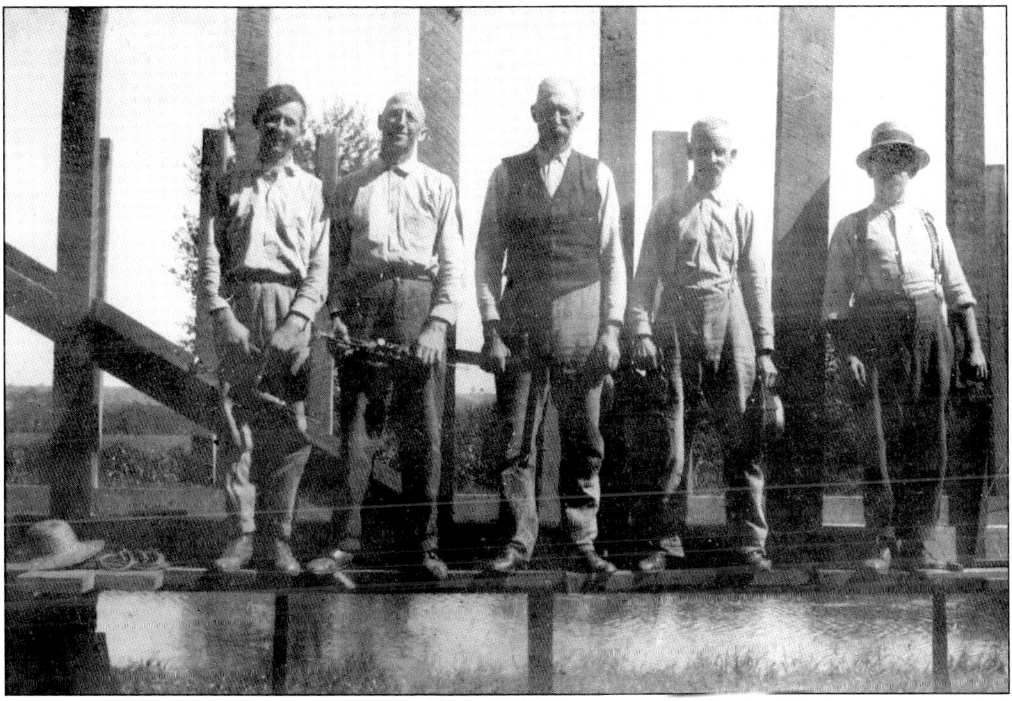

A boatbuilding crew stands before the ribs of its current project around 1920. Pictured from left to right are Grant Weaver, Samuel "Daddy" Reigle, foreman Luther Tettemer, John D. Weaver, and an unidentified worker. During the 1914 production of the silent film series *The Perils of Pauline*, these workers were hired to build flower boxes and other props for the scenes that were filmed in the Uhlerstown area. (WMS.)

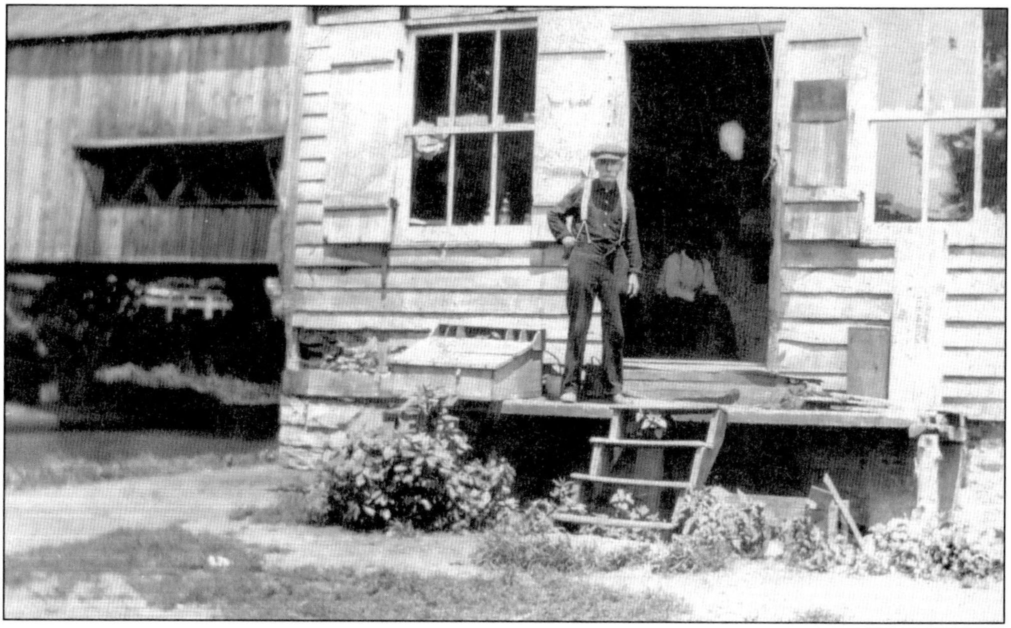

In the early 1900s, Billy Wells kept a shop in this shed attached to the house beside the covered bridge, which appears on the left. Wells made harnesses for the canal mule teams and was also a shoemaker. On the porch at his side is a portable desk, without legs, complete with cubbyholes and lift-top writing surface for recording his business transactions. The house continues to serve as a residence. (SIG.)

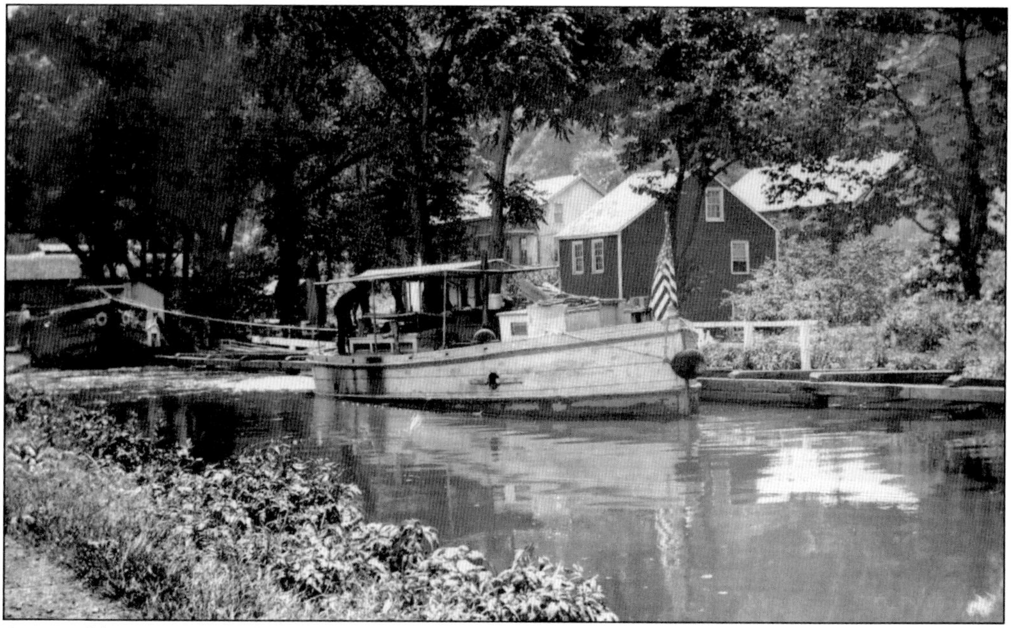

As canal business waned, the Lehigh Coal and Navigation Company searched for more efficient methods of towing barges. An experimental coal-powered tug pulls canal barges through the locks at Uhlerstown around 1912. Although these boats pulled five or six barges at a time, getting so many boats through the locks slowed the operation. In the background, from left to right, are the covered bridge, hotel, and lock keeper's shed. (SIG.)

Four

Religion, Education, and Fire Prevention

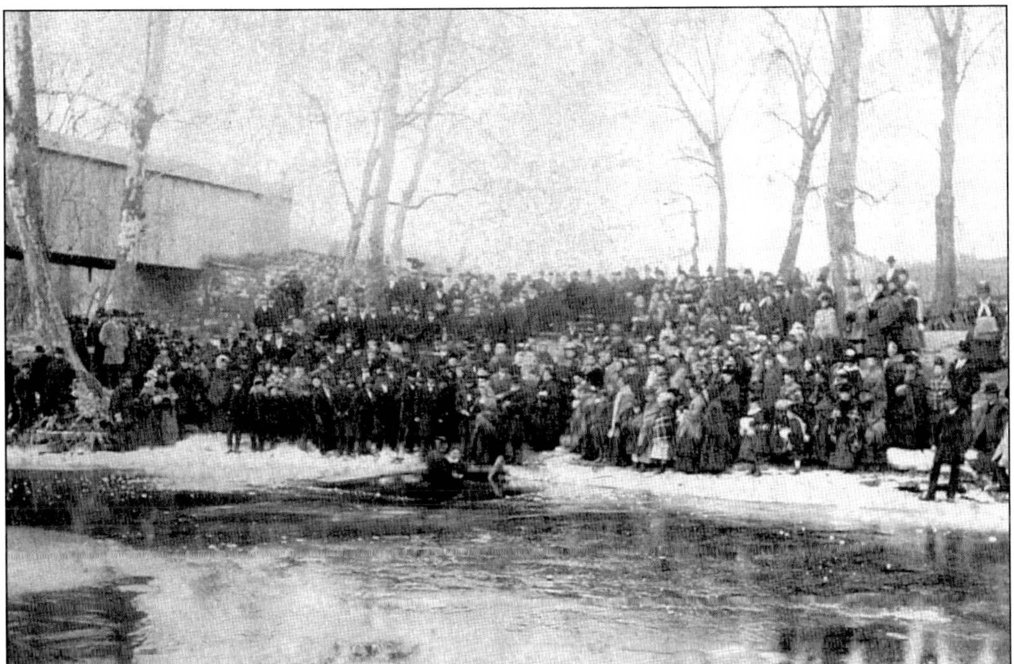

Members of the Point Pleasant Baptist Church were baptized in the Delaware River, regardless of the season. In February 1874, this large crowd gathers on the icy bank to witness a baptism. The Point Pleasant Covered Bridge appears in the background, and a skim of ice is visible in the foreground. (CPR.)

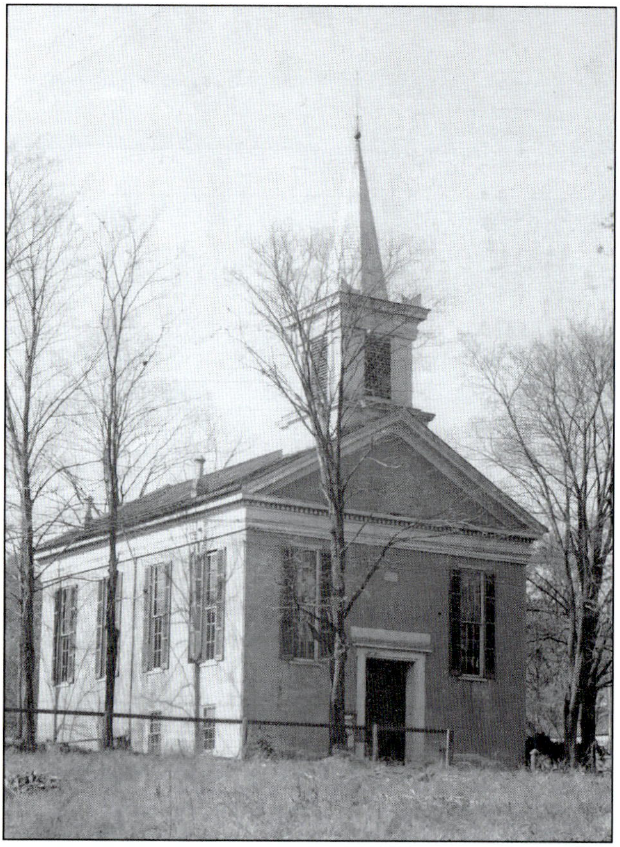

Ralph Stover donated the land for the church, and for the cemetery farther north along Cafferty Road. The congregation met in the adjacent Point Pleasant School, pictured on page 78, until it moved into the new church, pictured here, in 1853. (WLT.)

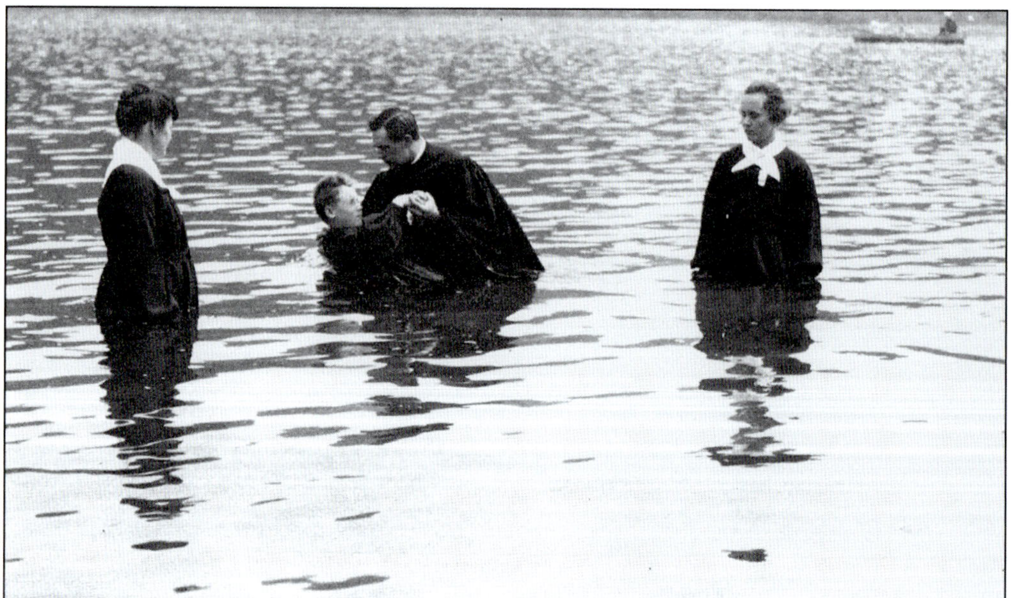

Boaters on the river witnessed this baptismal ceremony in more favorable weather, in August 1919. From left to right are Mary (Ingram) Walter, John Willis Walter Jr. being baptized by the Reverend Howard L. Zepp, and Helen Walter. (WLT.)

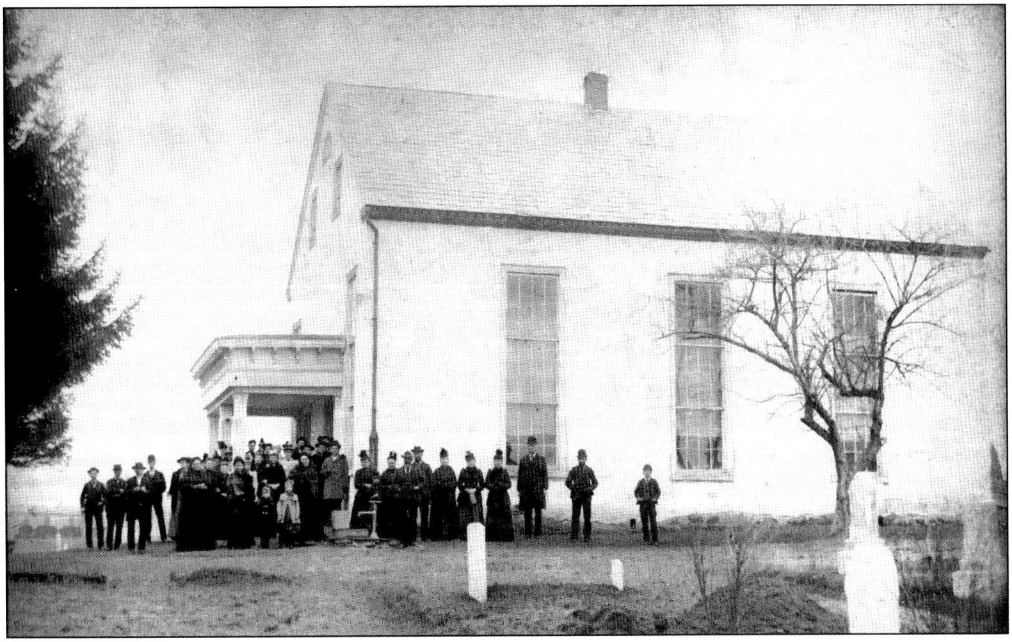

The Upper Tinicum Lutheran Church, located on the hill above Uhlerstown, near the intersection of Jugtown Hill and Upper Tinicum Church Roads, is pictured around 1890, before the church burned. It was rebuilt with several changes to the entryway and belfry designs. Church records include a suggestion that wasps be eliminated from the building during summer services. (HLB.)

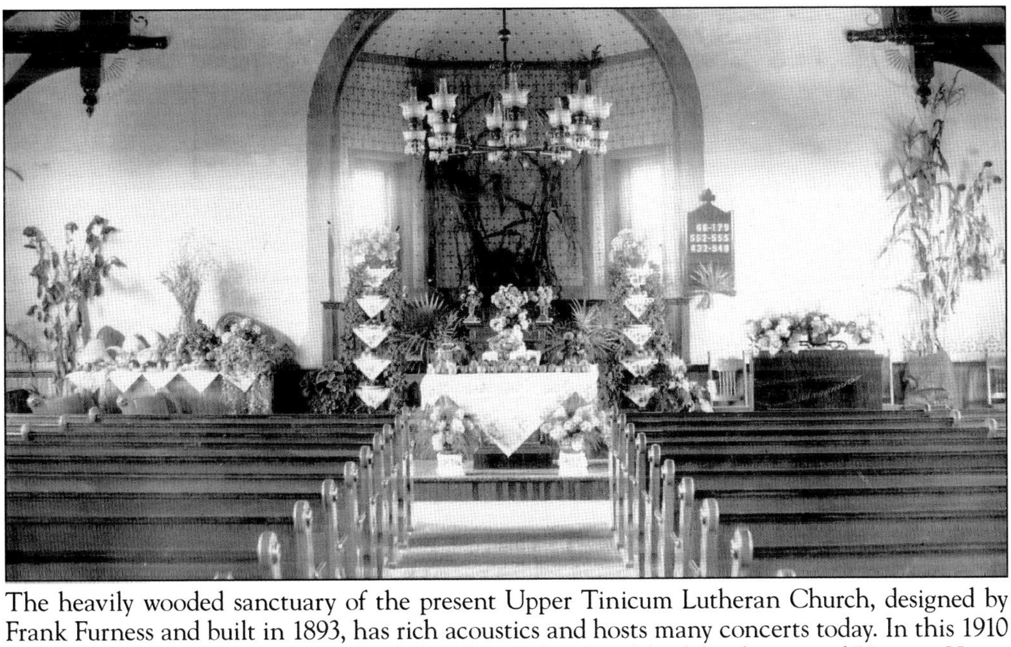

The heavily wooded sanctuary of the present Upper Tinicum Lutheran Church, designed by Frank Furness and built in 1893, has rich acoustics and hosts many concerts today. In this 1910 photograph, members have decorated the altar with gifts of food for the annual Harvest Home celebration, which included several days of services of thanksgiving for the bounteous harvest. The edible decorations were later donated to the pastor or to needy persons. (FRY.)

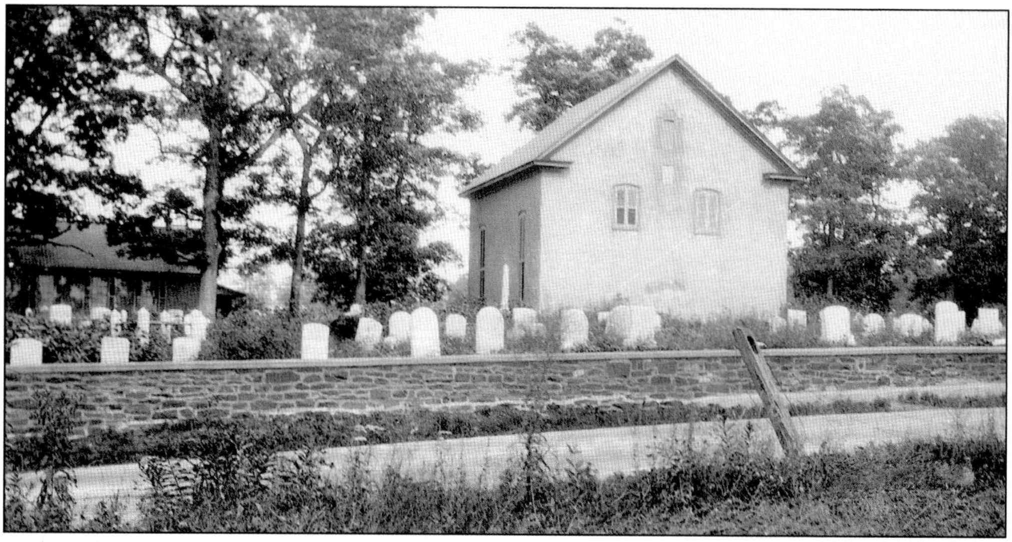

Red Hill Church, viewed from Durham Road in 1928, was built in 1761 by Scotch-Irish Presbyterians, whose original 1735 building had been located east of Ottsville. They later shared it with Lutherans, with sermons in German and English. Abandoned, then restored several times, today it serves the community as St. Luke's United Church of Christ. A small congregation of the Pillar of Fire Church also met near Ottsville in the 1930s. (OVP.)

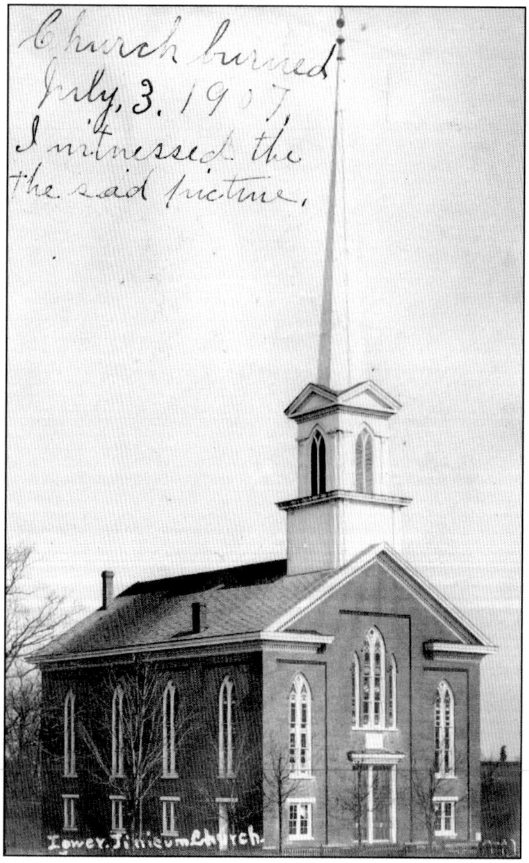

This church near Wormansville, known for many years as Brick Church, has a long history of serving Presbyterian, Lutheran, and German Reformed congregations, with two concurrent ministers at times, preaching sermons in German and English. As early as 1759, a log church was replaced by larger brick buildings over the years, with an 1876 building topped by the 160-foot steeple in this photograph. (RPK.)

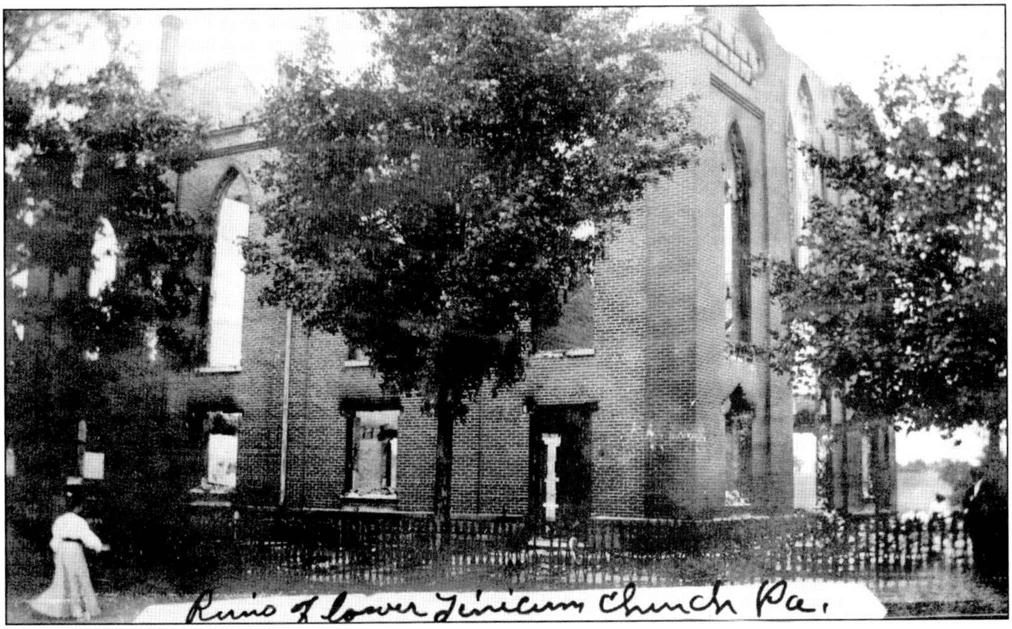

"Church burned July 3, 1907. I witnessed the sad picture," is the message scrawled on the previous photograph, sent to a friend before this, or any other pictures of the lightning-caused tragedy, was available. The Lutherans then decided to build a separate church, leaving the Reformed congregation to rebuild the present Brick Church. (RPK.)

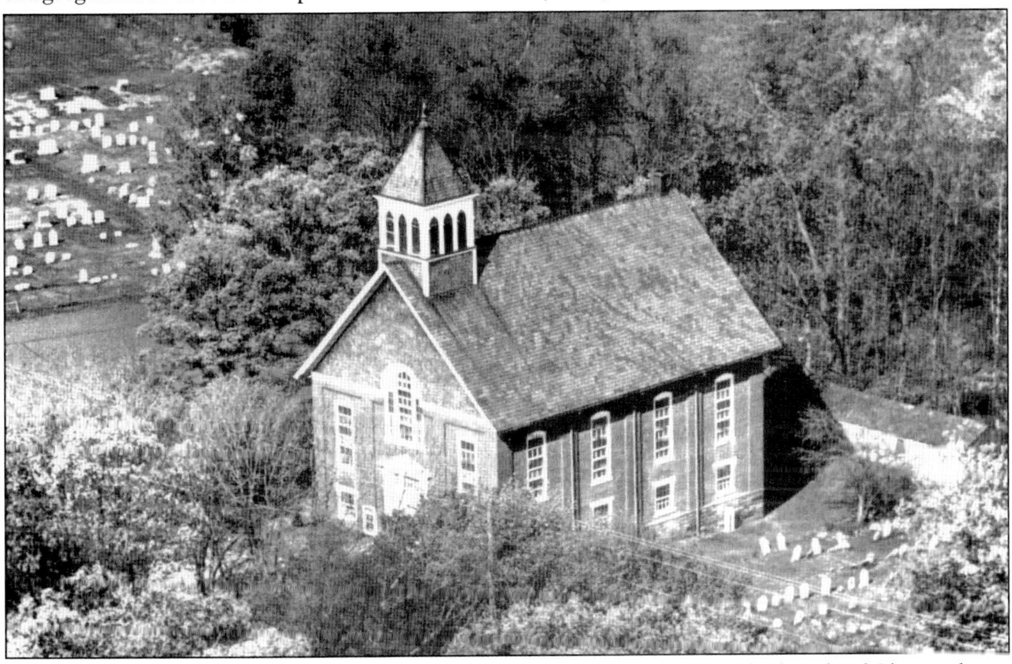

This 1984 aerial view of the rebuilt Brick Church, now Tinicum United Church of Christ, shows the surrounding cemeteries, in which many of the tombstones bear German inscriptions. The sanctuary is beautified by stained-glass windows in the memory of George Shull, benefactor and descendant of a long line of Shulls in Tinicum. The carriage sheds visible behind the church are now gone, and a parking lot for automobiles is beside the church. (EWH.)

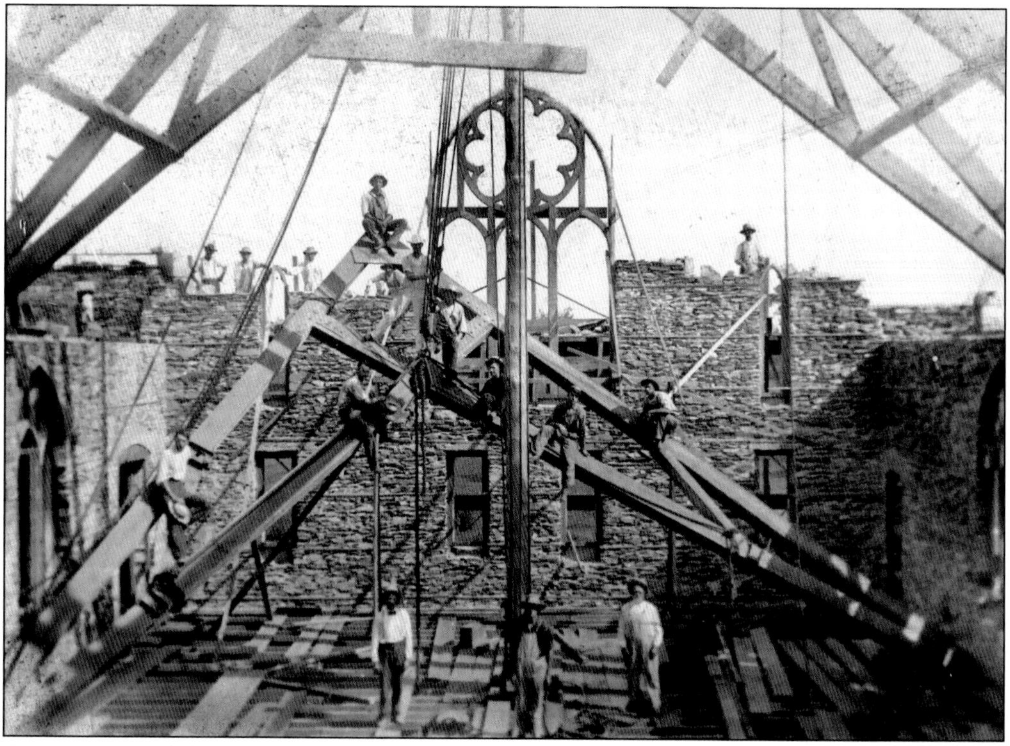

Construction of the new Lower Tinicum Lutheran Church was completed in a single year by Frankenfield Builders. From left to right in the foreground are George Frankenfield, wearing a bow tie; John Urban, right of the center beam; and Henry Frankenfield, who had been the contractor for the Upper Tinicum Lutheran Church and was called from retirement to supervise this project. (LTC.)

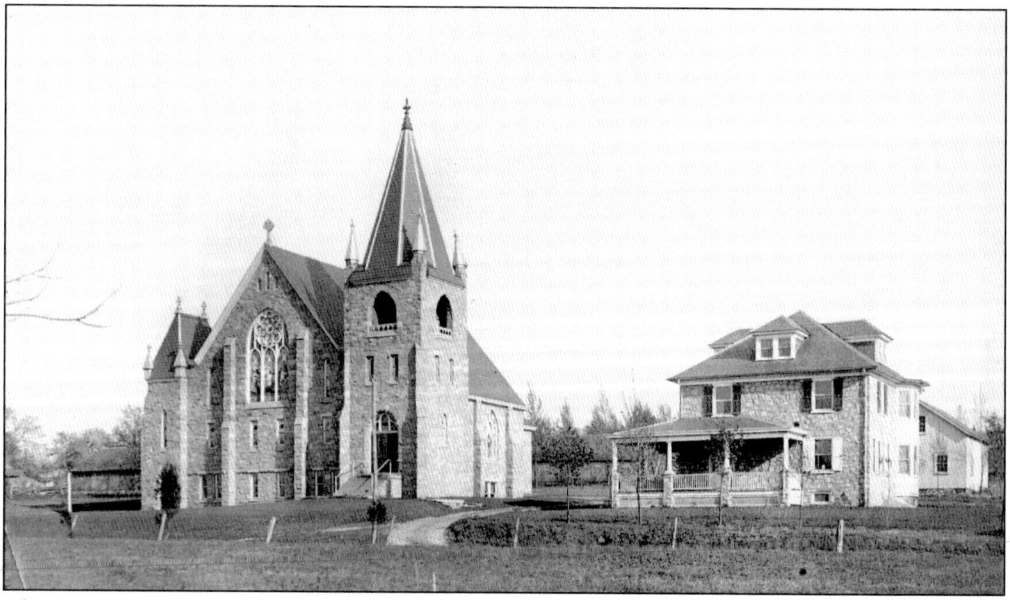

The new building, now officially Christ Evangelical Lutheran Church, in the village of Wormansville, was completed in 1908, and the parsonage was added in 1917. (LTC.)

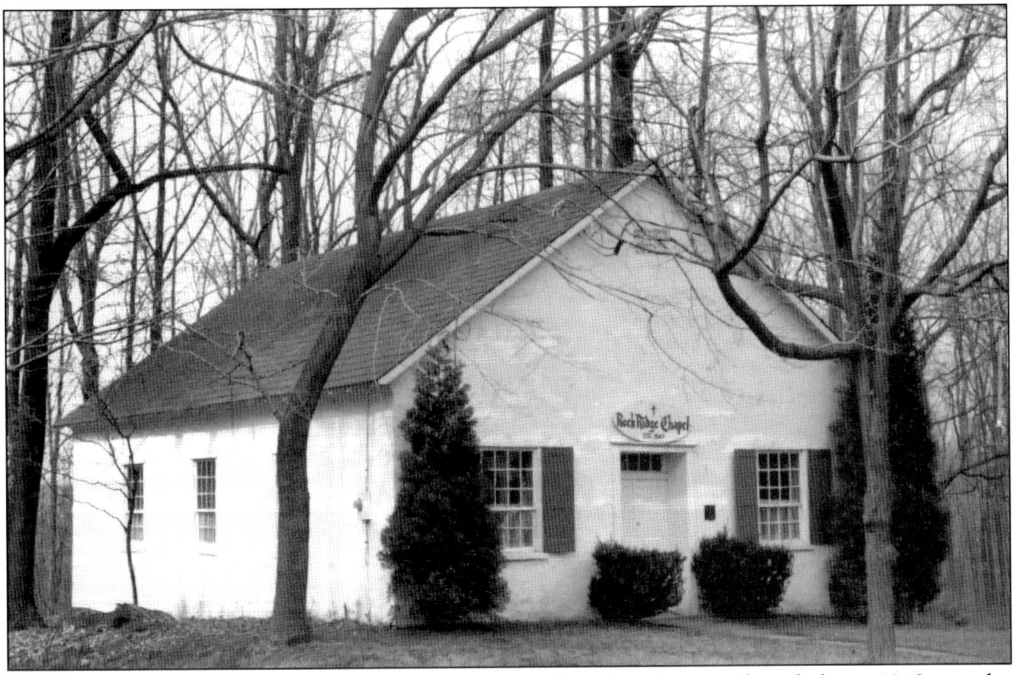

Rock Ridge Chapel, originally called Rope Walk Chapel, was founded in 1843 as the nondenominational canal men's chapel at the crest of Geigel Hill. From here a mile-long path, following most of present-day Rope Walk Road, was followed as canal men twisted strands of flax, produced by Isaac Stover's flax mill near the Erwinna covered bridge, to make the strong, inch-thick rope needed to haul the canal boats. (TTP.)

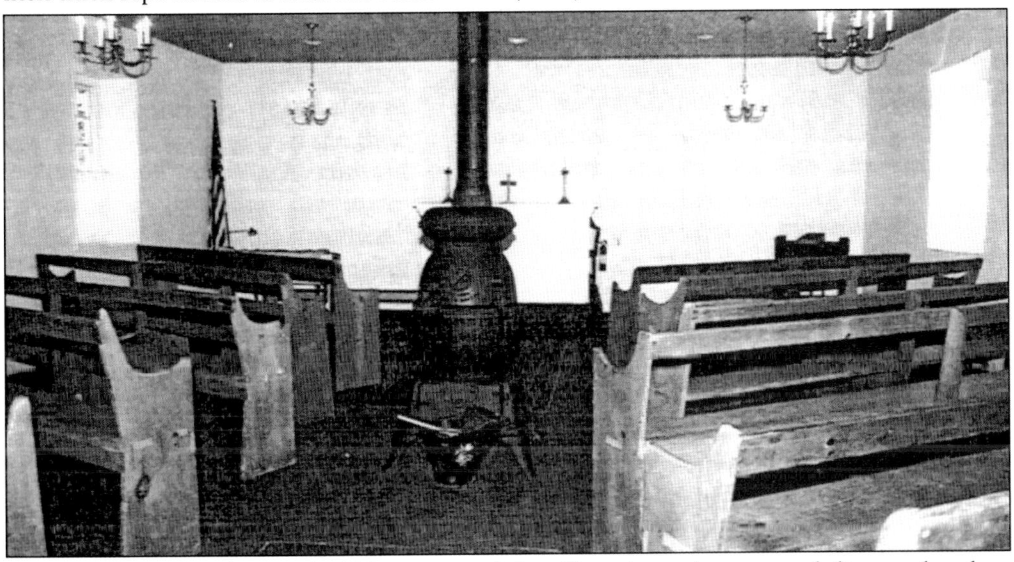

Attendance declined around 1925 as automobiles allowed people to attend distant churches. After the Tinicum Civic Association paid the back taxes in 1972, Victor and Eleanor Meierdierck, Bill and Anna Bickel, John Quinby, Carl Damm, and others donated labor and materials to restore the building for a Thanksgiving Eve service. Since then the chapel has held regular Thanksgiving Eve, Christmas Eve, and Easter sunrise services, as well as weddings, christenings, and memorial services. (KAB.)

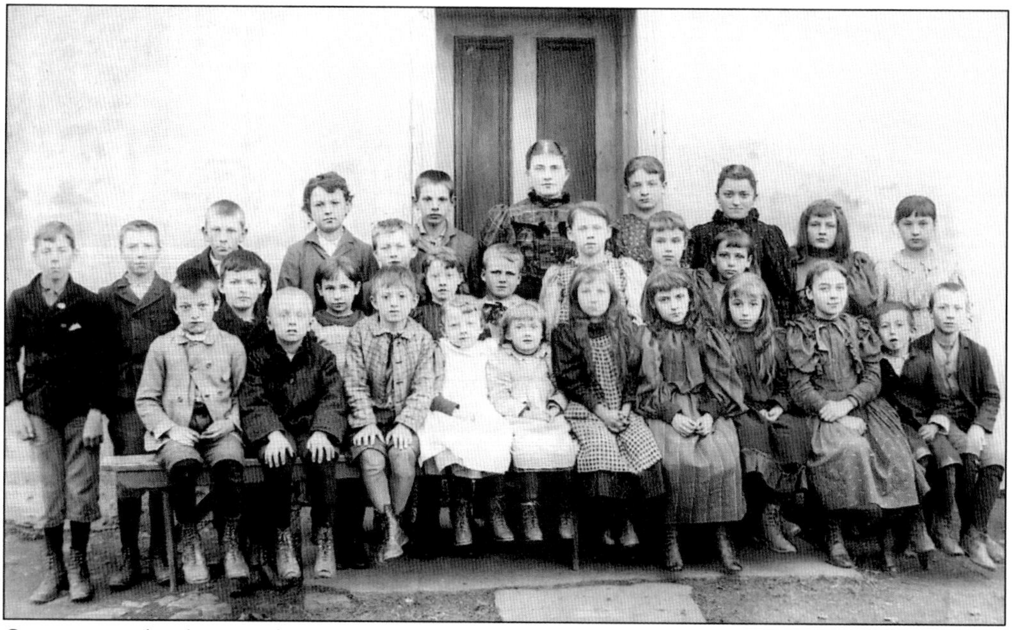

One-room schools served Tinicum from 1844 until 1958, providing a sound educational foundation that led some to future high academic and business successes. The annual school pictures from 1895 to 1943 show an interesting progression in clothing styles. In 1895, Minnie Allem's Red Hill School students wore high-top shoes and black stockings, with short pants on the boys, pinafores on the younger girls, and long skirts on the older girls. (LSG.)

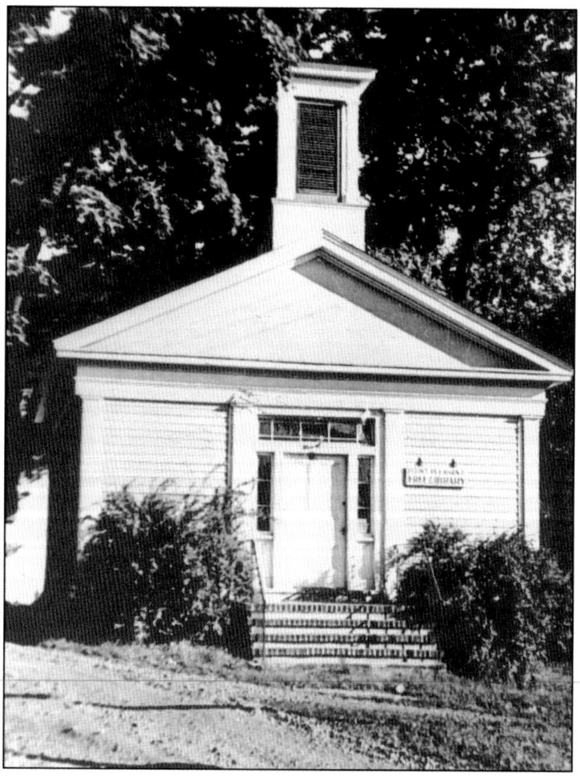

Point Pleasant School, at the intersection of Cafferty and River Roads, was decidedly more formal in style than the rest of Tinicum's one-room schools. Most were of simple one-story design like Clay Ridge School on page 10, while Erwinna and Uhlerstown, on page 83, were two-story buildings. Teacher Harriet Fabian recalled teaching resourcefulness, reasoning, respect, and responsibility in addition to the traditional three Rs: reading, writing, and arithmetic. (DBM.)

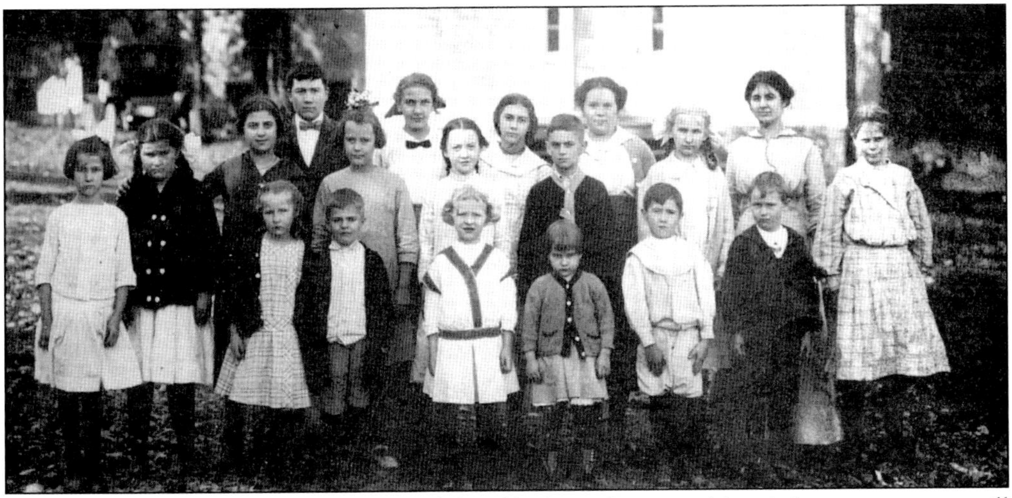

By 1913, girls' pinafores had disappeared, but black stockings and boys' short pants were still in vogue. Pictured in front of Point Pleasant School are, from left to right, (first row) ? Fulmer, Joseph Musselman, ? Black, Elsie Lerch, Clinton Lerch, and John Walter; (second row) Edna Lerch, Mildred Lerch, Priscilla Hicks, Helen Walter, Clara Lamborne, Lewis Musselman, Helen Lerch, and Emma Holtz; (third row) Weston Lamborne, Gertrude Utter, Ellen Musselman, Nellie Lamborne, and teacher Mary Fox. (DBM.)

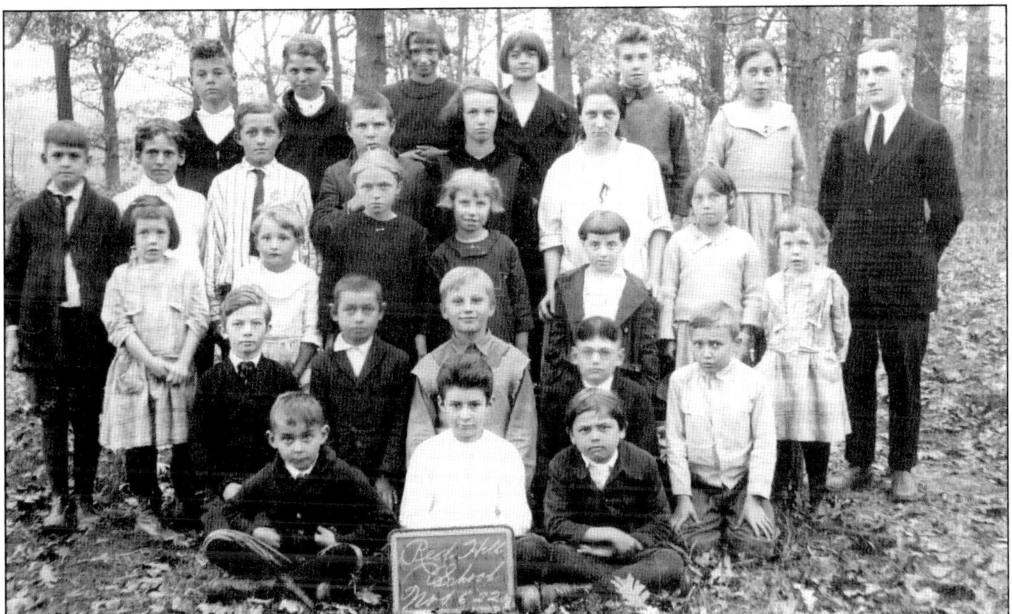

Earl Yost's 1922 Red Hill School students, still in black stockings, are, from left to right, (first row) Frances Hager, Arthur Hager, and Eddie Gerloski; (second row) Claude Mood, Steve Weinbel, Eddie Liss, Ralph Steeley, and Clarence Culp; (third row) Dorothy Mood, Blanche Weirbach, Anna Zuekow, Margaret Wehrung, Madeleine Weinbel, Florence Mathias, and Florence Mood; (fourth row) Floyd Szczepanski, Henry Weitzmann, Jake Schmidt, Marvin Sheetz, Eleanor Wittig, and Viola Steeley; (fifth row) Wayne Frankenfield, Tony Wentz, Florence Weitzmann, Aileen Hulsizer, Woody Wehrung, and Josephine Weinbel. (BWG.) The school building survives, beside the Red Hill Church.

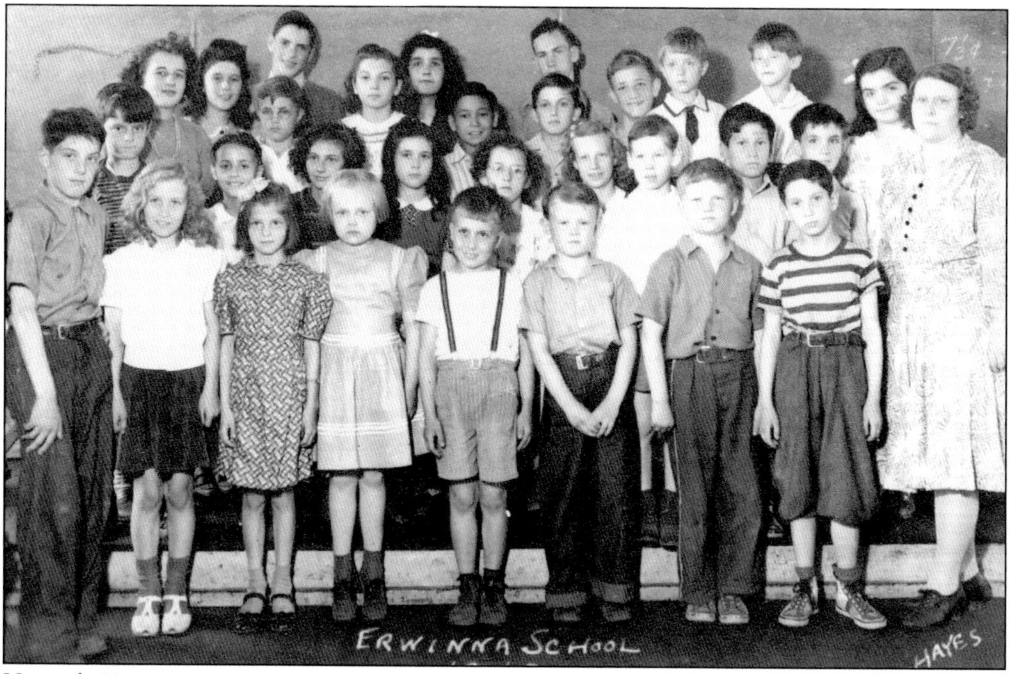

Hannah Hampton's 1943 Erwinna students, without black stockings, are, from left to right, (first row) Allan Goulding, Dottie Ridge, Virginia Bryan, Joyce Cochran, Frank Swope, Bob Bartleman, Roy Vanselous, and Larry Goulding; (second row) Calvin Bryan, Betty Schaible, Paul McIntyre, Beatrice Conrad, Jane Frankenfield, Jean Dillon, Betty Ridge, James Ridge, Larry Rillera, Chester Frankenfield, and Doris Burgstresser; (third row) Marion Hager, Esther Frankenfield, Walter (?) Goulding, Mary Herstine, Evelyn (?) Case, Charles Rillera, Stanley Herstine, Gene Ridge, Kenneth McIntyre, Ronald Geiser, and David Bryan. (GLD.)

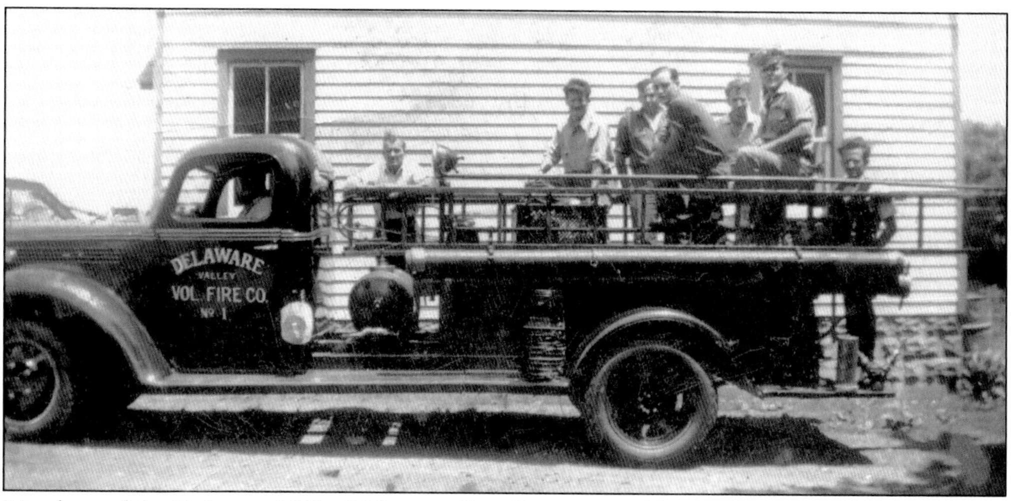

Members of the Delaware Valley Volunteer Fire Company in Erwinna are atop their fire engine in this 1939 photograph. They are, from left to right, driver C. Arthur Ridge, Frank Sispera, Charley Miller, Roy Cochran, Bill Fingledie, unidentified, Ed Sigafoos, and Ernest Schultz. The Ottsville Volunteer Fire Company was organized in 1940. Tinicum is also served by fire companies in Point Pleasant and Upper Black Eddy. (RLY.)

Five

Weather and Transportation over the Years

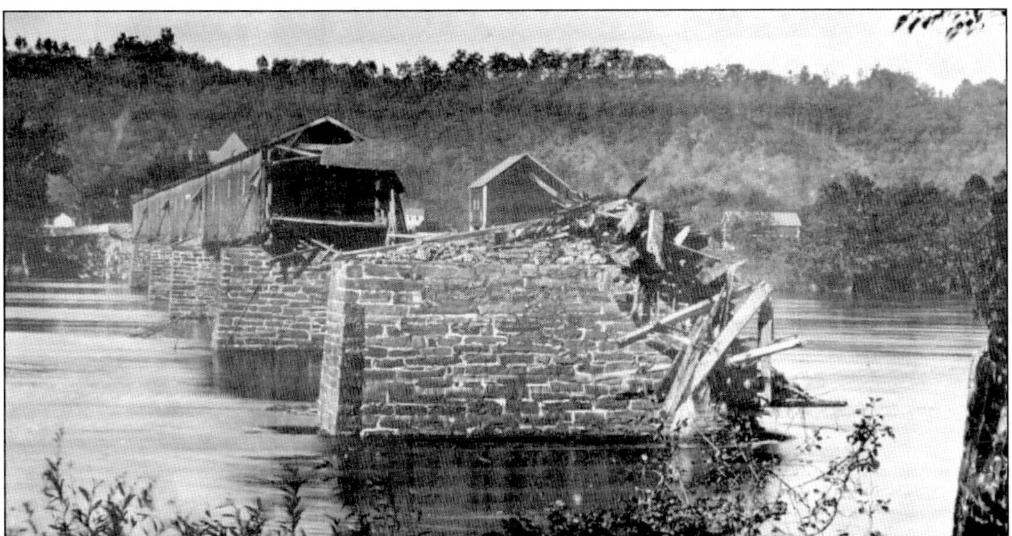

Weather and Tinicum's many hills and creeks have hampered transportation over the years. Floods have deposited prime agricultural soils along the Delaware River, sometimes covering the Erwinna area with five feet of water and depositing shad in a cornfield on Marshall's Island. A six-span covered bridge over the Delaware from Frenchtown, New Jersey, to Uhlerstown was built in 1844. When the 1903 flood washed away two spans, the crash was heard a mile downstream. (LDV.)

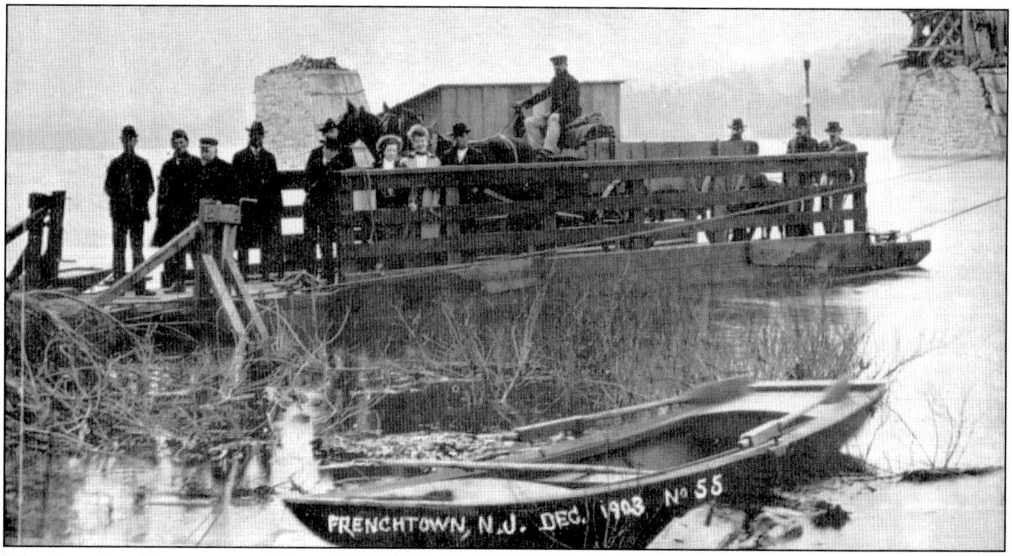

The London Ferry crossed from Frenchtown as early as 1699. George Washington's army crossed here during 1778–1780, and the ferry's Durham boats were used for his famous Christmas crossing. Temporary ferry service had to be resumed after the 1903 flood. Continuing development in the floodplain has led to increased flood damage in recent years. (LDV.)

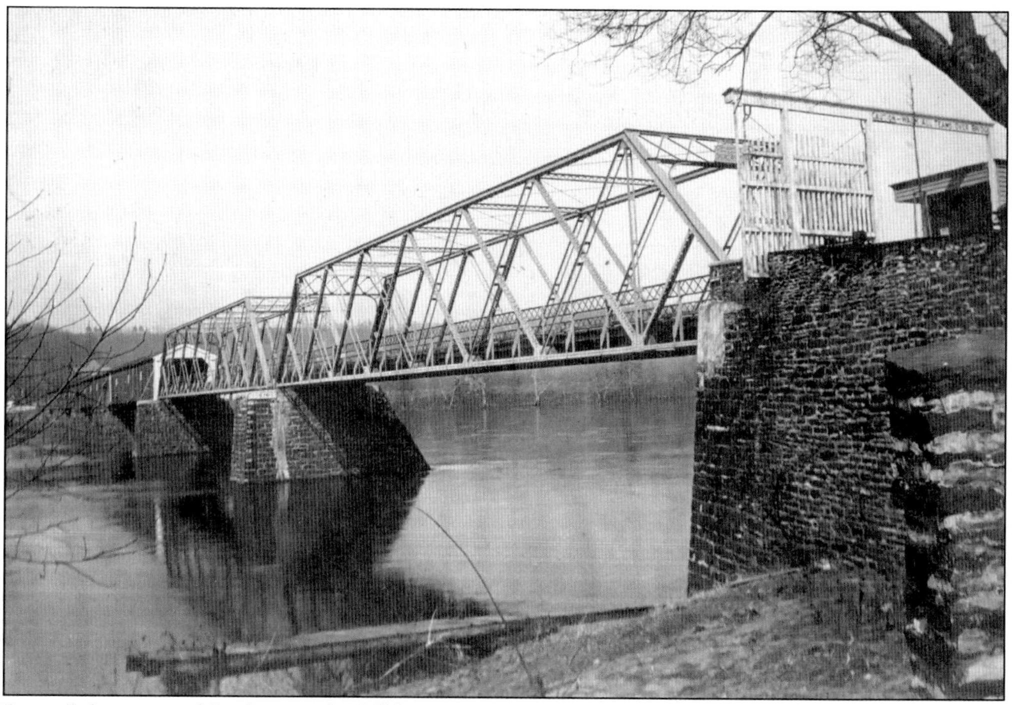

Part of the covered bridge on the Uhlerstown end remained until 1931, when the present steel bridge was built on the original foundations. Very little public transportation was available to Tinicum's residents. To get from Uhlerstown to Doylestown at the beginning of the 20th century, one had to walk over the bridge to Frenchtown, take the train north to Riegelsville, then walk across the bridge to take the trolley south to Doylestown. (EWH.)

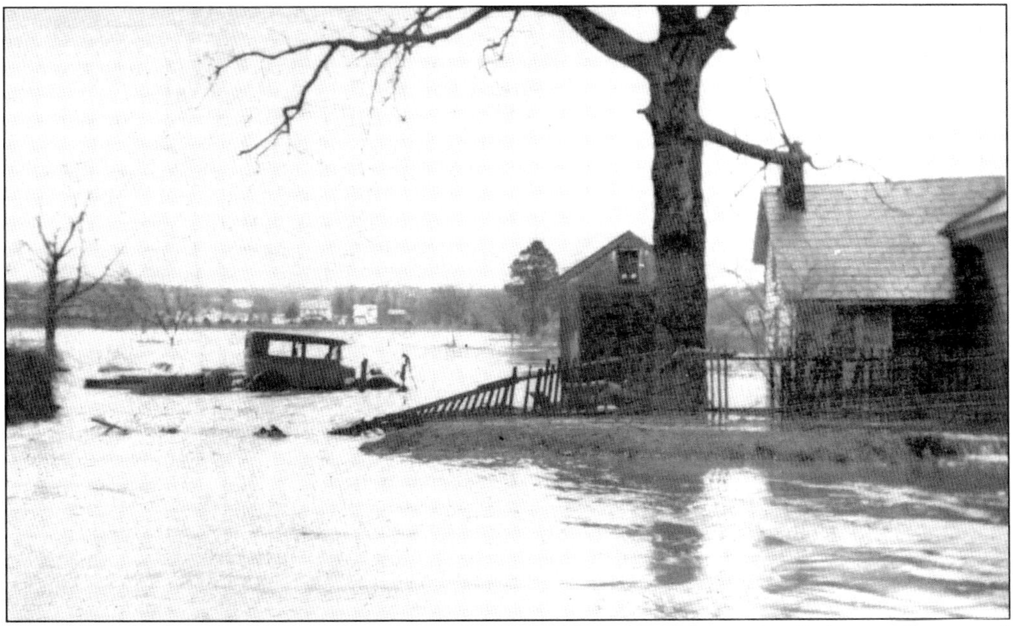

The St. Patrick's Day flood of 1936 sent huge chunks of ice down the Delaware River and surrounded the home of Harvey Lutz on the bank of the canal near Uhlerstown. Across the flooded fields of the Lewis farm, houses on River Road are on the bank of the Delaware, and Frenchtown is faintly visible on the distant New Jersey shore. (SIG.)

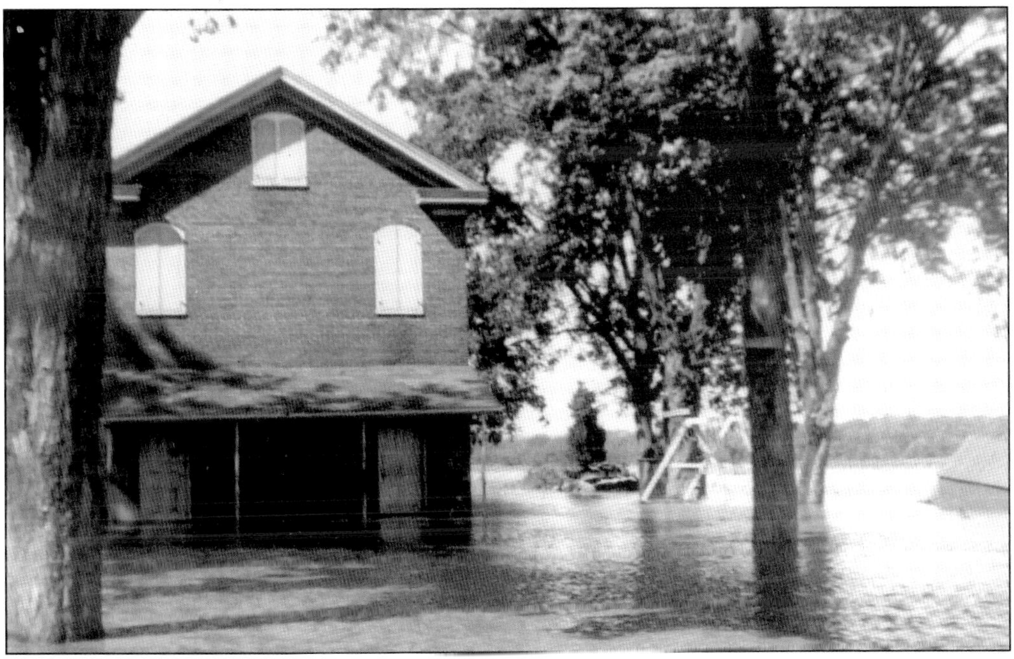

The August 1955 flood spared Erwinna but surrounded the Uhlerstown School up to the windowsills. Although books, a record player, and a piano were ruined, new furnishings, still stacked in crates atop one another, survived. Receding waters left two cottages in the middle of a road, and the school's coal shed landed at Oberacker's Tavern below Erwinna. The Red Cross fed 1,000 people and inoculated all residents against typhus. (RPK.)

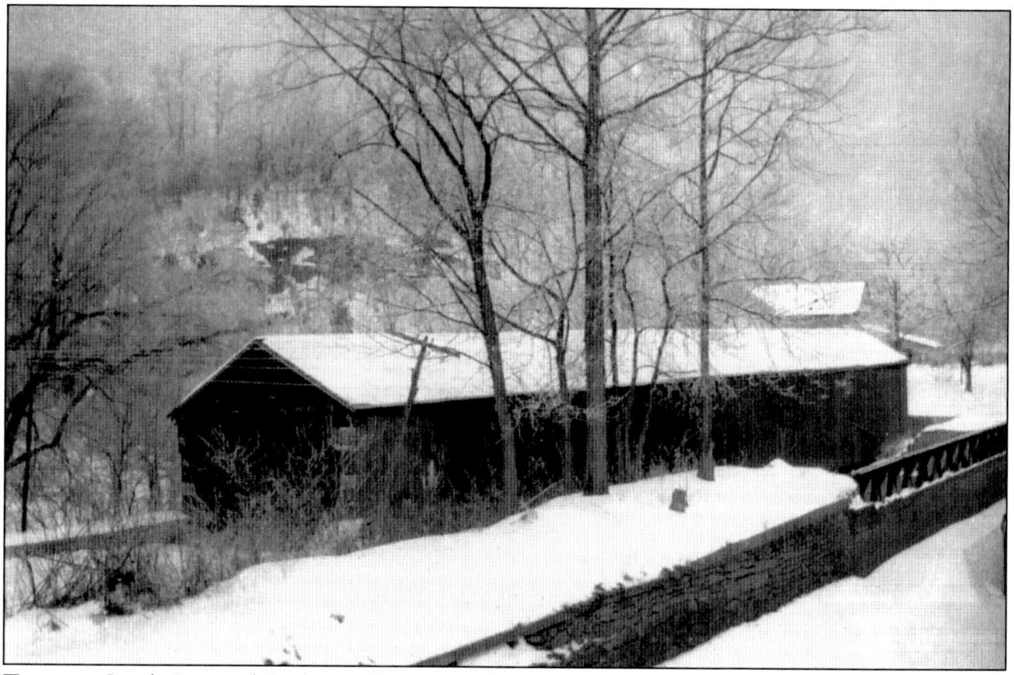

Tinicum Creek Covered Bridge on River Road was replaced in 1932. It was 160 feet long, which would qualify it as one of the "kissing bridges" favored by courting couples because their lengthy darkness afforded a brief respite from the watchful eyes of the chaperone. Another bridge tradition was to hold one's breath and make a wish during the crossing. Snow had to be shoveled onto these bridges to permit horse-drawn sleighs to cross. (GLD.)

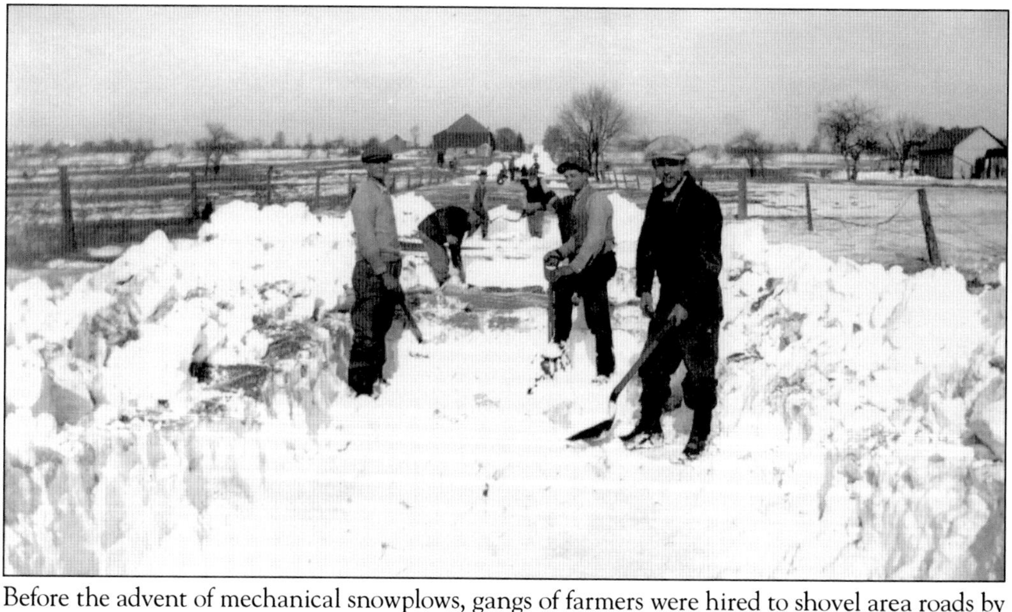

Before the advent of mechanical snowplows, gangs of farmers were hired to shovel area roads by hand. This provided additional income during the lean winter months. During a snowstorm in February 1925, expectant father Austin Haney drove his team back and forth all night between his Ottsville farm and the doctor's home in Revere to keep the road open. The doctor arrived in time to deliver baby Joseph. (SHV.)

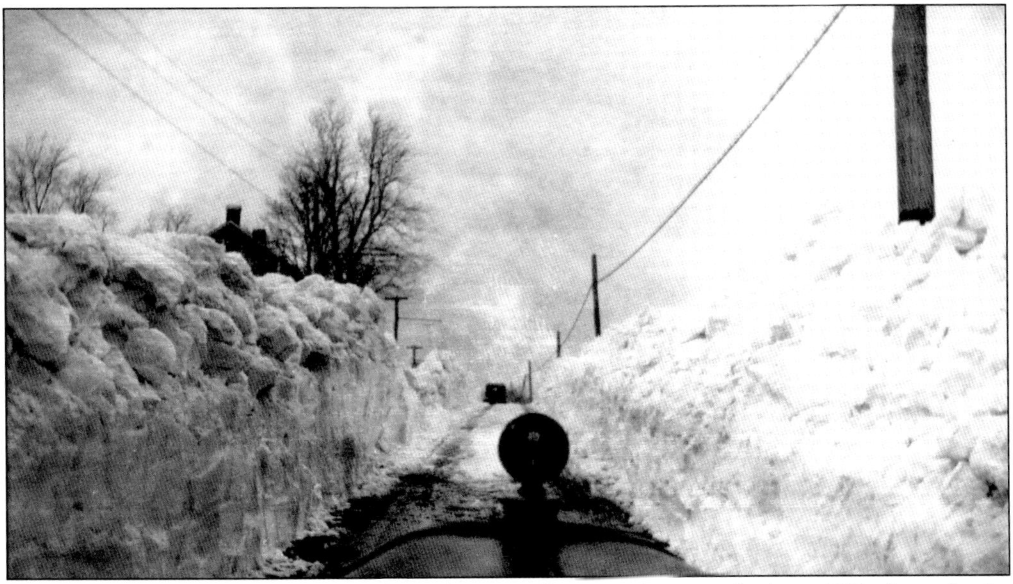

Deep snow along Durham Road through Ottsville was photographed in 1922 through the windshield of a 1920 Peerless automobile. A Herculean effort for hand labor, this road clearing may have been accomplished with the help of a snowplow attached to the front of the trolley. (LSH.)

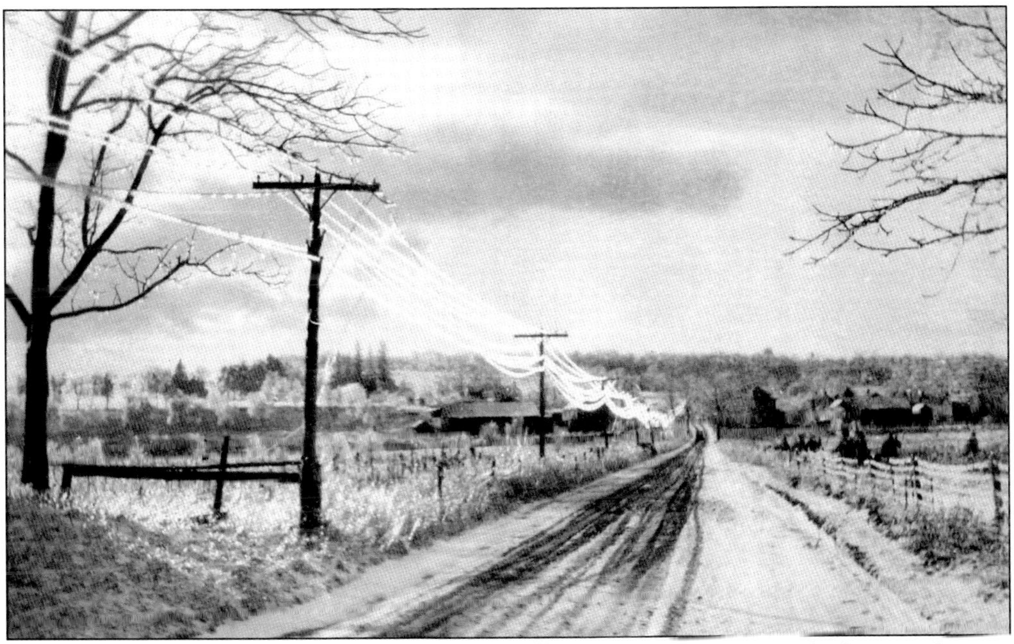

By 1945, when electricity was finally extended to all parts of rural Tinicum, the beauty of winter ice storms was tempered as downed power lines forced residents to resort to their old kerosene lamps. This view follows Headquarters Road from River Road to Erwinna. Although rural areas were slow to get electrical service, some farms had installed battery systems by the 1920s, while others used gasoline engines for power. (LSH.)

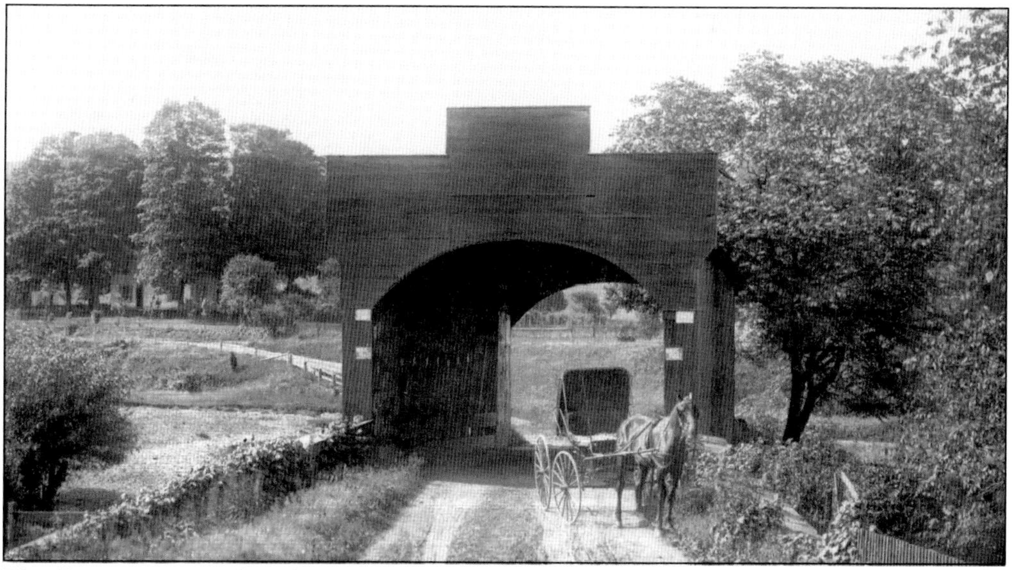

The Erwinna Covered Bridge is one of Bucks County's 11 surviving covered bridges. Three are in Tinicum. Materials required for its 1832 construction included whiskey for the workers. Its original squared facade, pictured here in 1908, was later modified. An 1892 sign warned of a $5–$30 fine for crossing this bridge faster than a walk. The Frankenfield Covered Bridge crosses Tinicum Creek near Sundale, and the Uhlerstown Covered Bridge is pictured on page 66. (EWH.)

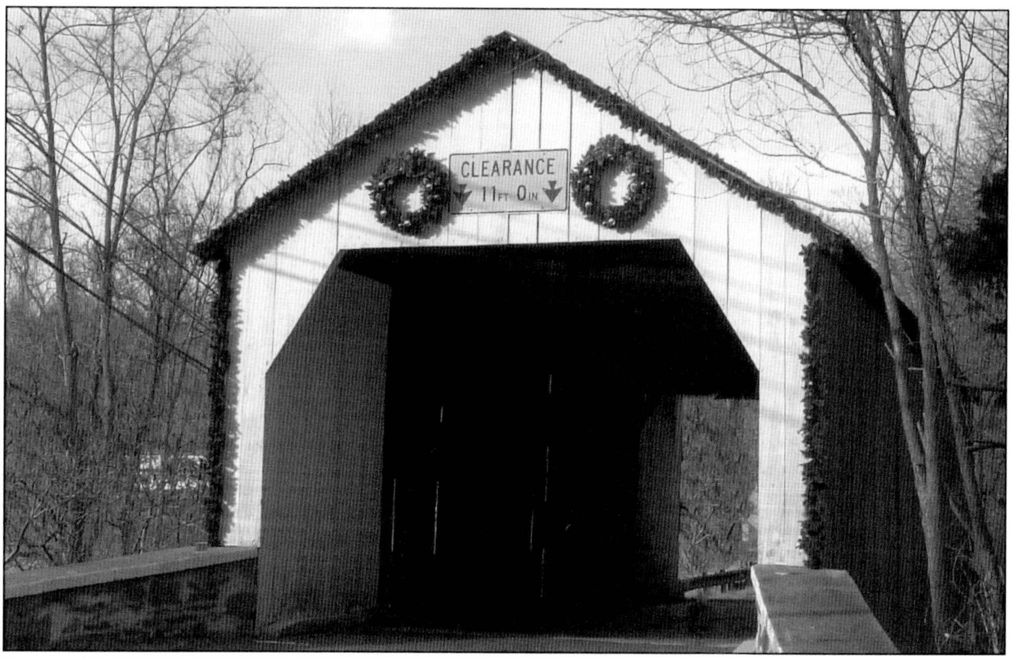

Beloved by its neighbors, the Erwinna Covered Bridge, with its later facade, has been decorated for Christmas for many years. In 1971, neighbors held a birthday party for it, complete with a parade and singing, "Happy birthday, dear bridge." Caught by a sudden summer storm, farmers with a load of hay sometimes sought shelter inside a covered bridge. (PYR.)

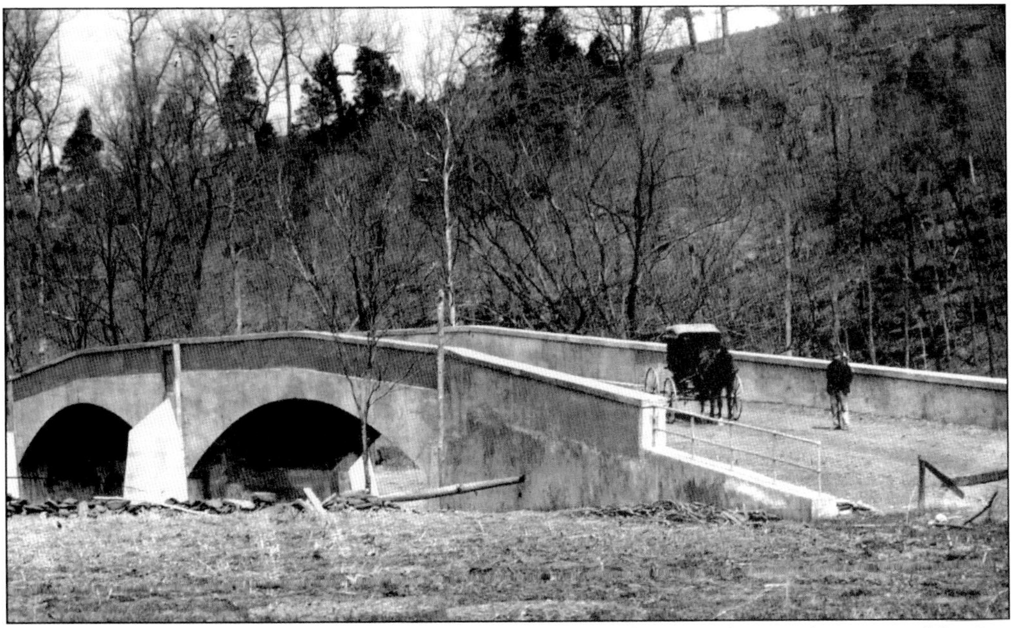

The 1906 Dark Hollow Road bridge, replaced in 2002, had replaced an earlier covered bridge, which burned in 1904. It crossed Tohickon Creek into Bedminster at Stover-Myers Mill. The earliest Tinicum road began at the mouth of Tinicum Creek in 1741, following an old Lenni-Lenape trail west along much of the route of Dark Hollow Road to Durham Road. The Lenni-Lenape word *Tohickon* translates to "place where we cross on driftwood." (FOX.)

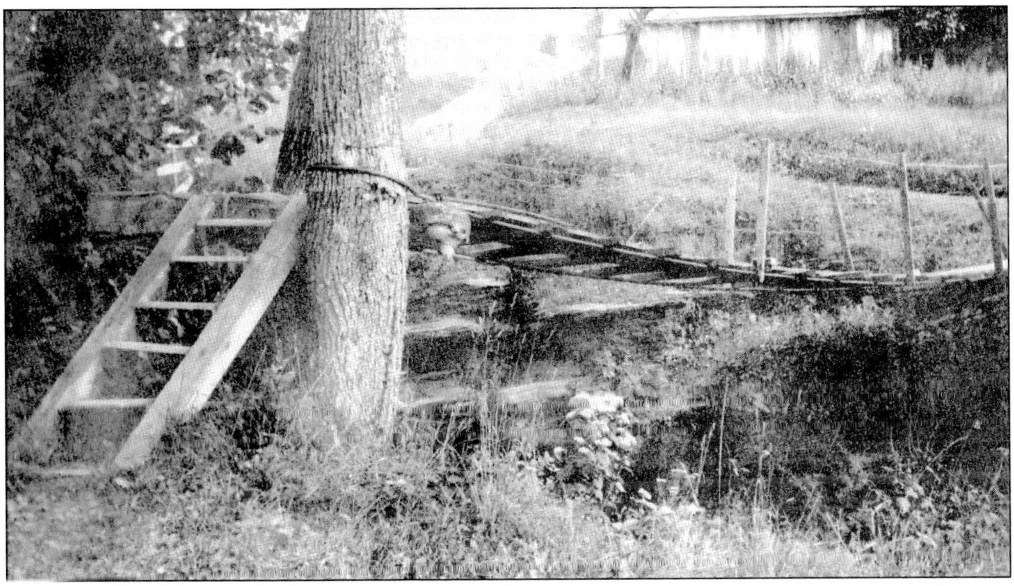

On less-traveled roads of Tinicum, primitive means of crossing creeks continues into the 21st century. For the swinging footbridge over Tinicum Creek along Sheephole Road, similar to that pictured here, wire cables anchored to sturdy trees supported a floor of wood slats for pedestrians, while wagons were driven through the stream. Traffic continues to ford the creeks at three locations, which has left occasional drivers stranded in midstream after misjudging water depth. (BCHS.)

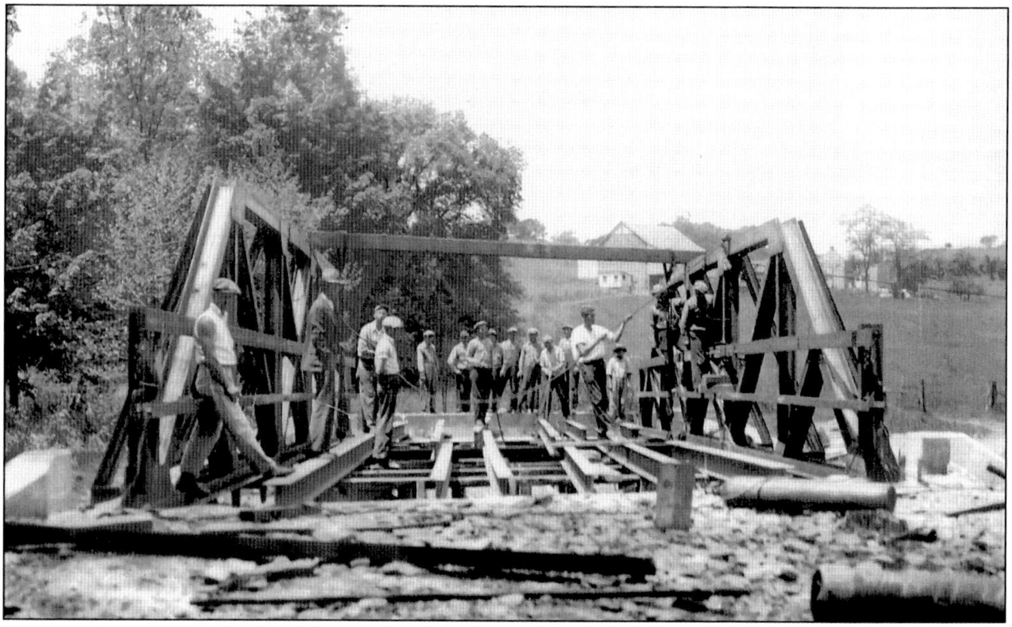

During the Depression, neighbors John Wexley, Alex Wittig, Cleveland Overpeck, and Russell Eichlin, tired of having to cross on a wobbly footbridge or drive through Tinicum Creek along Sheephole Road, petitioned the Works Progress Administration (WPA) for two bridges. The WPA construction, which was completed in 1936, brought income to a dozen local workers, who then boosted the local economy by purchasing from Ottsville businesses. (GBK.)

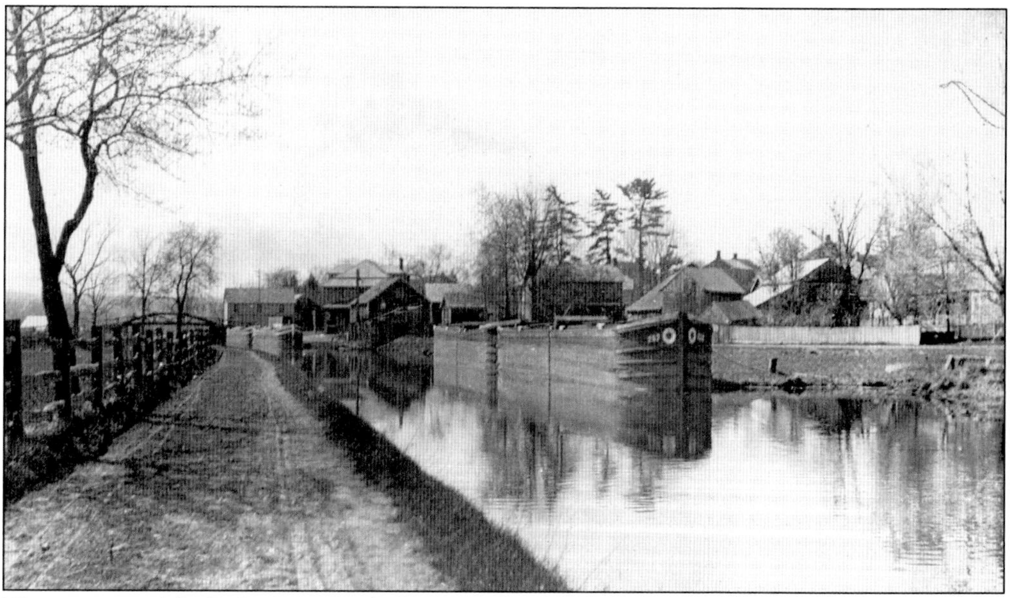

The opening of the Delaware Canal in 1832 vastly improved commerce, especially the transport of coal. Boating season ran from mid-March into November, when the canal froze. Entire families sometimes lived on the boats, which limited their children's school attendance to the winter months. On long stretches between locks, boatmen might stop at an inn for refreshment and to turn their grateful mules loose in an adjacent field. This *c.* 1915 view looks south to Erwinna. (LSH.)

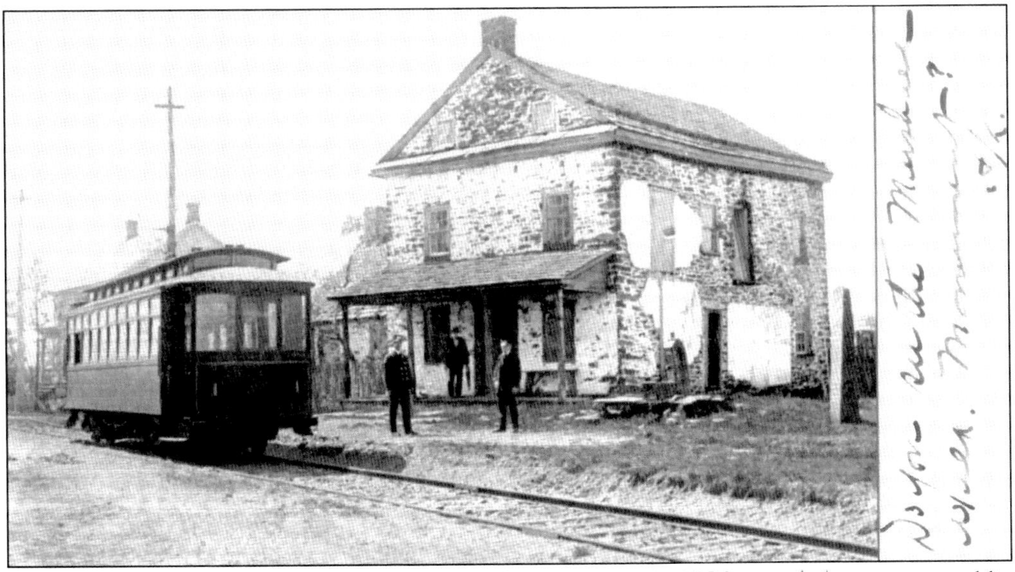

The extension of trolley service from Philadelphia to Easton in 1906 provided important public transportation. This early postcard portrays the Red Hill Inn, which, as a stagecoach stop, had been known as the Inn of the White Bear. Present Route 611 follows the trolley route, and that of the infamous 1737 Walking Purchase, commemorated by the stone marker right of the building and noted by the sender of the card. (BCHS.)

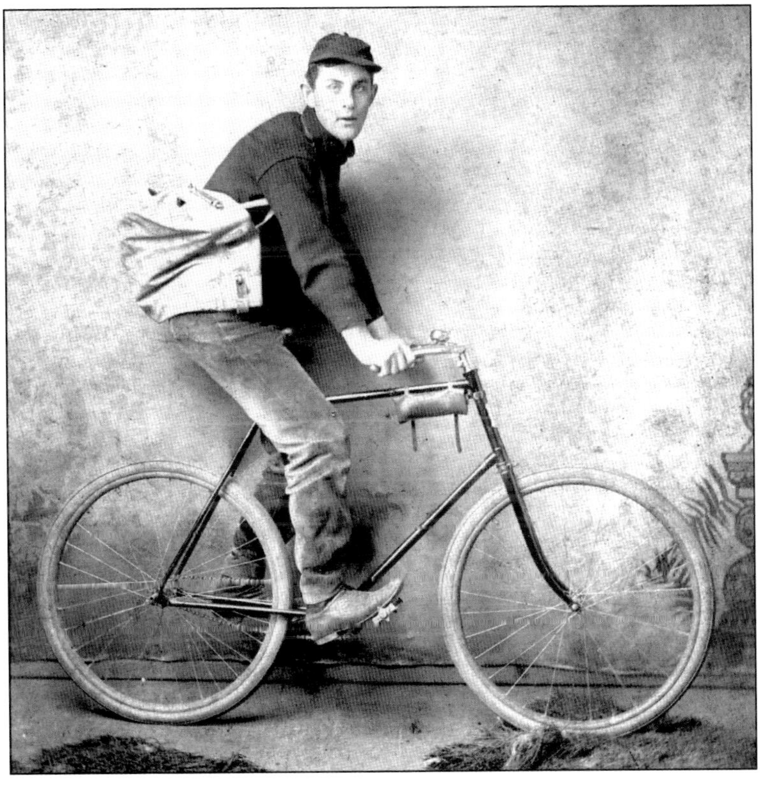

Bicycles have long provided transportation for all ages. Graduates of Tinicum's one-room schools biked to Nockamixon to attend high school. Boys biked to Easton to study newsreels of Babe Ruth. Percy Bryan, pictured here in 1897, carried mail from Erwinna to Frenchtown on his bicycle. Cycling is a popular pastime in Tinicum today, with the annual Tour de Tinicum, sponsored by the Delaware Valley Volunteer Fire Company, drawing cyclists from several states. (WVR.)

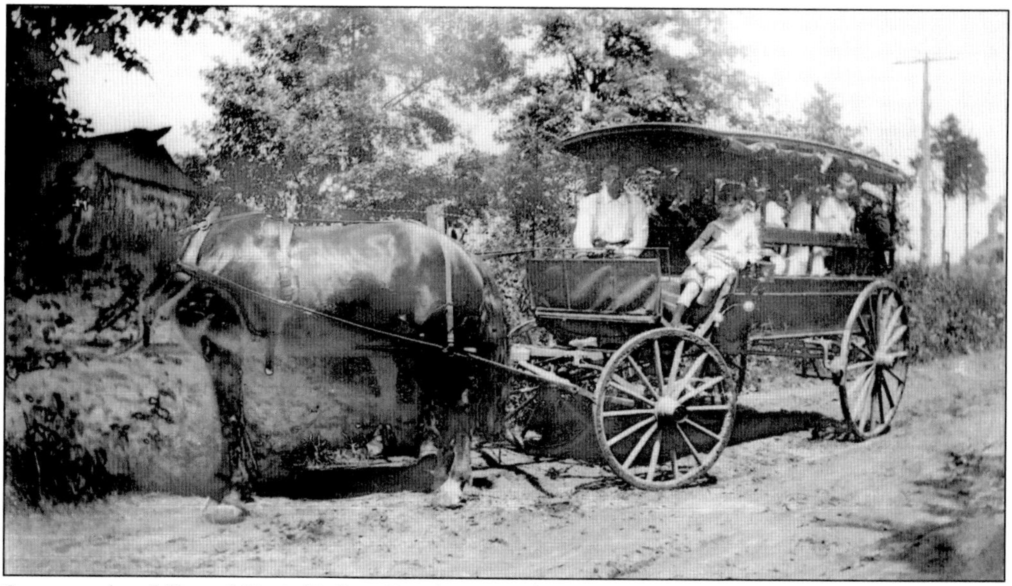

Stagecoaches followed Dark Hollow Road past Wilson's Tavern in 1767. When a rowdy Sunday morning crowd heckled James Carrell on his way to church, he took Wilson to court and had Wilson's license revoked. Red Hill had twice-daily service between Philadelphia and Easton in 1831. This stagecoach, which is pictured in 1914, brought guests from the Frenchtown train station to Riverside Farm. It now serves as the used book wagon at the annual arts festivals. (LSH.)

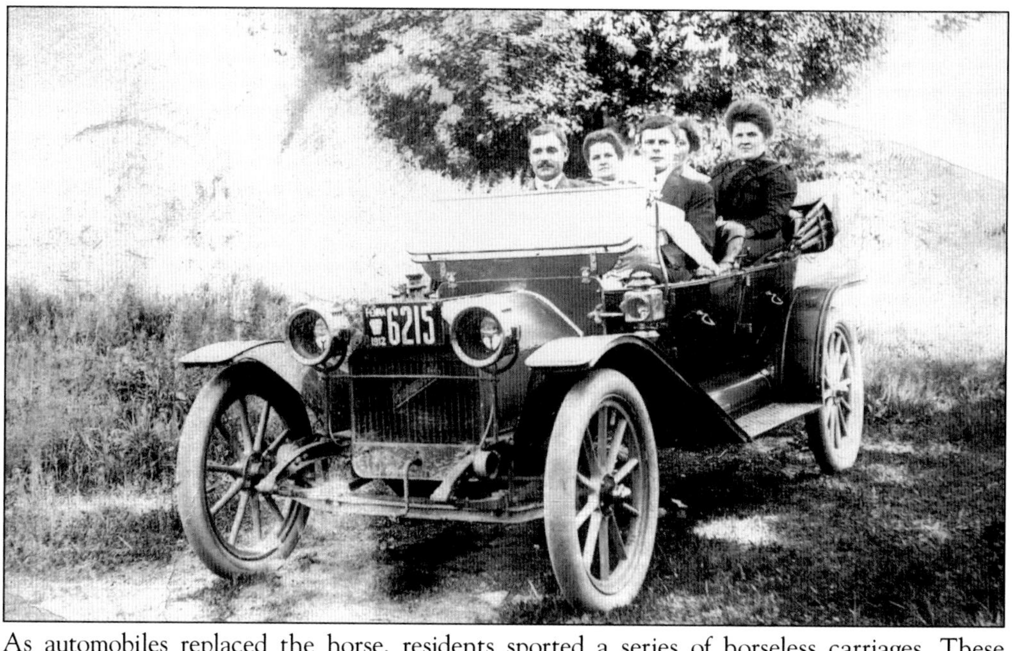

As automobiles replaced the horse, residents sported a series of horseless carriages. These required road improvements and maintenance, which in turn required road supervisors, the first form of municipal government. In 1912, the Sigafoos family enjoys an outing in their Hupmobile touring car. From left to right are Charles P. Breiner, Elizabeth (Dillon) Breiner, Harry Sigafoos, and Margaret (Dillon) Sigafoos. Two unidentified passengers are a child on Harry's lap and a partially hidden woman behind him. (SIG.)

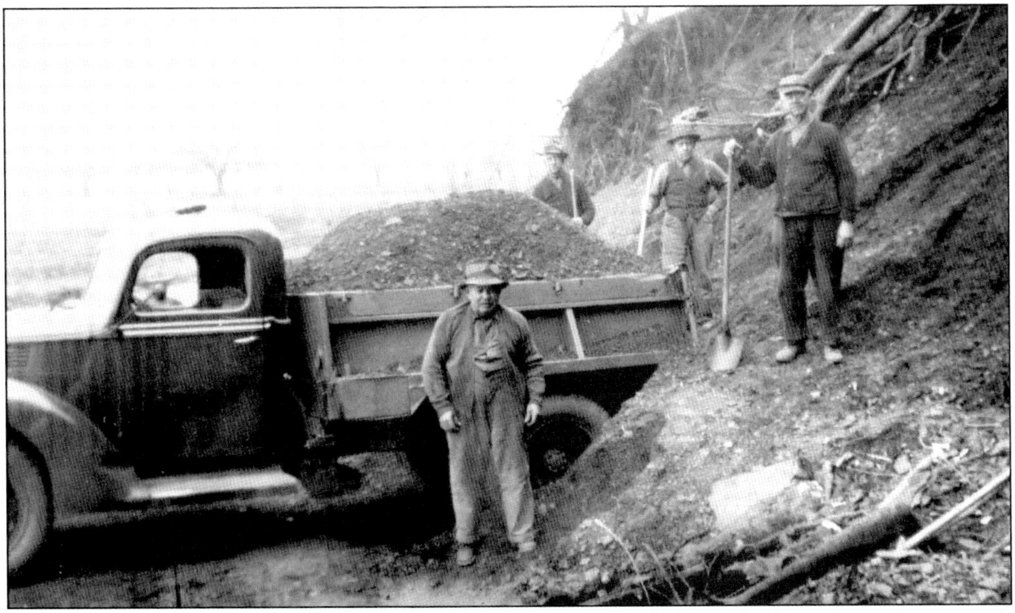

The Tinicum road crew fills its truck by the shovelful from a shale bank along Canal Lane north of Uhlerstown. From left to right are John Schaefer, uncle of Ottsville baseball player John Schaefer; Willis Steeley; Martin Bullich; and Harry Mood. Austin Haney, road supervisor, was directing road repairs elsewhere when this *c.* 1940 photograph was taken. (EWH.)

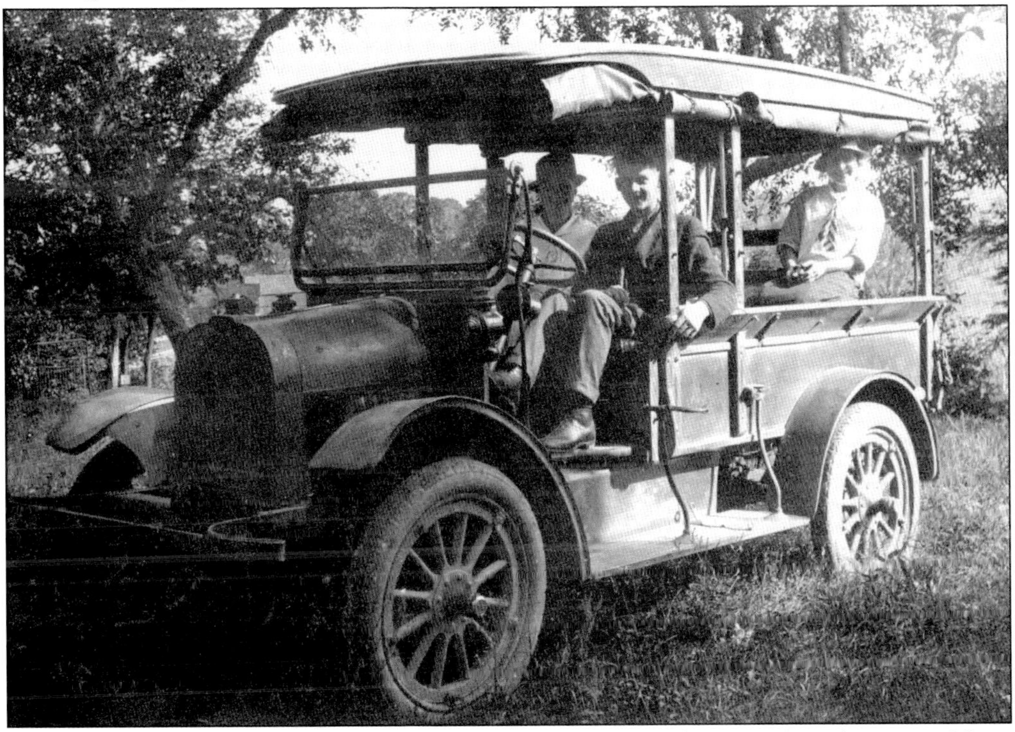

An early form of motorized public transportation was Schneider's panel truck, pictured here near Point Pleasant in 1920. It transported guests from the train station in Byram, New Jersey, across the bridge to Schneider's Inn on River Road. (LSH.)

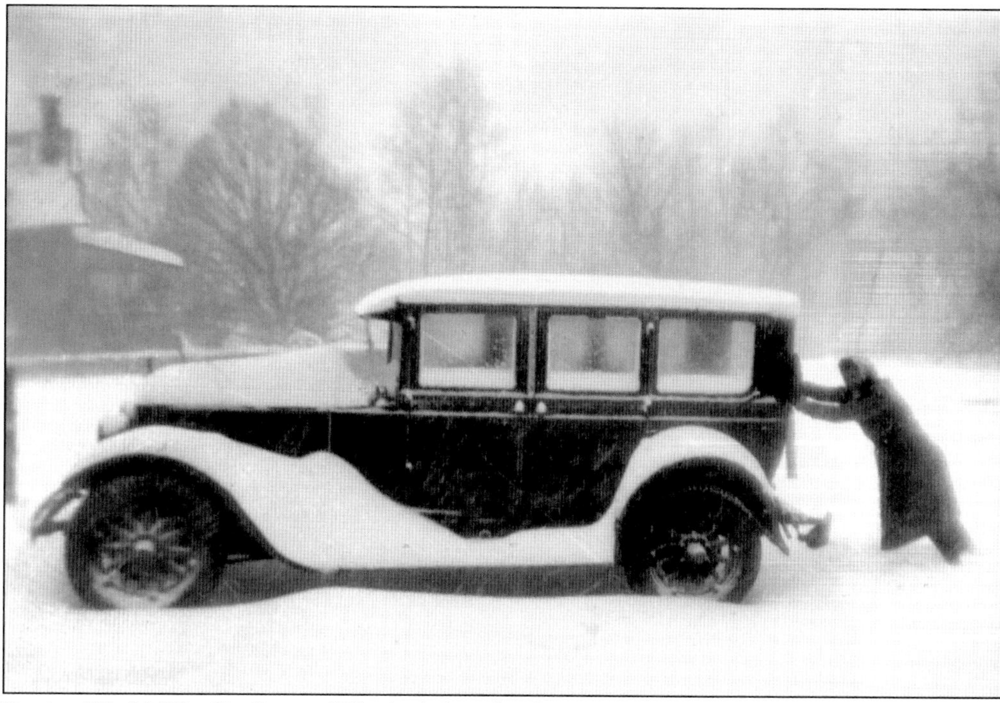

During World War II, George Whitlock bought this 1928 Buick, planning to convert it to a truck. He abandoned these plans upon discovering that it was a gas-guzzler, a particular problem during gas-rationing days. In 1944, his daughter, Evelyn, demonstrates the only economical way to operate the vehicle. (EWH.)

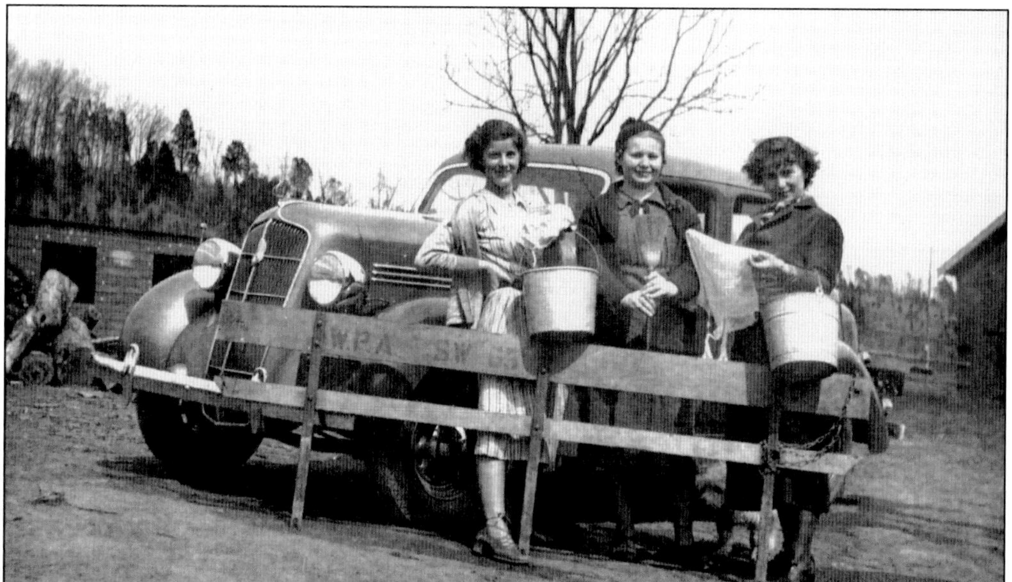

During World War II, the top halves of headlights were painted black to reduce visibility during possible enemy attack. From left to right, Pearl, Della, and Anna (Kothstein) Bickel prepare to wash the family car. The barrier with the letters WPA was a leftover from the senior Sam Bickel's work on the Sheephole Road bridge construction project described on page 88. (BBK.)

Six

Leisure Activities for All Ages

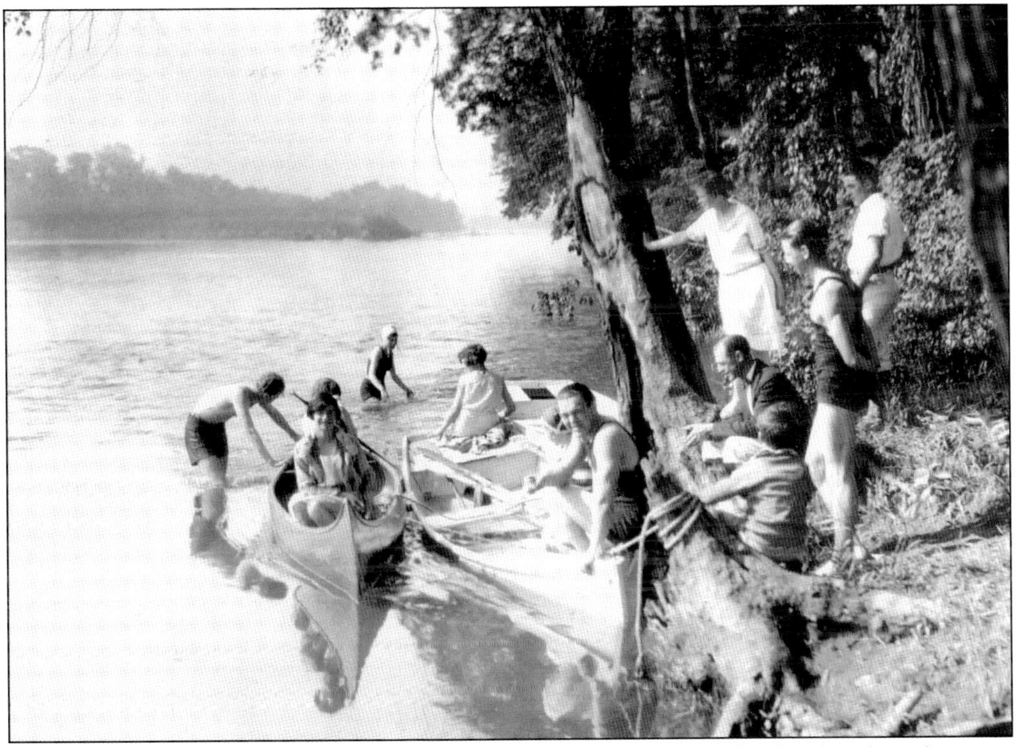

The Delaware River, which forms 10 miles of Tinicum's eastern border, has long been an attraction for a variety of leisure activities for both residents and visitors. Swimsuit styles in this group of swimmers and boaters at Erwinna date the picture to the 1930s. (LSG.)

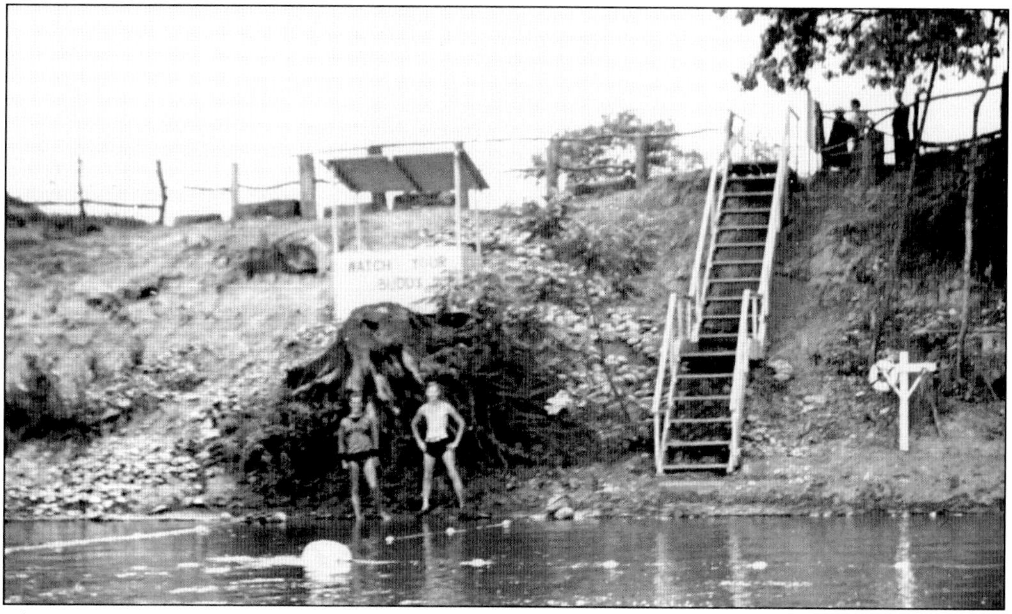

The message on this postcard, mailed from Erwinna in 1940, reads, "Dear Grandma, I am having a swell time up here. This is a picture of our swimming section which is the Delaware. The current is very swift and is hard to swim against." The sign warns, "Watch Your Buddy." (DBM.)

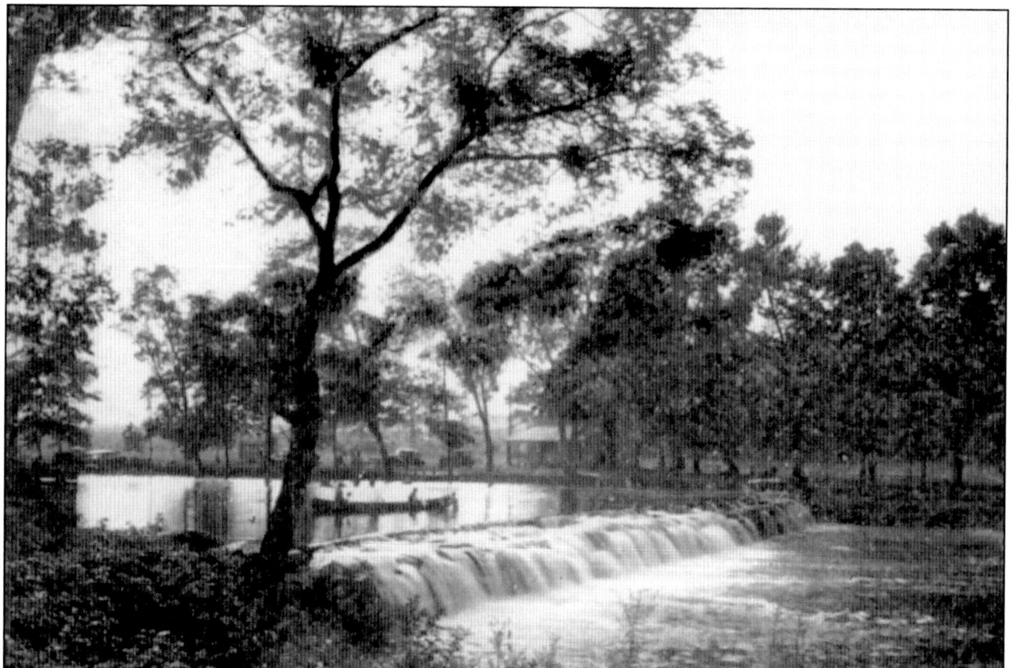

Trauger's Park, a picnic grove on Tohickon Creek at Myers Dam on Dark Hollow Road, was a favorite gathering place of families and the high school crowd from the 1930s to the 1960s. The dam for adjacent Stover-Myers Mill provided boating, fishing, and swimming, and a snack bar sold refreshments. The 68-acre property, now owned by residents of summer cabins here, is permanently protected from further development by a conservation easement. (RPK.)

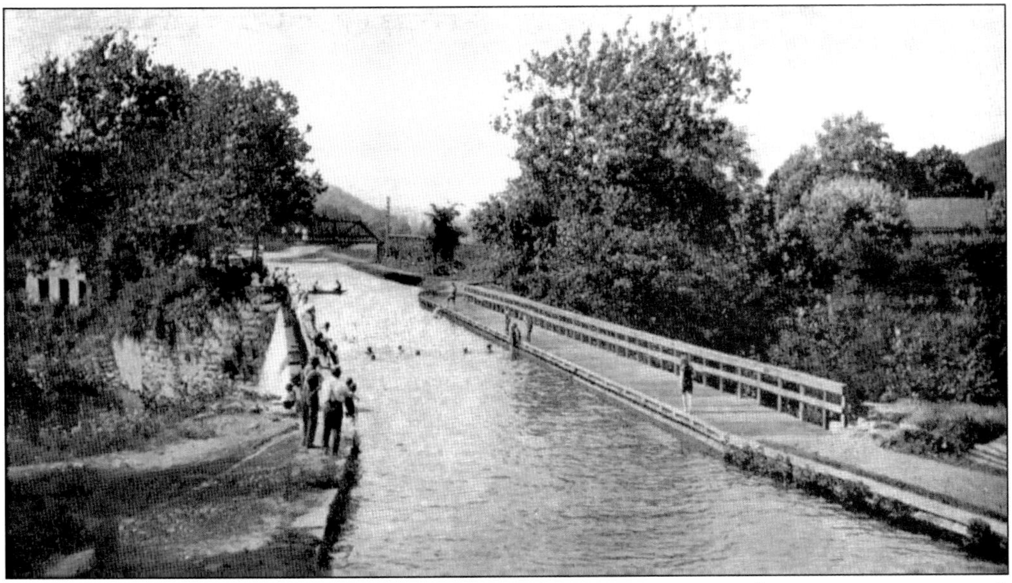

As the state-owned canal declined in commercial use, its attraction for recreation increased. Swimmers enjoy the water of the aqueduct over Tohickon Creek at Point Pleasant in this *c.* 1915 view. First called Theodore Roosevelt State Park to honor Roosevelt's leadership in promoting conservation programs, it is now the Delaware Canal State Park, designated a national historic landmark, and the towpath is a national recreation trail. (LDV.)

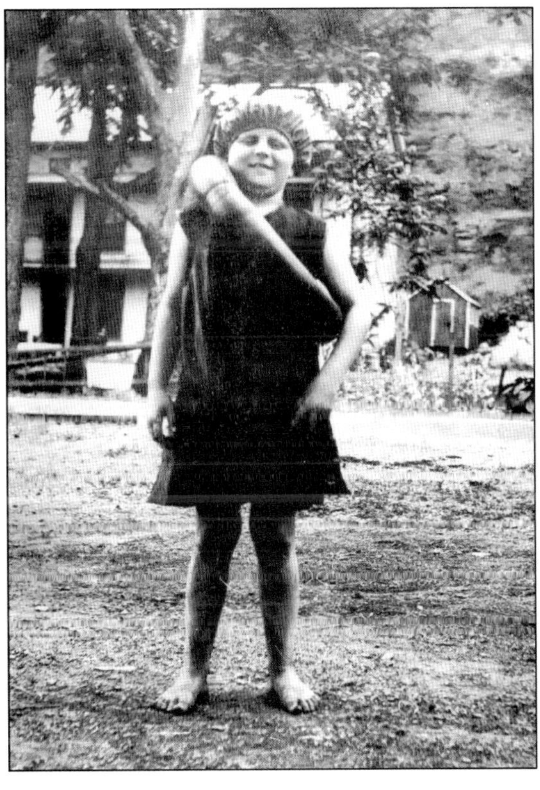

Thelma Sigafoos prepares for a swim in the canal in front of the Uhlerstown Hotel in 1925, equipped with the narrow inner tube of an early automobile tire. Whether or not she could swim, the inner tube could help her avoid touching the unpleasant muddy bottom with her feet. (SIG.)

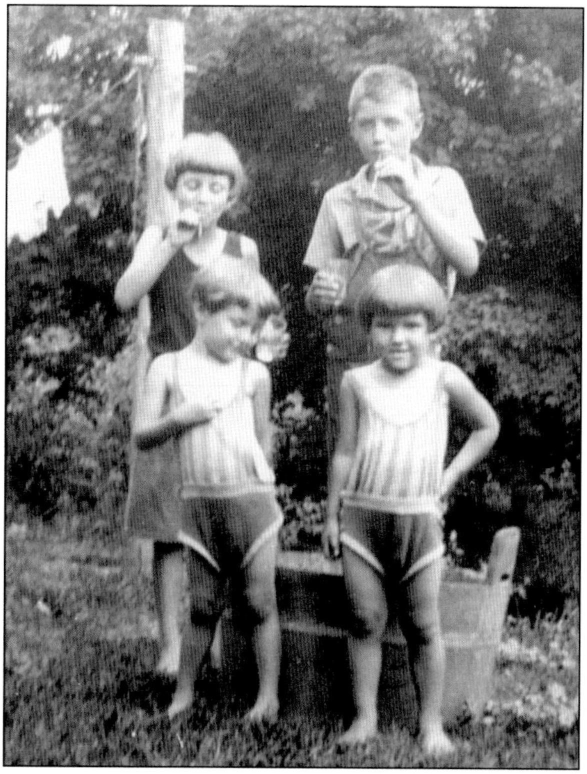

Summer was a time for sailing paper boats in ditches, blowing dandelions, and dressing paper dolls. Violet Gruver recalled learning to balance on stilts built by older brothers, then racing one another. In 1932, the Whitlock children blow bubbles and cool off in a washtub. In front are twins Elsie (left) and Evelyn, with Edith and George behind them. At dusk, they chased lightning bugs, filling jars to light their bedrooms. (EWH.)

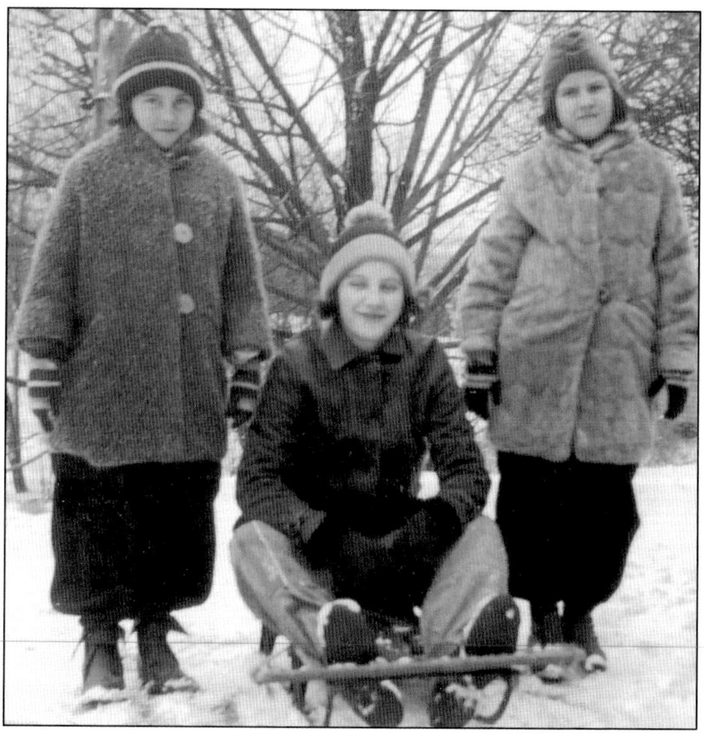

Tinicum's sloping landscape made sledding a popular winter pastime. Scraps of tin roofing sometimes substituted for toboggans, and the ramp to the threshing floor of the John Stover barn provided a suitable slope for sledders living in the flatlands along the river. Pictured in 1939 are, from left to right, Elsie, Edith, and Evelyn Whitlock. (EWH.)

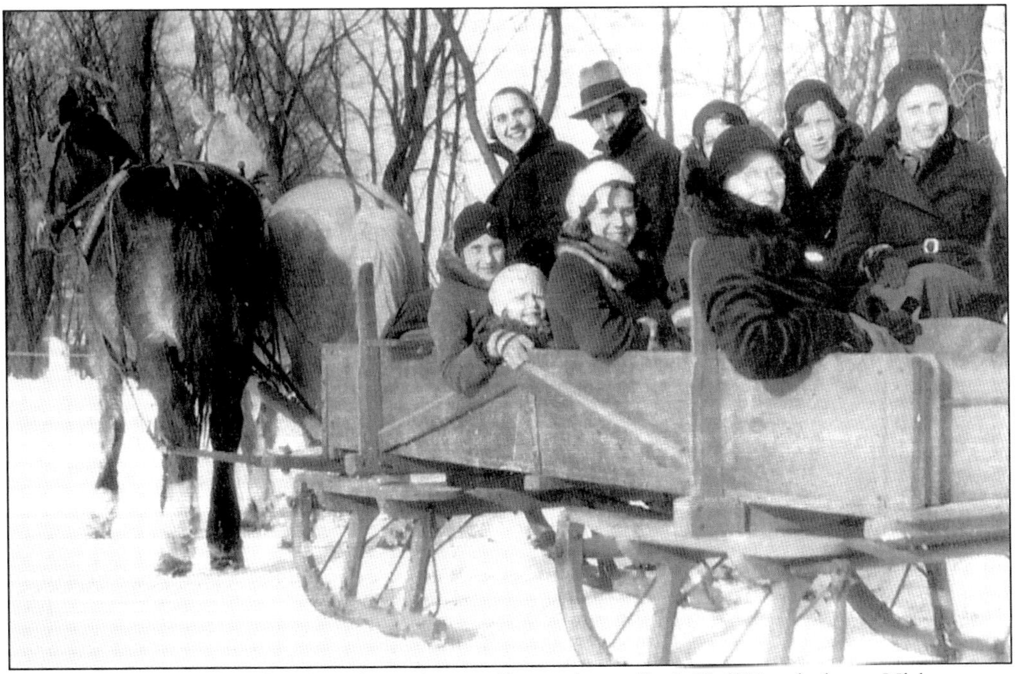

The Stanford Sigafoos family, whose farm still stands on Red Cliff Road above Uhlerstown, enjoys a 1933 sleigh ride. In the front row, from left to right, are Dorothy, Jean, Bertha, and Stanford's wife, Kathryn. Behind them, from left to right, are Margaret, Arthur, Laura, Elsie, and Bessie Sigafoos. (QBY.)

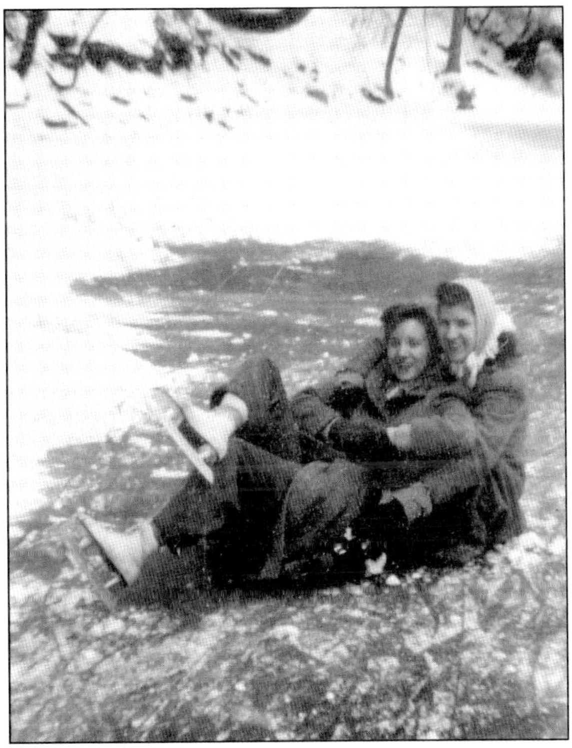

After clearing snow from a frozen stretch of Tinicum Creek, skating was an up-and-down experience for Edith (left) and Evelyn Whitlock in 1945. One challenge for skaters before shoe-skates were available was keeping the skates securely strapped to the feet. (EWH.)

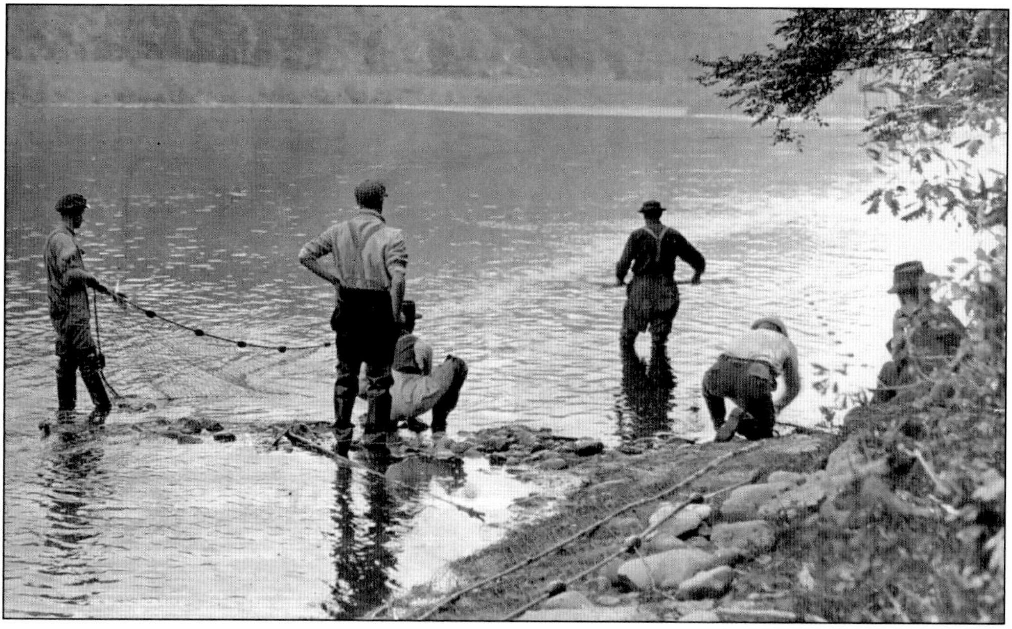

Sportsmen and commercial fishermen looked forward to the spring run of shad up the Delaware River. The men pictured here are setting nets in front of the Stovers' Riverside Farm, while others pursued the fish with rod and reel. The numbers of fish declined in the mid-20th century when pollution of the lower Delaware River prevented their return from the ocean. Thanks to water quality controls, the fish have returned in recent years. (DRD.)

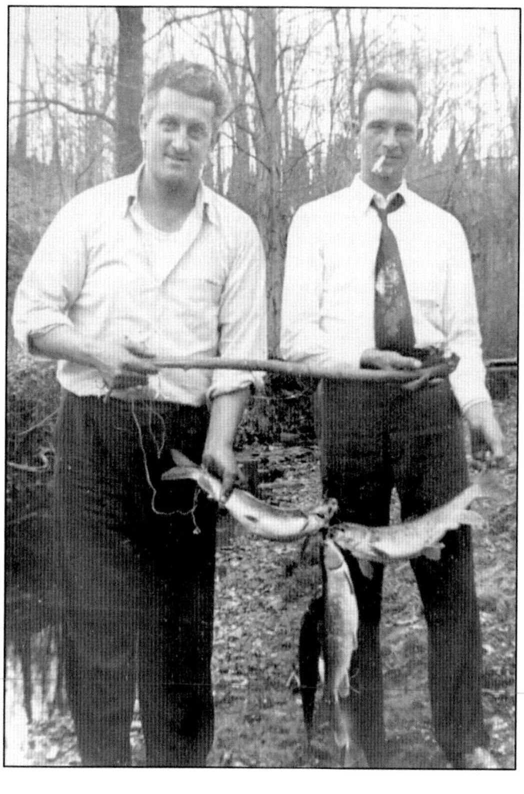

John Biresch (left) and George Dexheimer display the trout they caught in Tinicum Creek, near the Headquarters Road Bridge around 1930. After years of pollution from upstream sources, the creek has been restored to health, earning Exceptional Value rating, and trout once again swim in its clear waters. A large section of the creek flows through the Ridge Valley Rural Historic District. (BBK.)

Brothers Al (left) and Ernest Schaible Sr. admire the snapping turtles they caught in the canal. Turtle soup is such a delicacy that some former residents return annually to help catch a new crop of these canal dwellers. Snappers must be handled carefully; their powerful jaws can amputate a finger in a few seconds of inattentiveness. (TCA.)

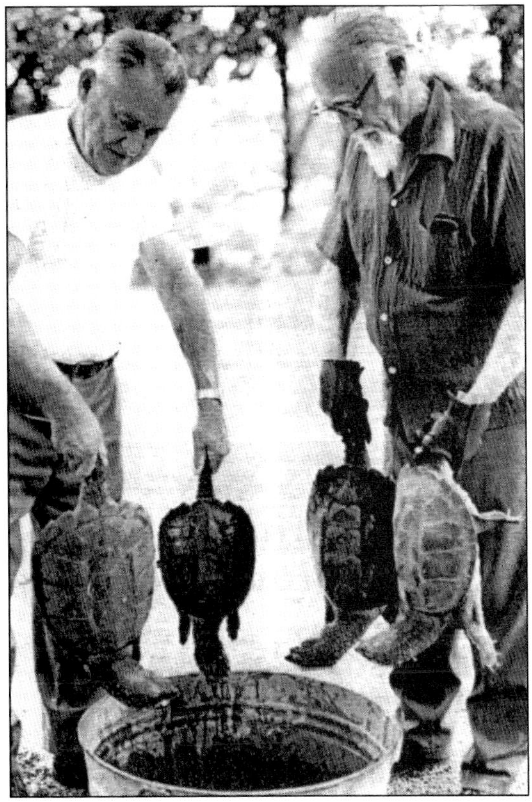

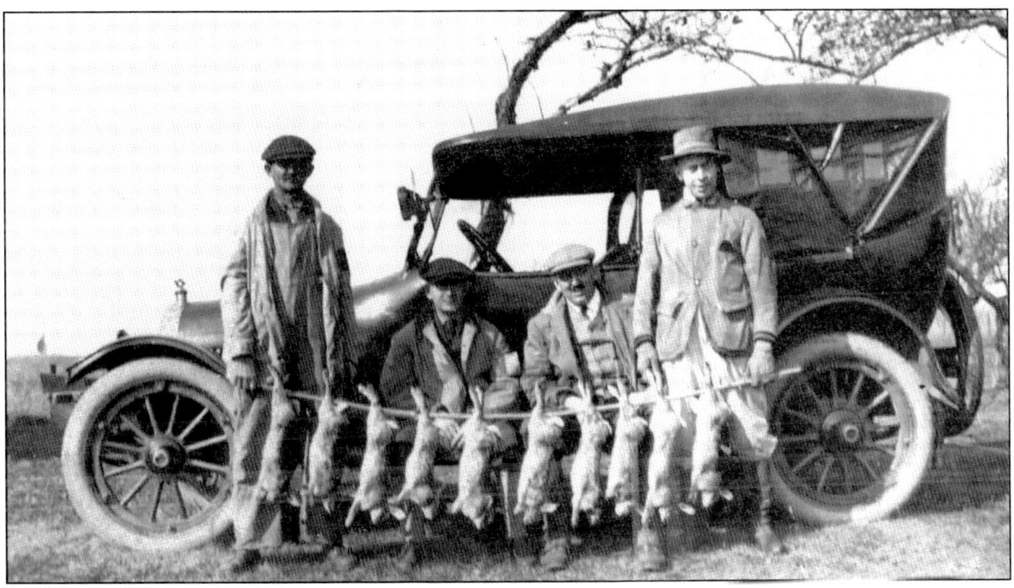

For Austin Haney (left) and companions, rabbits were plentiful in the 1920s, when much of Tinicum land was cleared for agriculture. As old fields have reverted to forest, it would be difficult for present-day hunters to bag such an impressive display, although wild turkeys and deer have proliferated to the point of threatening the environment with their numbers. Foxes have reduced the numbers of rabbits but have also reduced the pheasant population. (EWH.)

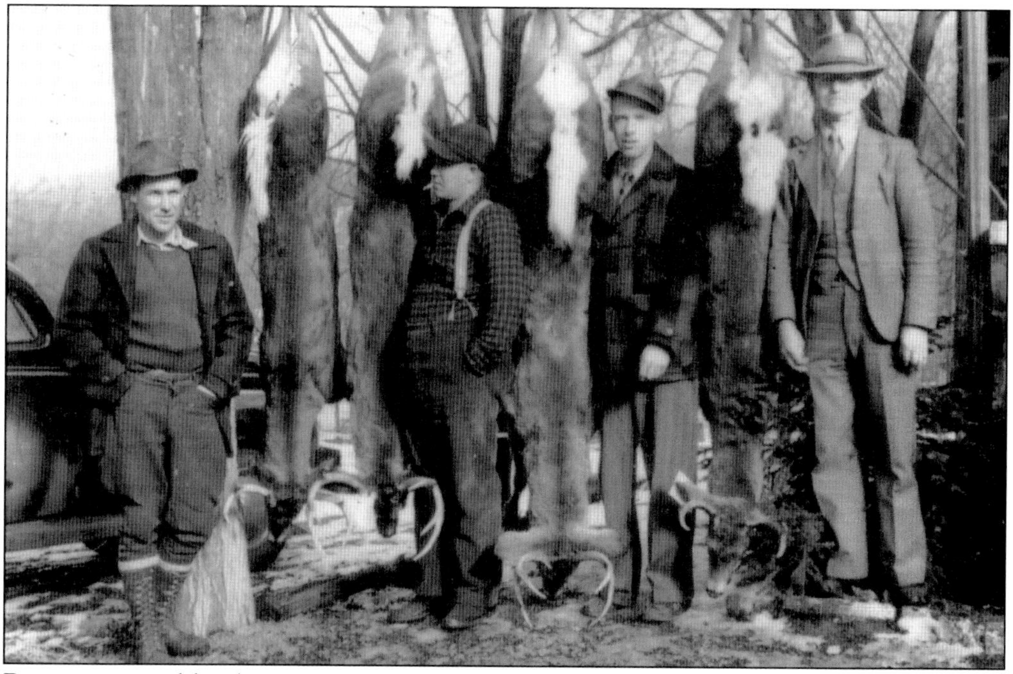

Deer were prized by the Lenni-Lenapes, who lived in Tinicum for thousands of years before white men arrived. After consuming or preserving the meat, they tanned the hides for clothing and created useful tools from the antlers and bones. Today deer may be picturesque, but they are also a menace to vegetation and to motorists. Deer hunters in 1941 are, from left to right, John W. Walter Jr., Hugh Allshouse, Brownie ?, and Phil Bowe. (WLT.)

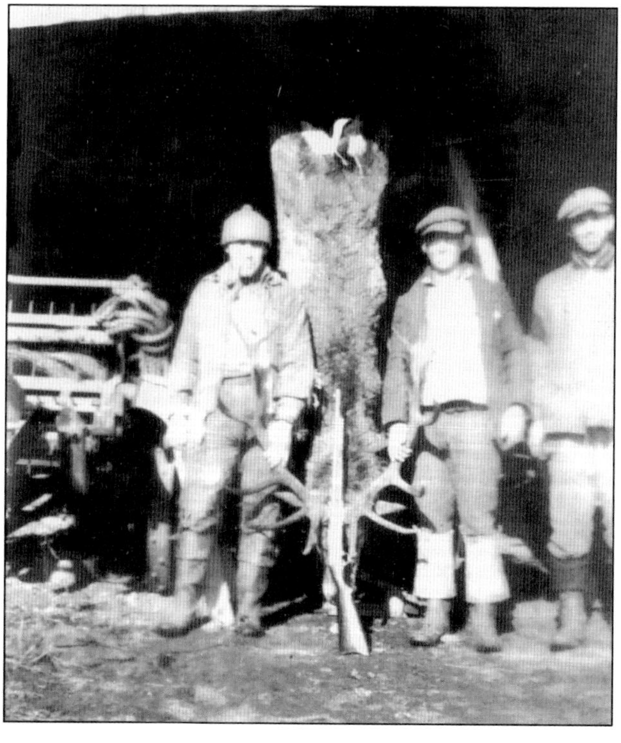

This 400-pound, 14-point elk had been terrorizing local cattle and raiding cornfields until it was shot by Walter Goulding in 1923 as it swam from Marshall's Island to Erwinna. It was such a rare sight in Tinicum that the local press mistakenly identified it as a moose. Posing with the trophy are, from left to right, Goulding, with Walter Weaver and Wilson Victor Hager, who helped haul the animal to shore. (GLD.)

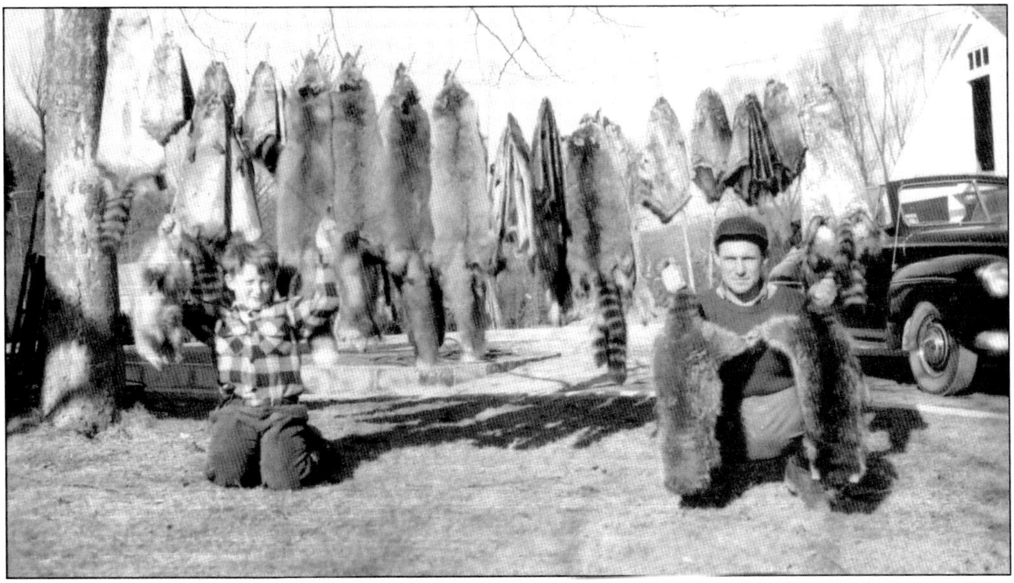

Trappers rose before dawn to check their trap lines before heading to school or work. Some of the pelts provided funds for the purchase of baseball equipment from Sears, Roebuck and Company. Inadequately wrapped packages containing skunk pelts might be rejected by the post office as "too strong." John J. Walter (left) and John W. Walter Jr. display their 1947 catch. (WLT.)

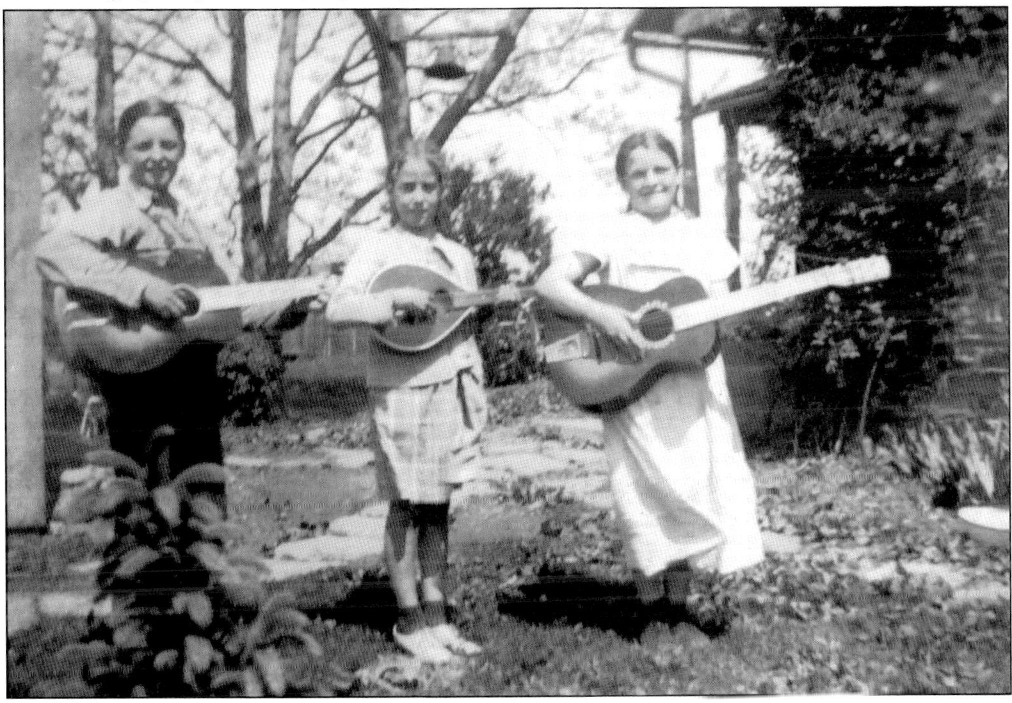

Music, in various forms, has played a role in leisure activity since time immemorial. By the 20th century, Tinicum parlors frequently had either a pump organ or a piano, perhaps a player piano, which required no talent other than pumping the pedals to propel the piano roll. Before youngsters had iPods or karaoke video games, from left to right, John, Viola, and Rose Timochenko enjoyed making their own music in the 1930s. (DTS.)

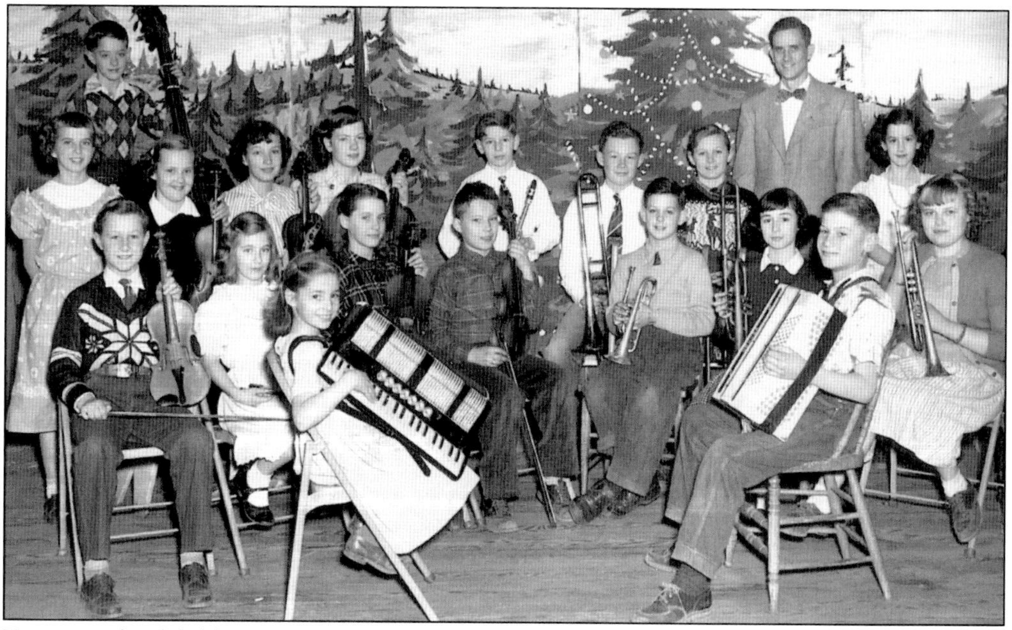

Tinicum schoolchildren received instrumental music instruction, leading to performances such as this 1949 Christmas presentation. From left to right are (first row) Arleen Bickel and Johnny Biresch; (second row) Wayne Hobson, Sonja Ridge, Emma Templeton, Billy Beer, Fred Budd, Jean Frankenfield, and Joyce Cochran; (third row) Sylvia Bohlman, Norma Schaible, Helen Beer, Doris Cromwell, Bill Bickel, Bob Bartleman, Victor Hobson, and Jean Biresch; (fourth row) Jimmy Biresch and music teacher John DeSilver. (LSG.)

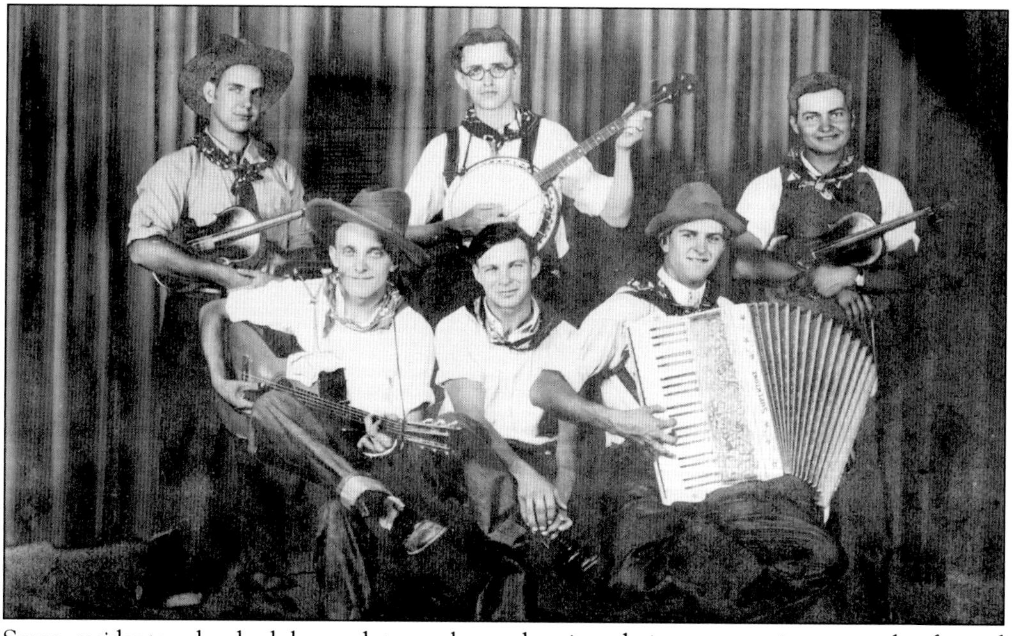

Some residents who had learned to make and enjoy their own music as youths formed semiprofessional groups as adults. This country and western band, pictured around 1933, includes, from left to right, (first row) Willis Myers, guitar; unidentified; and Floyd Szczepanski Stevens, accordion; (second row) unidentified; Granville Sterner, banjo; and unidentified. (PST.)

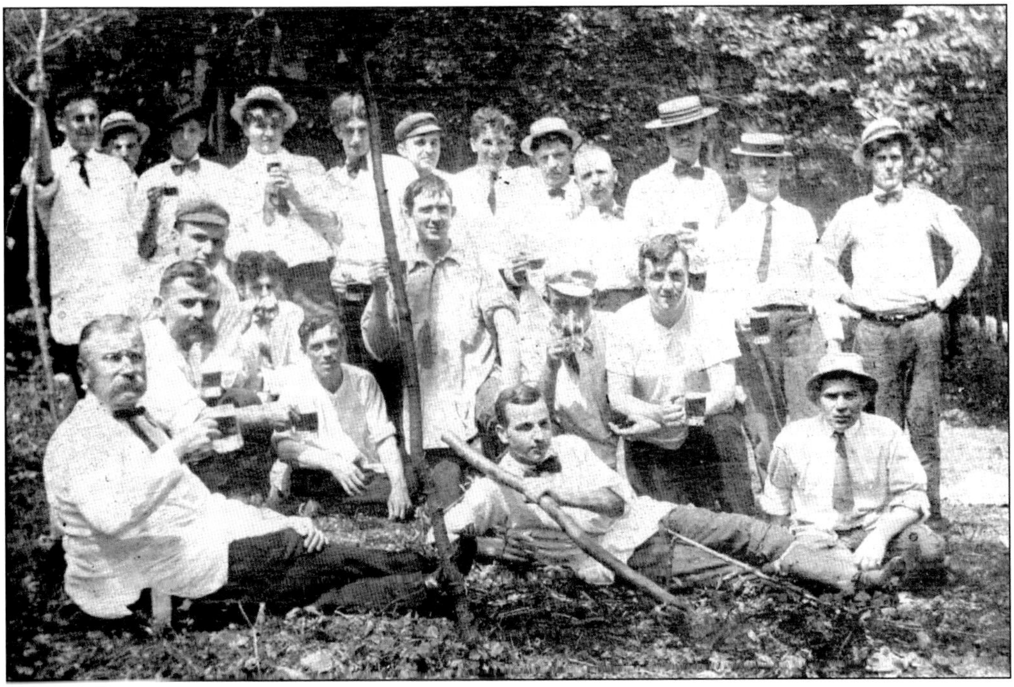

Vocal music was another form of artistic expression. This *maennerchor*, or German men's choir, composed of residents of the Tinicum area, used to hike up Haycock Mountain to practice singing. Pictured around 1910, they pause, hiking staffs in hand, to soothe their throats. Edwin Becker, with mustache, is seated in front left with beer stein raised. Similar groups across America today continue to preserve German music, language, and traditions. (WNR.)

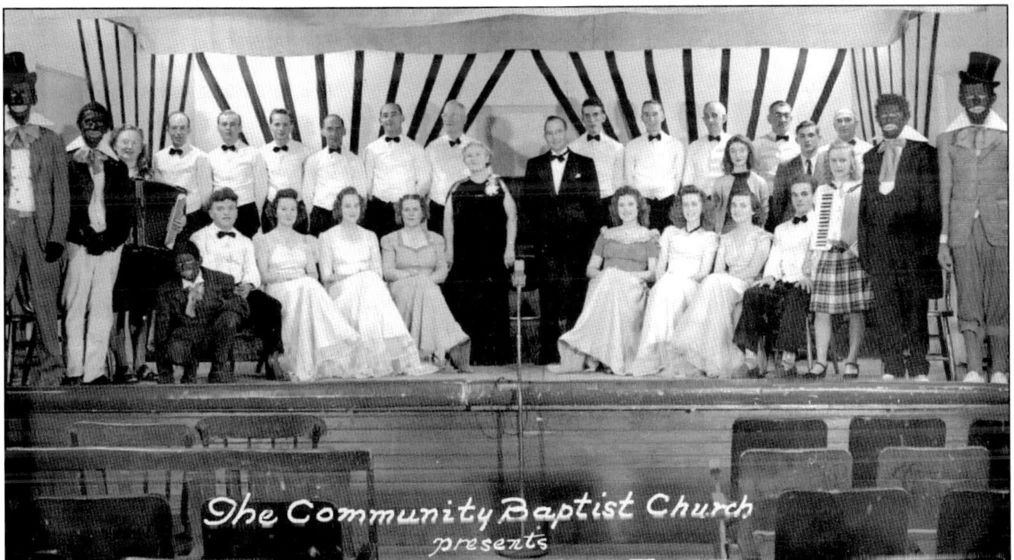

The Community Baptist Church in Point Pleasant presented this minstrel variety show in 1946. In the chorus are members of the Dobron, Fautz, Goulding, Hicks, Housley, Howarth, Keller, Lord, Myers, Naylor, Ott, Robinson, Schneider, Slotter, Stroh, Wilson, and Yansik families, with Joseph Mathews, pastor. (DLD.)

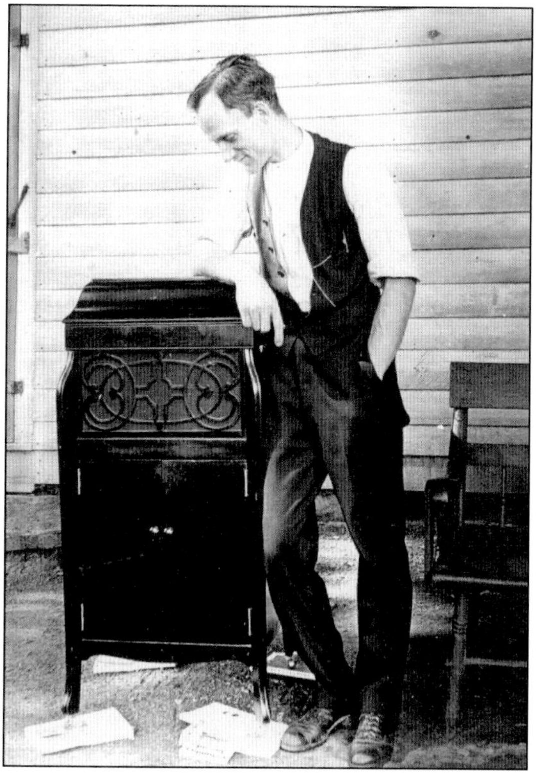

Thomas Edison's invention of talking machines produced musical entertainment without the hours of practice necessary to learn to play live music. Schultz son-in-law Fred Brandt admires one of these modern miracles of sound at the Ernst Schultz home in 1920. (LSH.)

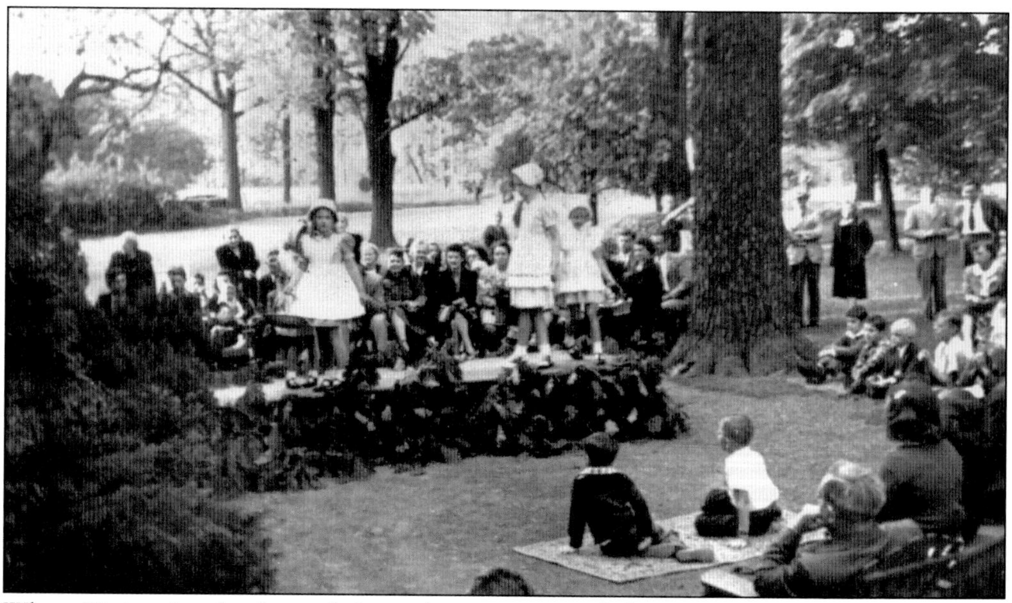

When Tinicum's schools needed supplies in 1946, Gladys Powell proposed a community fund-raiser, which evolved into the annual Tinicum Arts Festival. The first event, held in the Erwinna School, featured a fashion show of period clothing from residents' attics. Among the door prizes were a dozen baby chicks and a bushel of shelled corn. In 1947, the event, shown here, moved to the lawn of Riverside Farm, the Henry S. Stover homestead on River Road. (LSG.)

Known as Miss Tillie, Matilda Stover, seen here in 1946, had saved a lifetime of her fashionable clothing, which she loaned for several of the shows. Peggy Powell wears one of Miss Tillie's childhood outfits. Felicia Wittig wore the wedding dress she had brought from Germany in 1910. In the second show, Lorraine Rudy and a partner exchanged a spontaneous dialog in Pennsylvania Dutch dialect. The Tinicum Civic Association–sponsored event now draws a crowd of 5,000 annually. (ALX.)

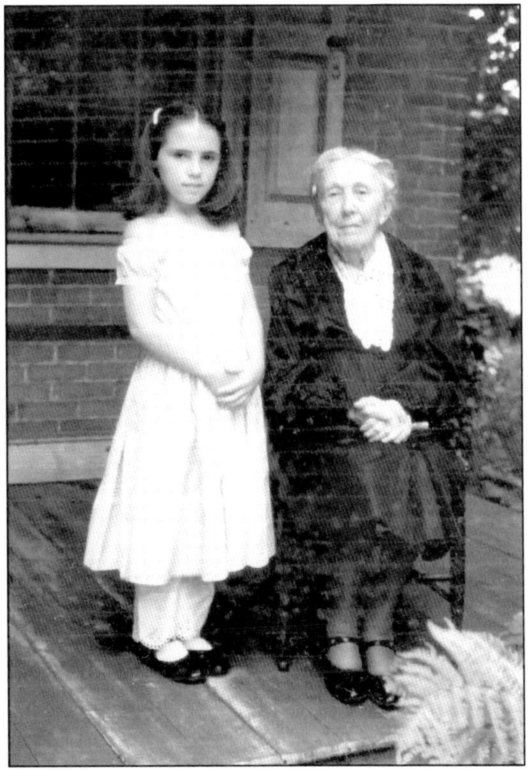

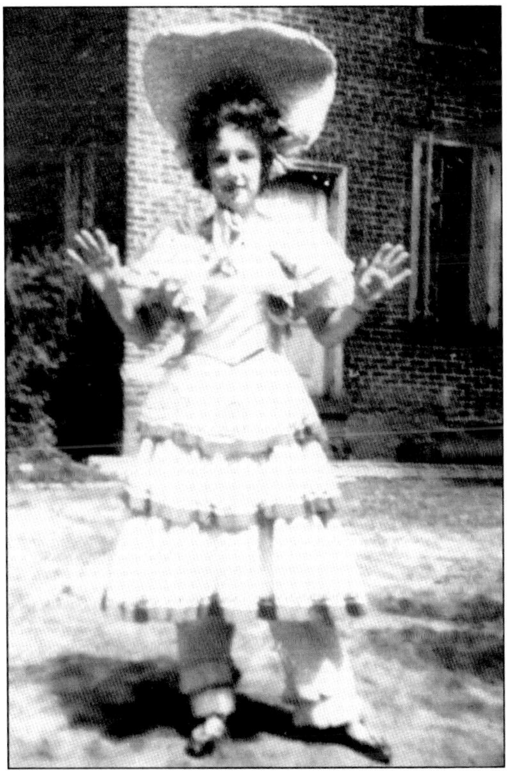

As the event grew in popularity, it moved again to the John J. Stover farm, which had become Tinicum Park in 1955. In this 1959 photograph, Shelly Goulding models another of Miss Tillie's childhood outfits. As Mrs. Dale Maddux, Shelly later served as Tinicum's tax collector. Early art shows included works by now-famous Bucks County artists Ranulph Bye, Walter S. Baum, Edward Redfield, and Daniel Garber. (LSG.)

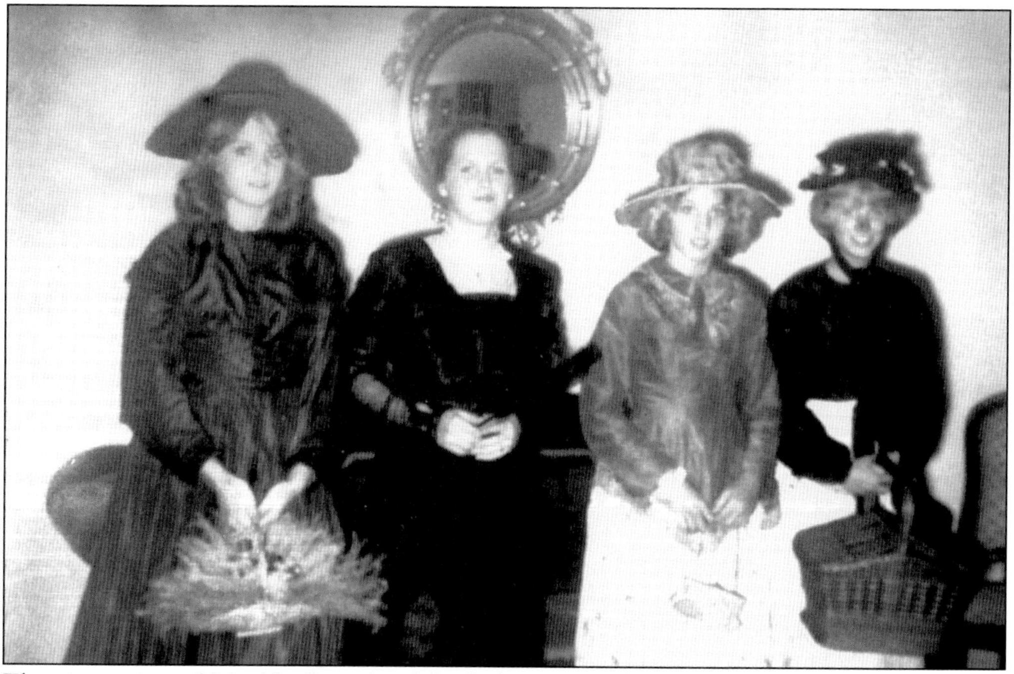

The tiny waists of Matilda Stover's adult clothes required local Girl Scouts to model them. In 1979, the Stover clothes were presented again, but since then they have been retired for conservation. Four of the models that year are, from left to right, Karen Lutz, Amy Stover (in her grandmother's dress), Karen Sailer, and Elizabeth Kallenbach. (LSG.)

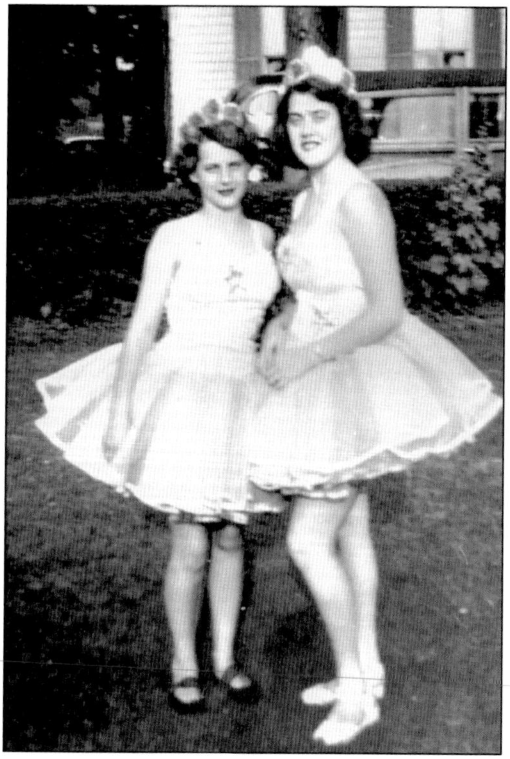

A highlight of the festivals for many years was the stage show. A presentation of *Swan Lake* one year featured all male "ballerinas" in pink tights. The ballerinas shown here, however, are Emma (Templeton) Roberson (left) and her sister, Hattie (Templeton) Fretz, who circulated among the gathered guests selling cigarettes at early festivals. No such enterprise would be condoned by today's health-conscious community. (LSG.)

The Tinicum Follies stage shows became more polished in appearance in 1952, when summer and weekend resident Jerome Cargill, inspired by the philanthropic efforts of the Tinicum Civic Association, donated his professional help, with costumes, staging, choreography, and a director. In 1967, costumed members greeted arrivals at the Flemington, New Jersey, train station. Sabina Cavanaugh and Leon Stem are in front of, from left to right, Robin Bernstein, Joyce Gilmore, and Kathy Kelly. (LSG.)

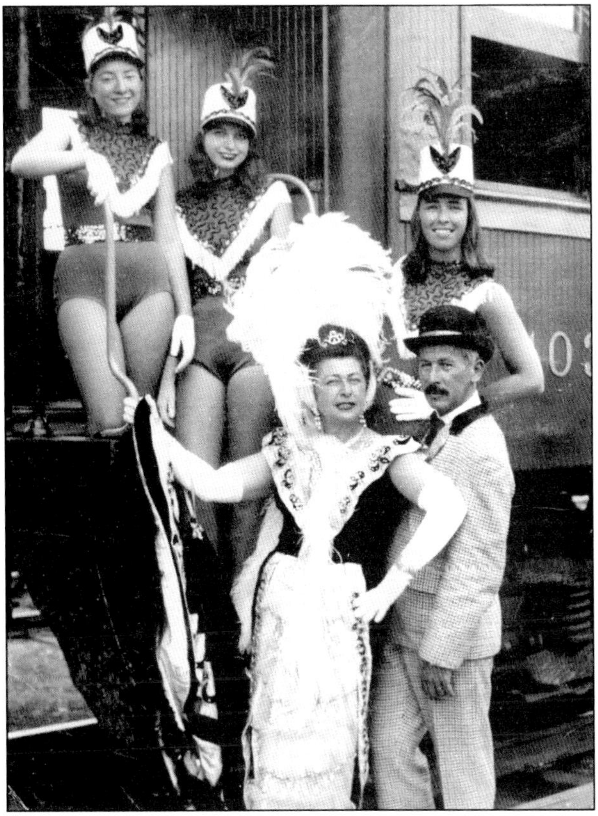

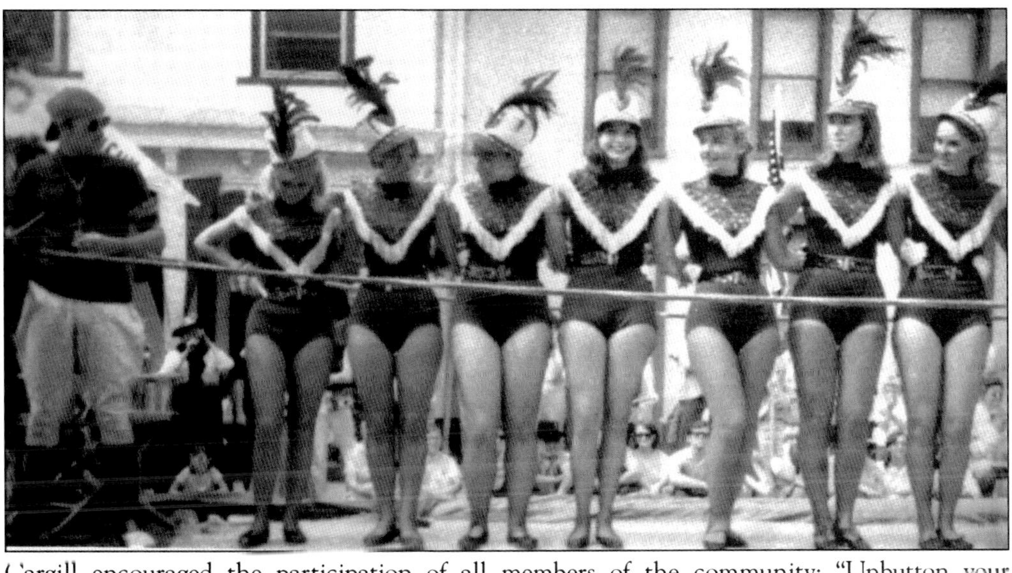

Cargill encouraged the participation of all members of the community: "Unbutton your inhibitions and rub elbows with the artist, the plumber, the farmer, the teacher—no previous stage experience necessary." These amateurs wowed audiences with their professional-quality performances. In a 1967 Frenchtown parade, this chorus line includes, from left to right, director Tony Townsend, Cindy Taylor, Barbara Jensen, Robin Bernstein, Joyce Gilmore, Diane Ditchman, Kathy Kelly, and Carol Moninghoff. (DVN.)

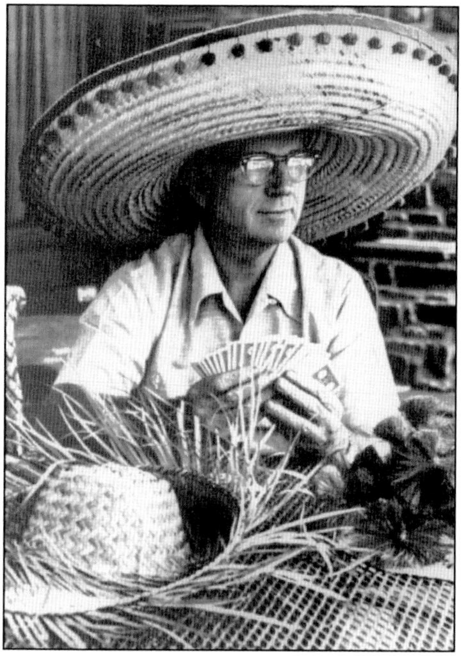

James Michener employed his storytelling talents to concoct outrageous fortunes as Mitch the Witch, before a backdrop of ailanthus branches resembling South Pacific palms. Asked by Matilda Stover, known as Miss Tillie, if she would meet a man, she reportedly reacted to his positive reply by buying a new outfit for the predicted occasion. Author S. J. Perelman wandered about the grounds with his pet mynah bird perched on his shoulder. The bird startled people by calling, "Hello, Hel-lo!" (INT.)

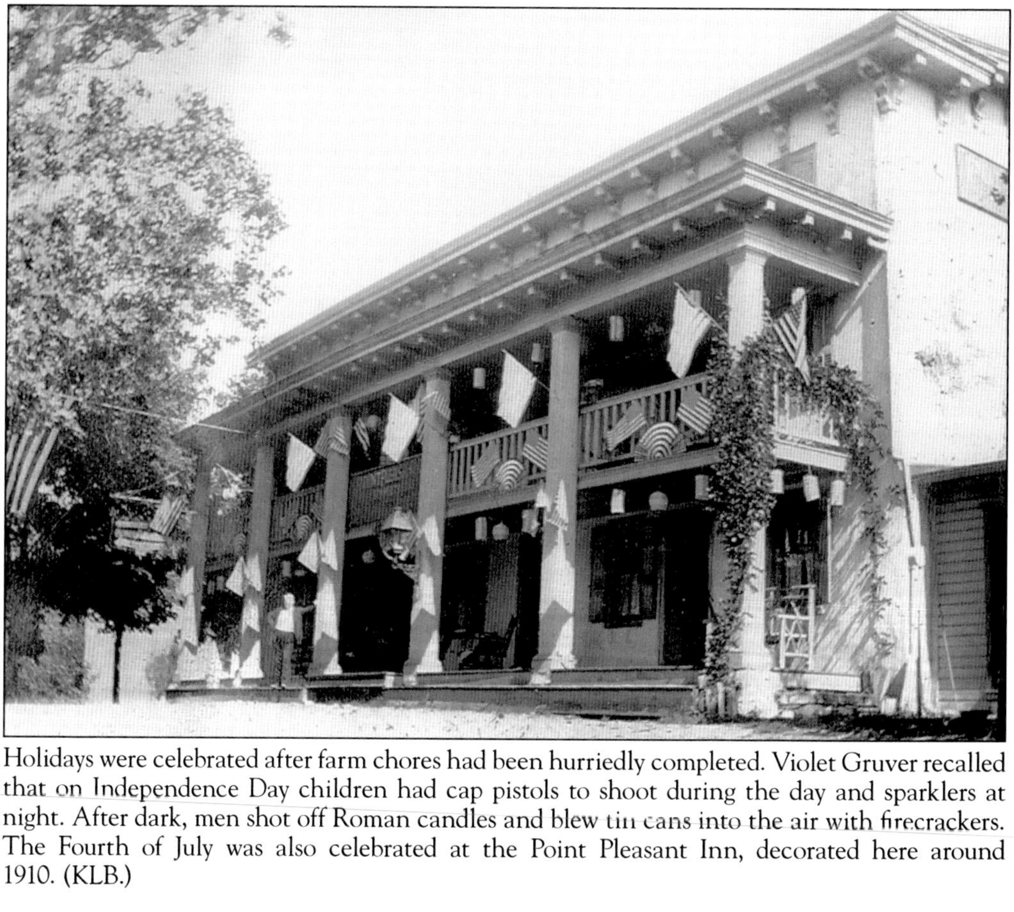

Holidays were celebrated after farm chores had been hurriedly completed. Violet Gruver recalled that on Independence Day children had cap pistols to shoot during the day and sparklers at night. After dark, men shot off Roman candles and blew tin cans into the air with firecrackers. The Fourth of July was also celebrated at the Point Pleasant Inn, decorated here around 1910. (KLB.)

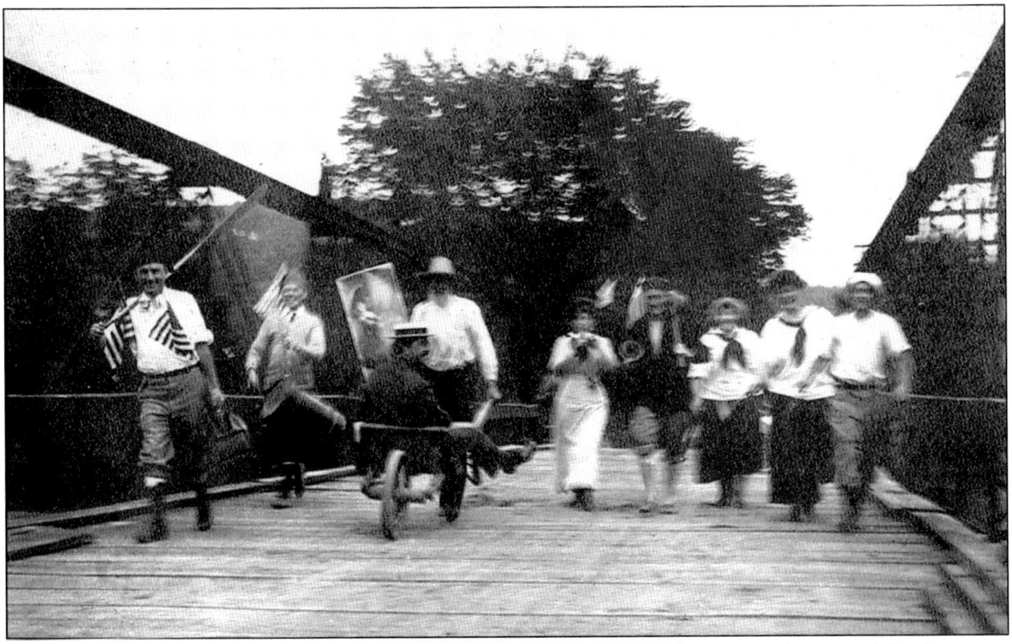

Guests at the Point Pleasant Inn formed an impromptu parade across the canal bridge near the inn to celebrate Independence Day around 1910. Marching to the drumbeat on a kerosene barrel, the revelers blow horns and wave flags. This bridge is now listed on the National Register of Historic Places. (KLB.)

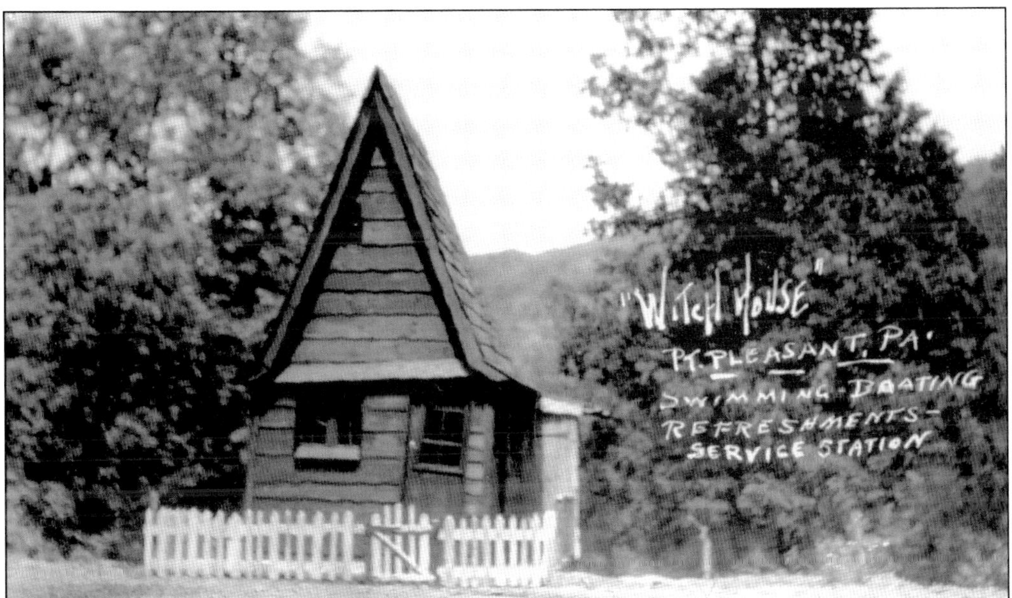

On Halloween, around 1910 to 1920, children were bused to the Witch House on River Road near Point Pleasant. Suddenly screams would erupt as a witch came flying off the top of the hill on her broom, crossing the road and landing in the yard. The children never noticed the wire strung by owner Joseph Aaron, who ran his business, a gas station and refreshment stand for swimmers and boaters, into the 1940s. (DBM.)

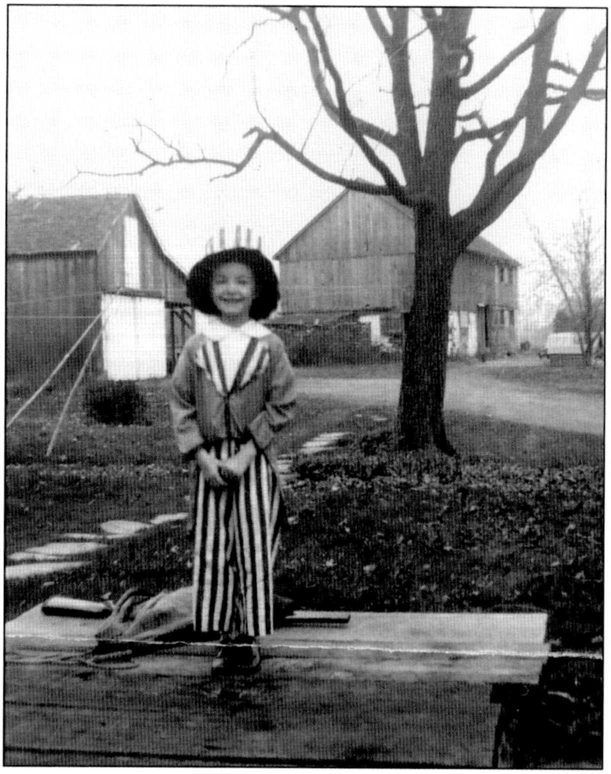

During World War II, Barbara Lowry dressed as Uncle Sam on Halloween, posing here on her family's Cafferty Road farm. Children wore costumes to school and played games like bobbing for apples, until concerns about the spread of polio ended that fun. Violet Gruver recalled that older youths used "trick night" to tip over outhouses or move equipment to strange places, as when a farmer's hay rake appeared on the schoolhouse porch roof. (DBM.)

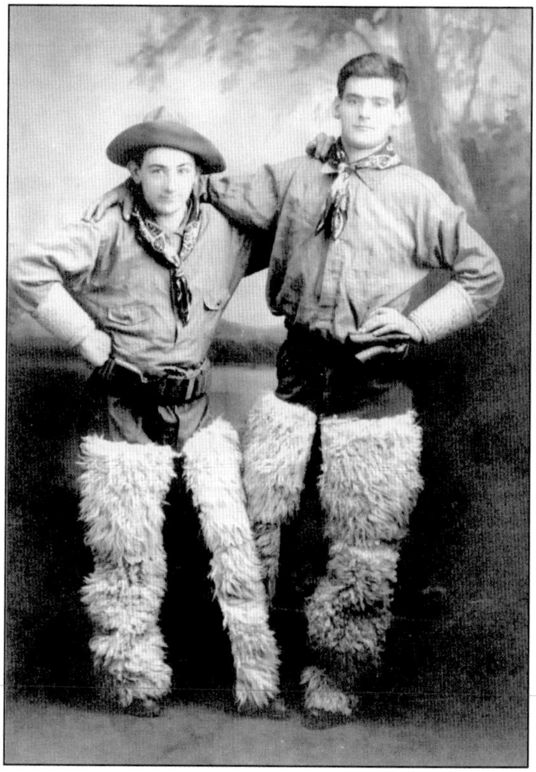

Sometimes people, including adults, enjoyed dressing in costumes regardless of the season. Brothers John (left) and Jake Wampfler duded up as cowboys for this 1911 studio portrait during a break from their farming routine. (LSH.)

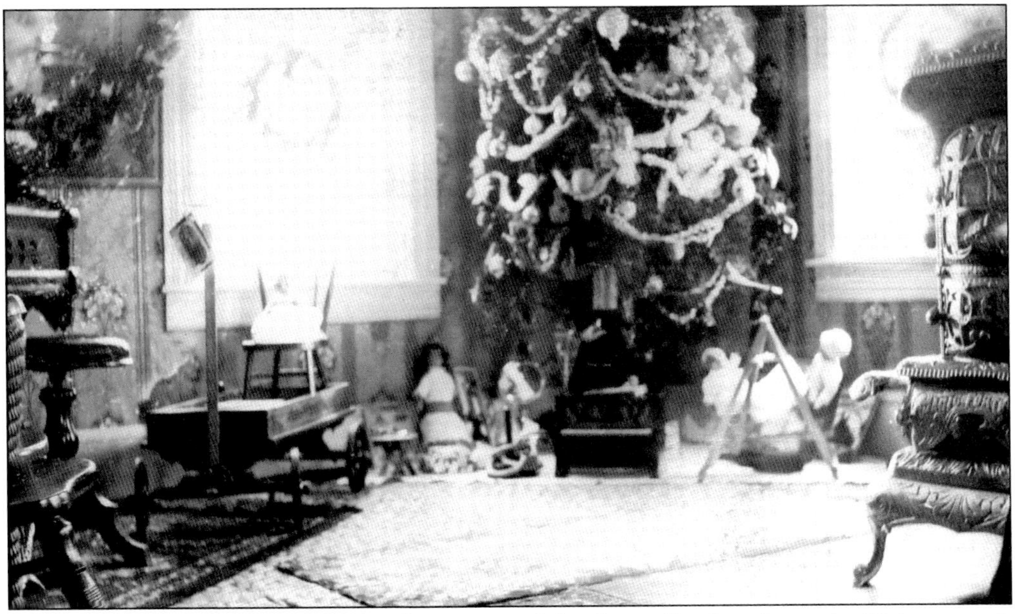

The 1914 cedar Christmas tree in the corner of the Jonas Sigafoos home in Uhlerstown is surrounded by a large assemblage of toys. The predominance of dolls indicates that girls outnumbered boys in the family, although a boy must have been thrilled to discover the wagon awaiting him. The ornate parlor stove, seen on the far right, and a parlor organ, partly visible on the left, indicate that the Sigafoos store was supporting the family quite comfortably. (SIG.)

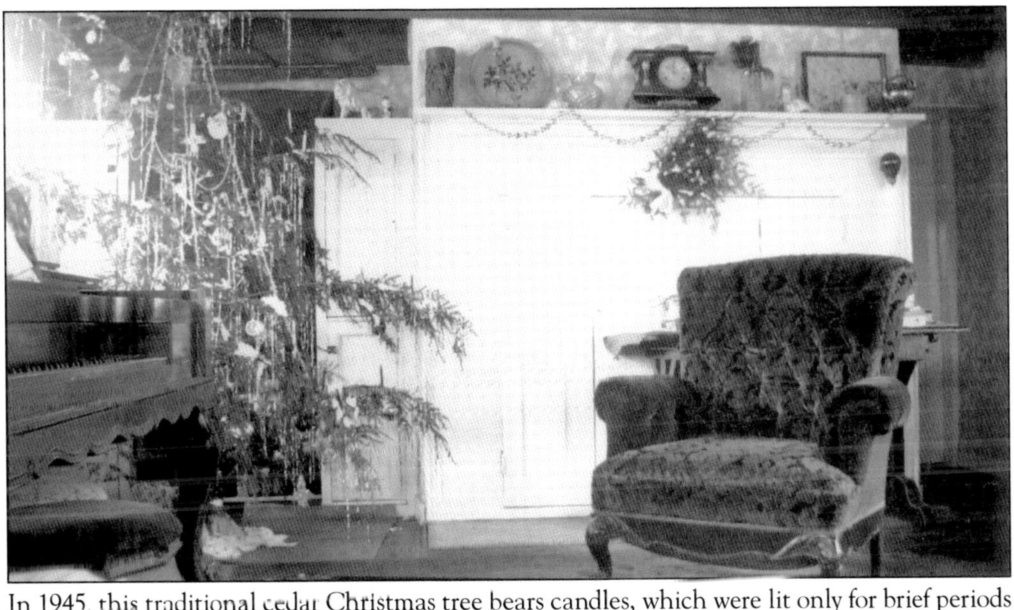

In 1945, this traditional cedar Christmas tree bears candles, which were lit only for brief periods because of fire danger. Shutters on the fireplace of the Krebs farm are a regional feature that sealed the opening from cold drafts when no fire was burning. The installation of chimney dampers later became a more efficient solution, or the doors remained closed when stoves and furnaces replaced open fires for heating. (EWH.)

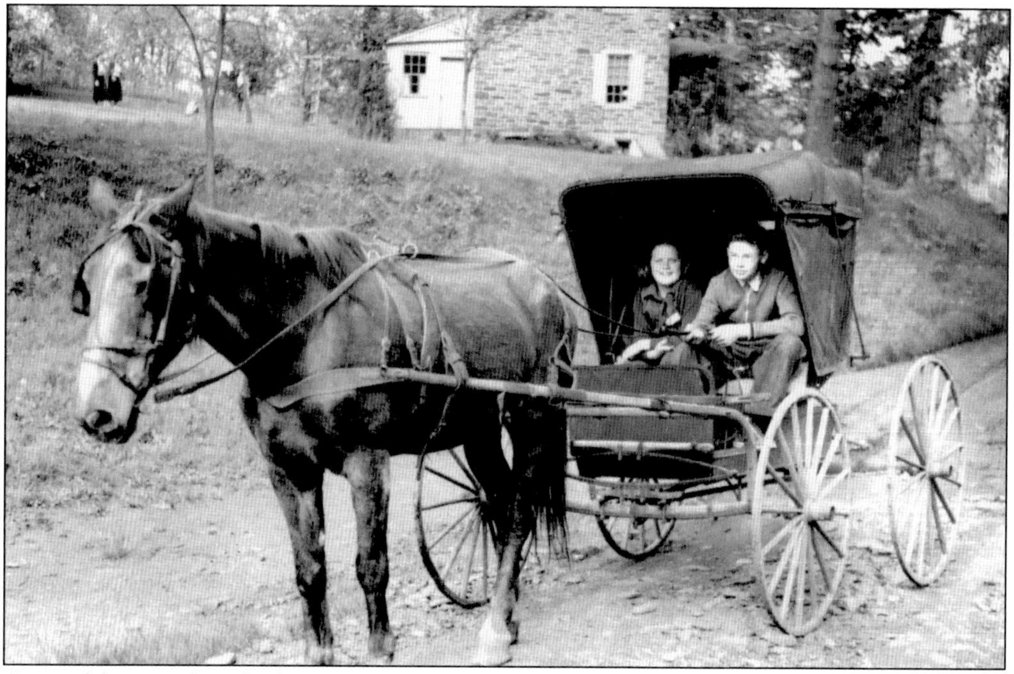

One celebration for which there was no season was a wedding, which followed a period of courtship. In early times, a drive in what is sometimes referred to as a Mennonite Courting Buggy was one way for a young couple to discover if friendship would lead to marriage. This unidentified couple traveled down Sheephole Road in a buggy borrowed from Alex Wittig around 1920. (HAL.)

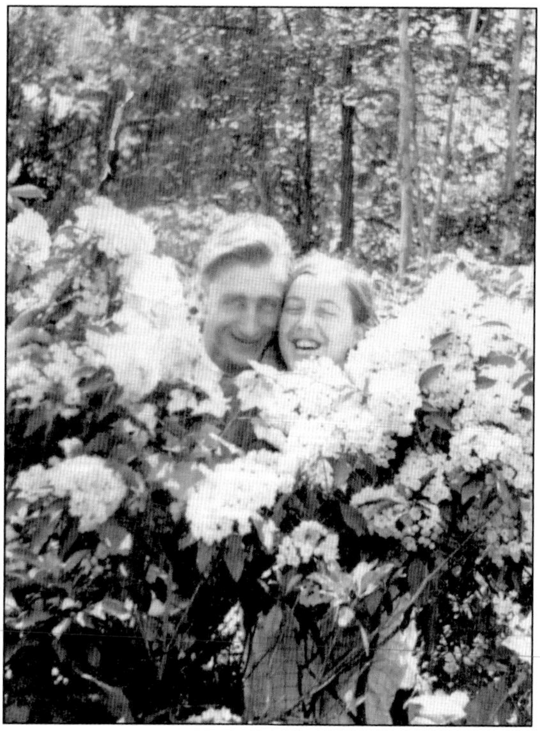

After a period of courtship, which included romantic strolls along woodland paths, Floyd Templeton and Helen Bickel were married in 1935 and enjoyed many years of living happily ever after. Many former Tinicum schoolchildren remember Floyd as their school bus driver. (FTZ.)

Courting couple Joe Heaney and Elsie Whitlock, friends since their Clay Ridge School days, enjoyed horseback rides and hikes in the hills. They perch here on a rock beside Tinicum Creek before their marriage in 1947. (EWH.)

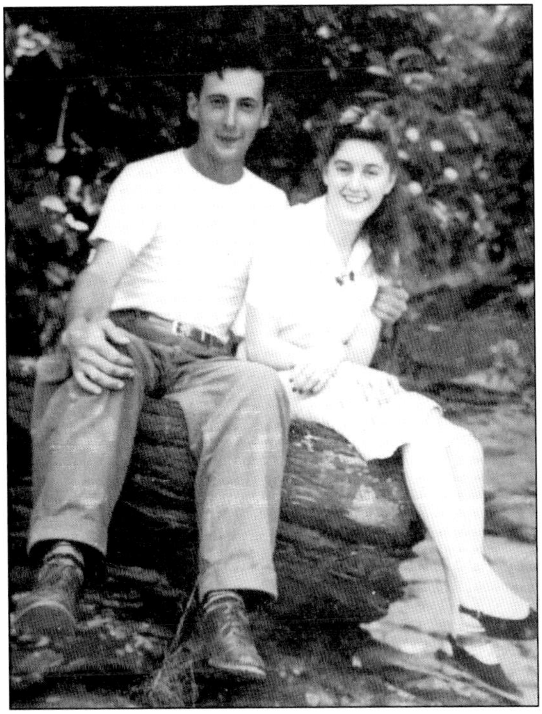

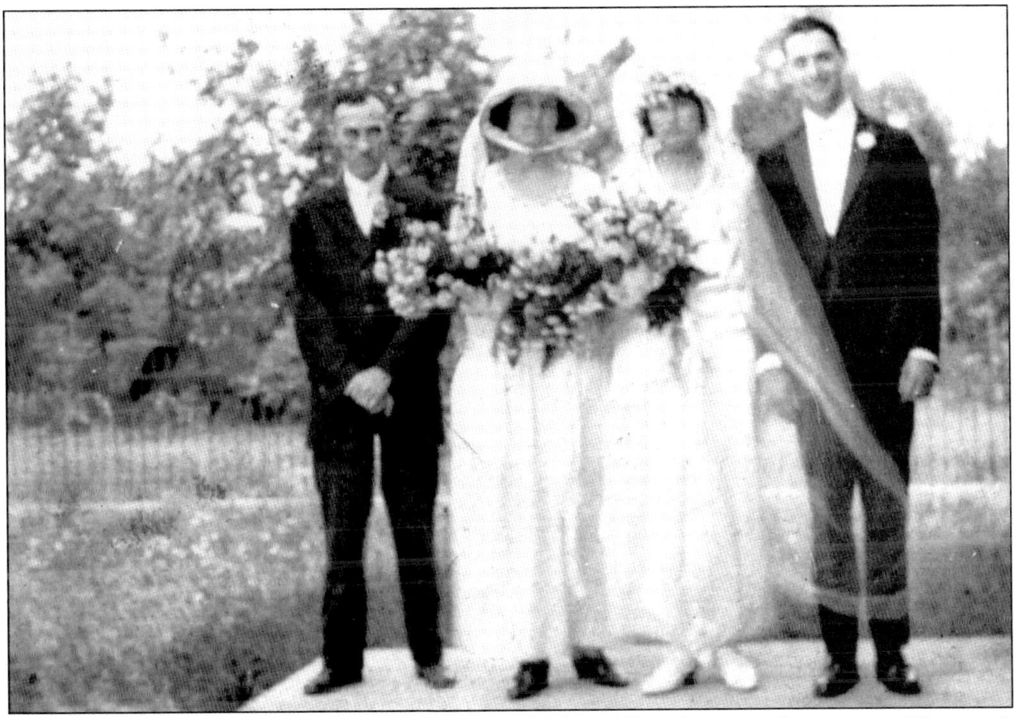

A friendship that had begun when Anna Free and Edward Bowden were classmates at Tinicum's one-room Rock Ridge School resulted in their 1923 wedding. Attendants John Boyd and Madeline Free (left) pose with the bridal couple (right) as a breeze carries the bride's long veil in front of her groom's dark suit. (HAS.)

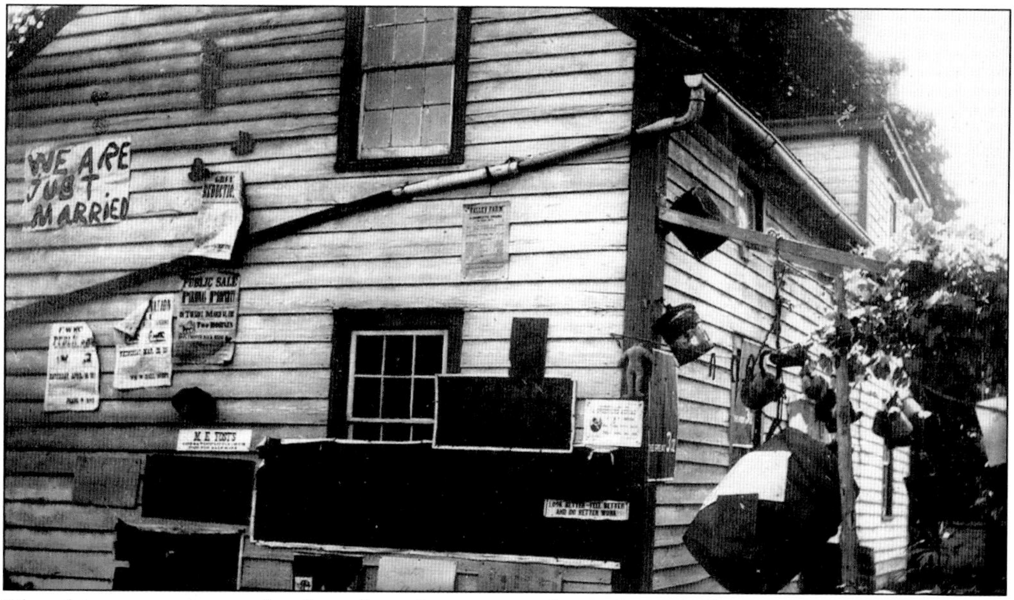

The chivaree, or serenade of newlyweds, was a tradition brought by European immigrants to America. Shortly after the wedding, a noisy crowd of well-wishers paid a surprise midnight visit to the home of the couple, beating pots and pans, ringing cowbells, and shooting firecrackers until they were invited inside for refreshments. In this c. 1910 scene, the serenaders have left house decorations as evidence of their visit. (KLB.)

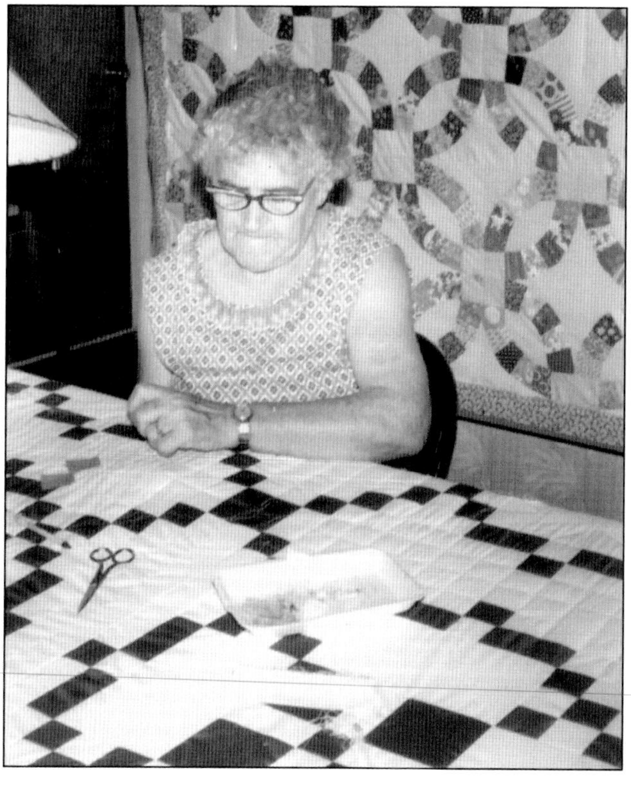

Some residents spent their leisure hours creating practical art, such as hooked rugs and patchwork quilts, from scraps of fabric. A prized wedding gift would have been one of Esther Weaver's quilts, which were widely admired and eagerly sought by collectors. In this 1975 photograph, she is working on a quilt in the Homespun design, while a completed Double Wedding Ring quilt is displayed behind her. (WVR.)

When baby carriages had outlived their usefulness, older children and adults rescued the wheels to create imaginative go-carts. Leslie Weaver devised the vehicle seen here in 1923 for his son, Robert. (EWB.)

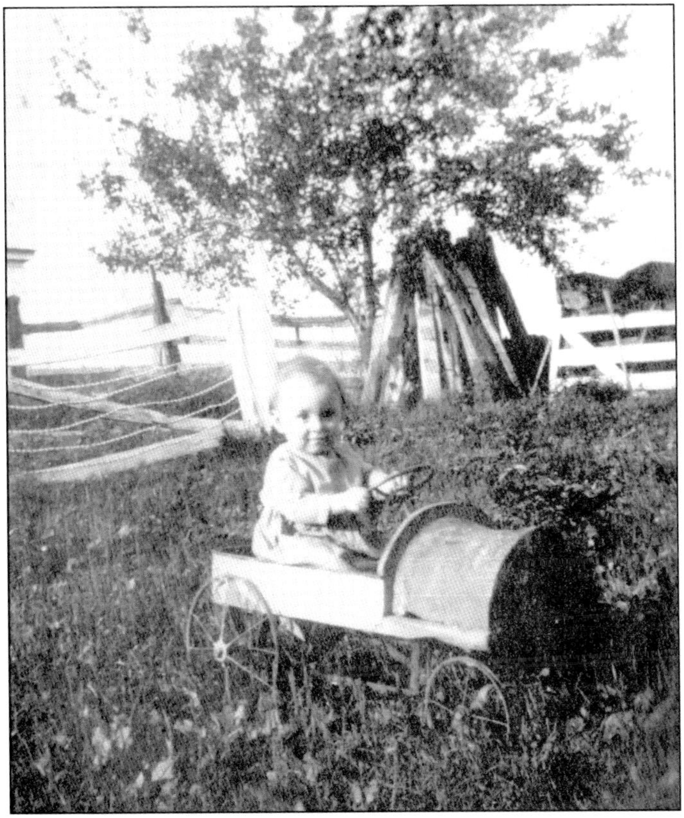

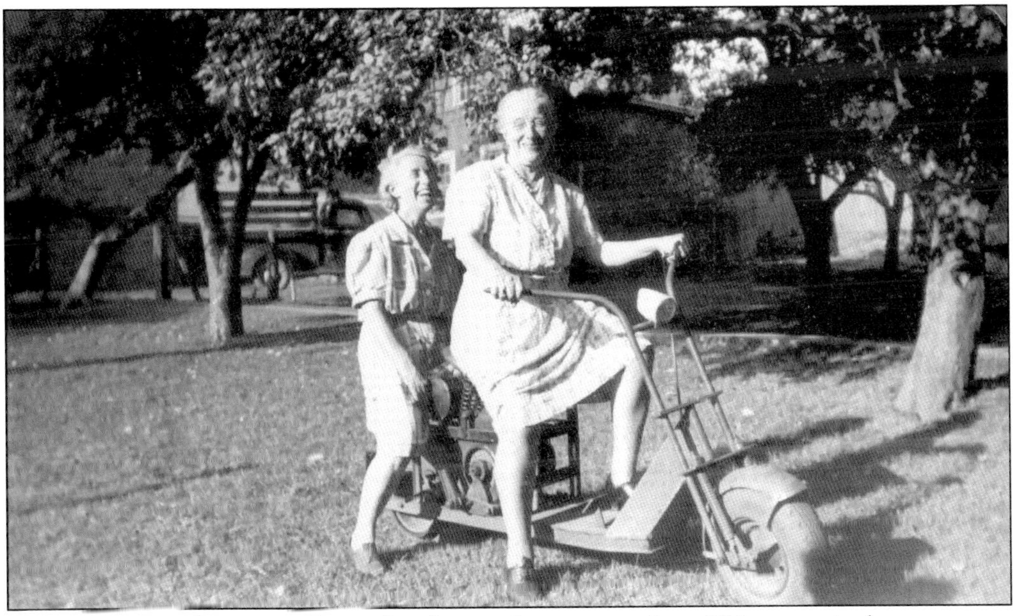

Senior citizens also enjoyed novelty forms of transportation. This motorized scooter was assembled from a commercially available Cushman kit. Sisters Emma (Overpeck) Bickel (left) and Bertha (Overpeck) Koplin share a laugh as they prepare for a test drive around the Bickel farm in 1947. (FTZ.)

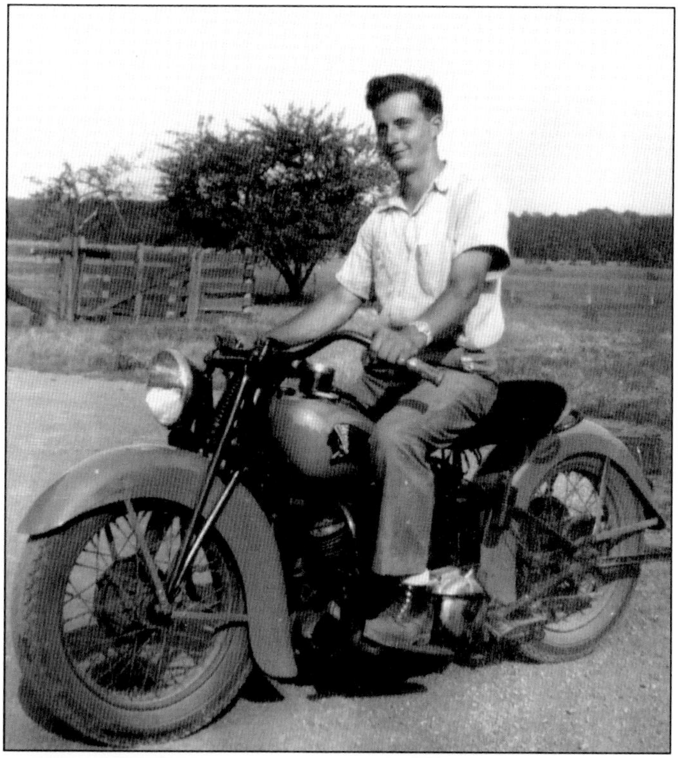

Newlywed Joe Heaney splurged on this Indian motorcycle in 1948, but his enjoyment was short-lived when he realized that it was more important to save the money to build a house. (EWH.)

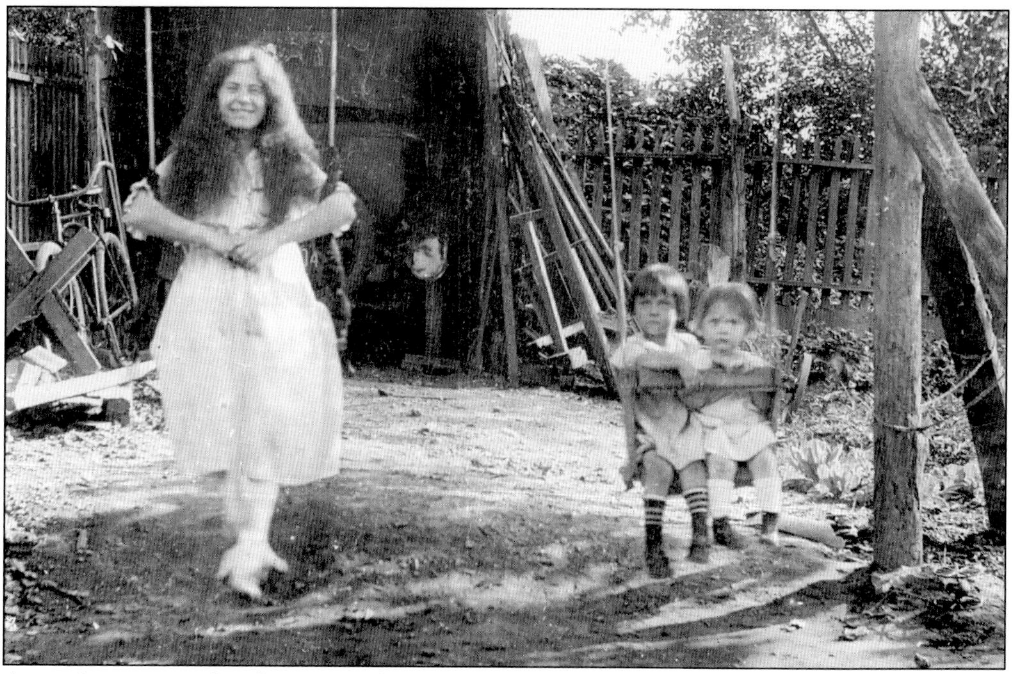

A carefree pastime for all ages was floating through the summer air on a swing. Bertha Schultz Brandt is clearly enjoying her swing, but her daughters Gertrude (left) and Amelia appear to be a bit dubious about the experience in 1923. Later generations took the concept of floating through the air to new heights as aviation caught the imagination of the nation. (LSH.)

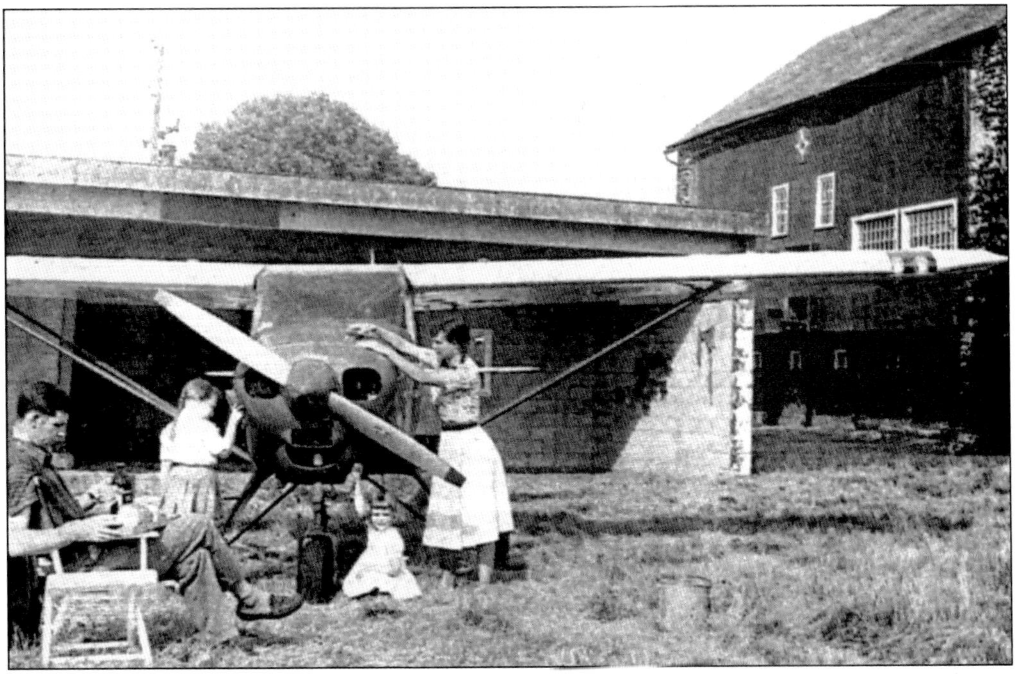

Tinicum residents became fascinated by aviation as early as 1918, perhaps inspired by the daring feats of World War I pilots. Six private fields were in use by 1960. Fred Bell studies an owner's manual in 1961, while his wife, Marge, and daughters polish their Piper Tri-Pacer. Bell's airfield was on his 133-acre farm near Sundale, now permanently protected from development. The barn survives but is not visible from the road. (LSG.)

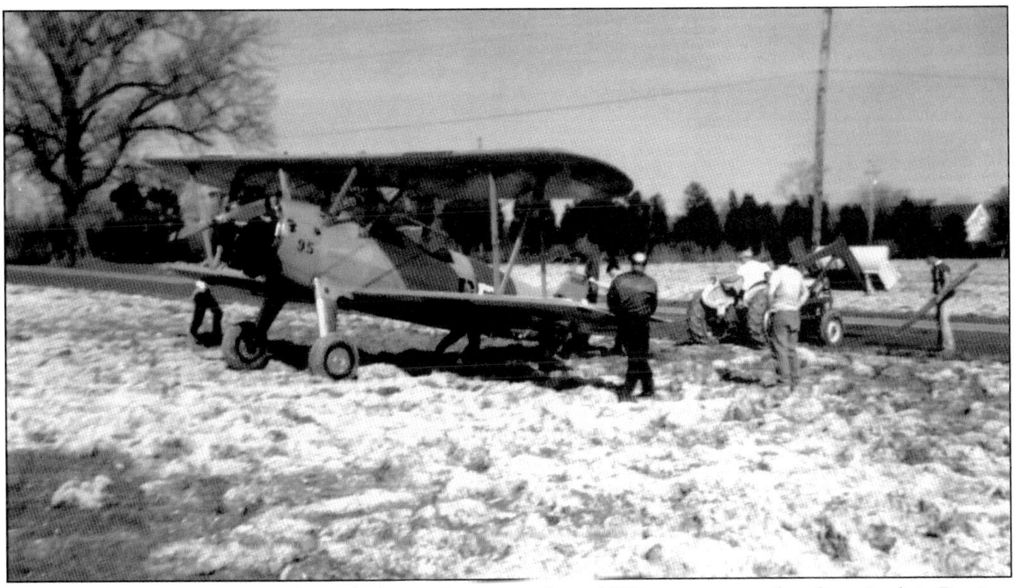

When John Posey, pictured in dark clothing, made a 1982 emergency landing in his Boeing Model 75 Stearman in a plowed field at the Haney farm, brothers Jim Haney and Joe Heaney, whose name was misspelled on his birth certificate, towed the plane to another location so that it could be trucked away. The large white oak on left still stands beside the Cafferty Road entrance to the 59-acre Haney farm, which is permanently protected from development. (EWH.)

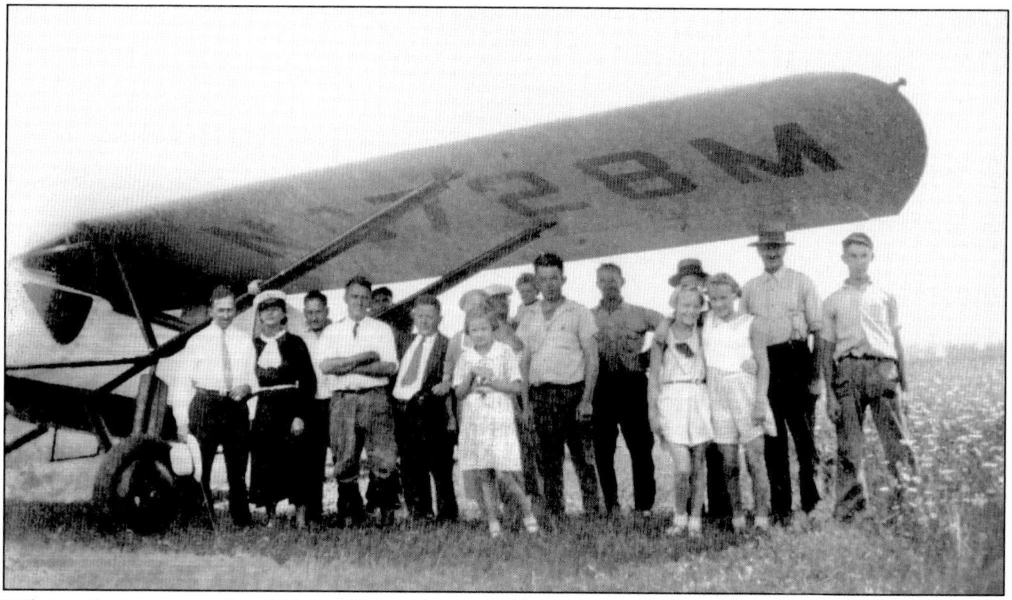

When a barnstormer landed in 1933 at the airfield opposite where the Ottsville Post Office now stands on Route 611, residents flocked to inspect the Ryan/Brougham aircraft, the commercial version of Charles Lindbergh's *Spirit of St. Louis*. Of those assembled in this photograph, Christian Wehrung stands with hands on hips beneath the number 28, and his son, Woody, stands on the far right. The site was also the Ottsville baseball field. (DWG.)

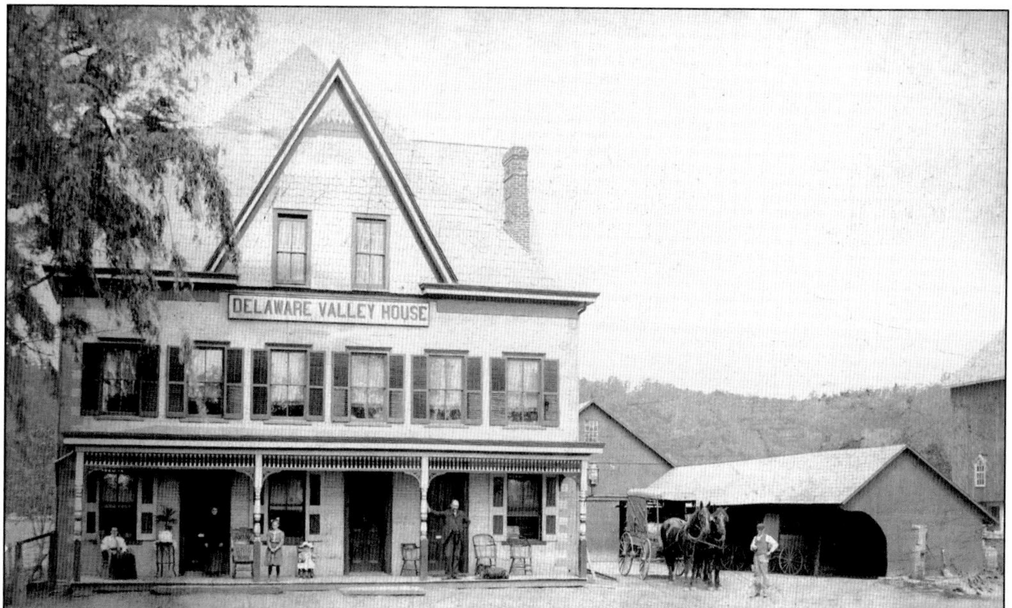

Tinicum has enjoyed a thriving tourism business along the Delaware River since earliest times, with stagecoach stops and country inns. When a bridge replaced a century of ferry service from Frenchtown, New Jersey, in 1844, the Delaware Valley House, a tavern since 1797, was expanded to accommodate guests, including Pres. Grover Cleveland, an avid fisherman, who stayed here and at the Point Pleasant Inn. Michael Uhler leans against the post to the right of the door. Now vacant, the building is part of the Uhlerstown Historic District. (WSW.)

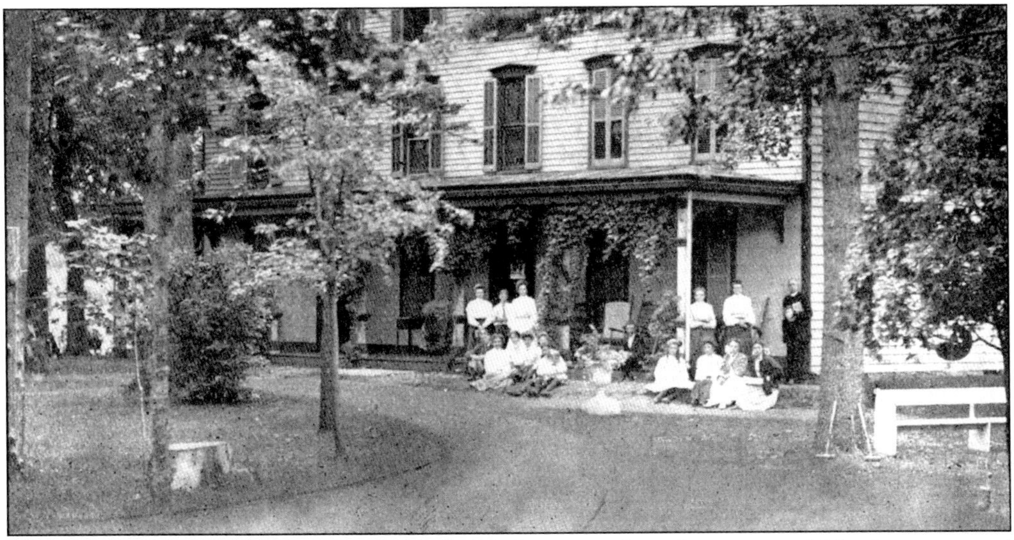

About 1880, Jordan Stover opened the family homestead at the corner of Headquarters and River Roads for summer boarders. The theatrical Barrymore family, who were from Philadelphia, were regular visitors to Riverside Farm, amusing themselves by playing charades in the kitchen. Members of the Stover family played music for singing in the parlor. Croquet mallets rest against a tree in this 1906 picture of the house, which is on the National Register of Historic Places. (DBM.)

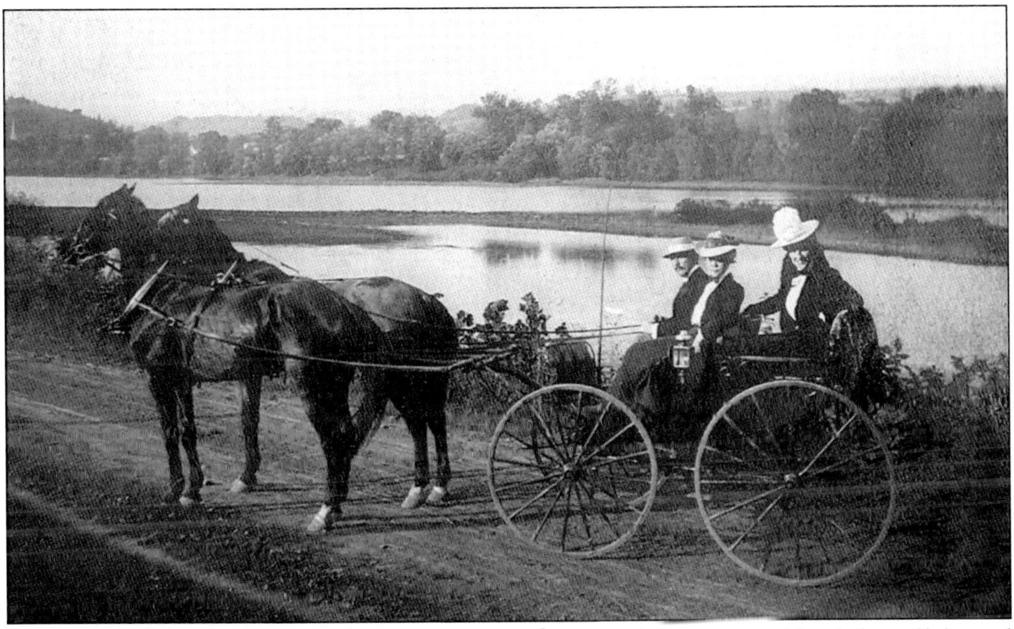

Fashionably dressed guests were driven on scenic rides around the countryside while staff cleaned their rooms back at the inn. The messages on postcards sent by visitors give an interesting insight to their thoughts and experiences. One somber reminder of the treatment of tuberculosis in earlier times was addressed to a resident of the Sunnyrest Sanatourium: "Am very glad to hear you are improving so much . . . Hope you are soon able to come home." (KLB.)

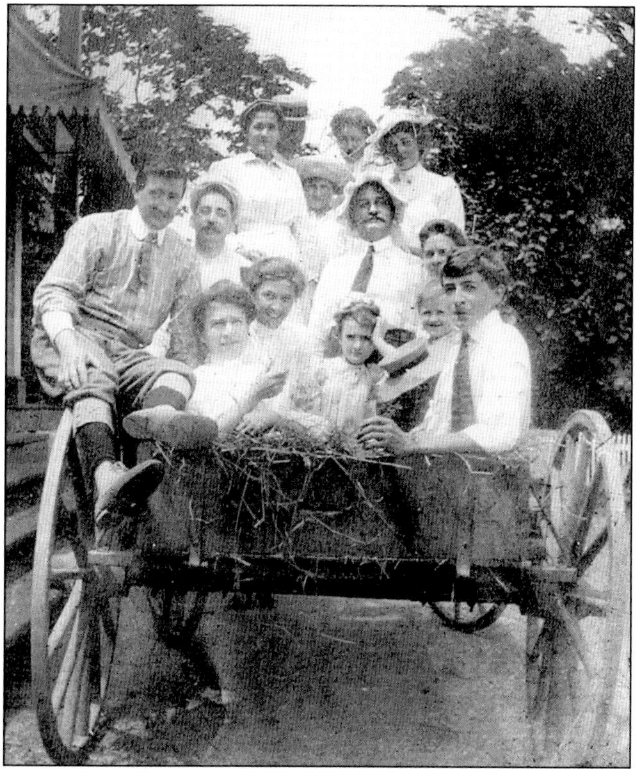

A hayride was a more casual form of entertainment for these jolly guests at the Point Pleasant Inn in 1912. A man in the center has donned a lady's hat. One postcard message read, "Yesterday we took a three mile walk and gathered the grandest flowers and had them for our table." (KLB.)

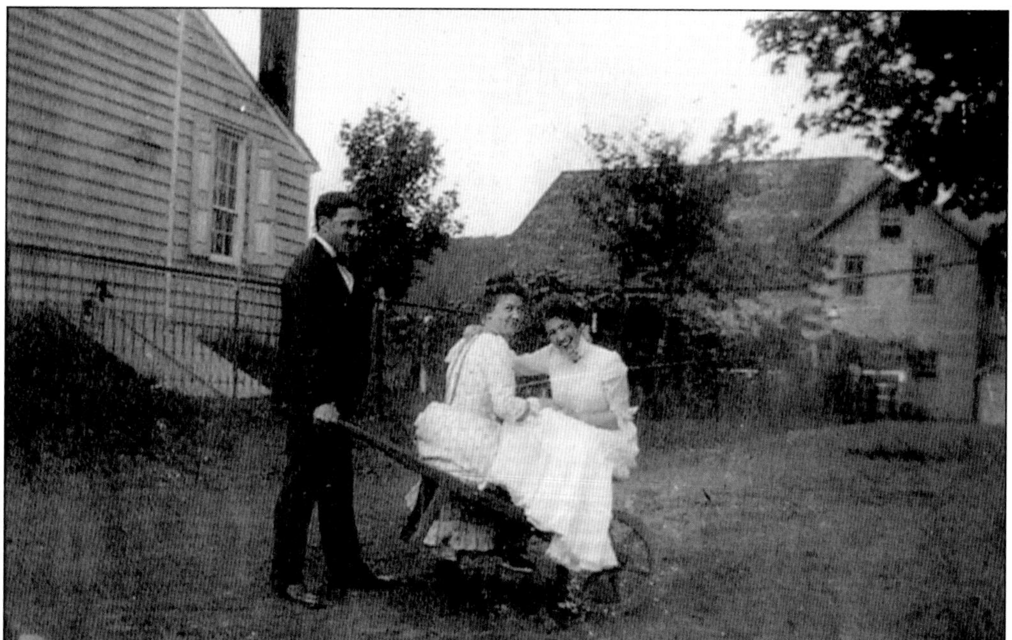

Guests clown with a wheelbarrow ride around the grounds of the Point Pleasant Inn, overlooking the scenic canal. A card postmarked 1917, and addressed simply to "Miss E. Reid, c/o Kresges 5 and 10¢ Store, Trenton, NJ," bore the message, "We are having the grandest time. It is much nicer than working." Another writer added, "I hope to learn some new songs." (KLB.)

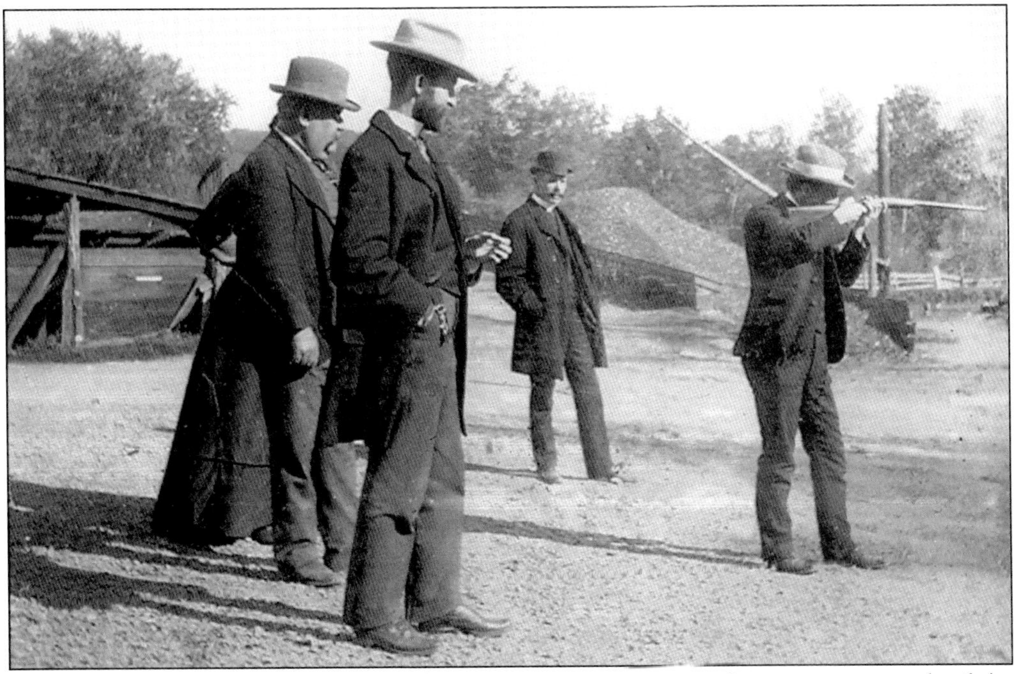

Gentleman guests, and at least one lady, enjoy target practice on the spacious grounds of the Point Pleasant Inn around 1912. A 1927 postcard message read, "Wish I could stay here a month. The scenery is beautiful—hills and trees and all." Eighty years later, the same message might accurately be sent by a visitor to Tinicum. (KLB.)

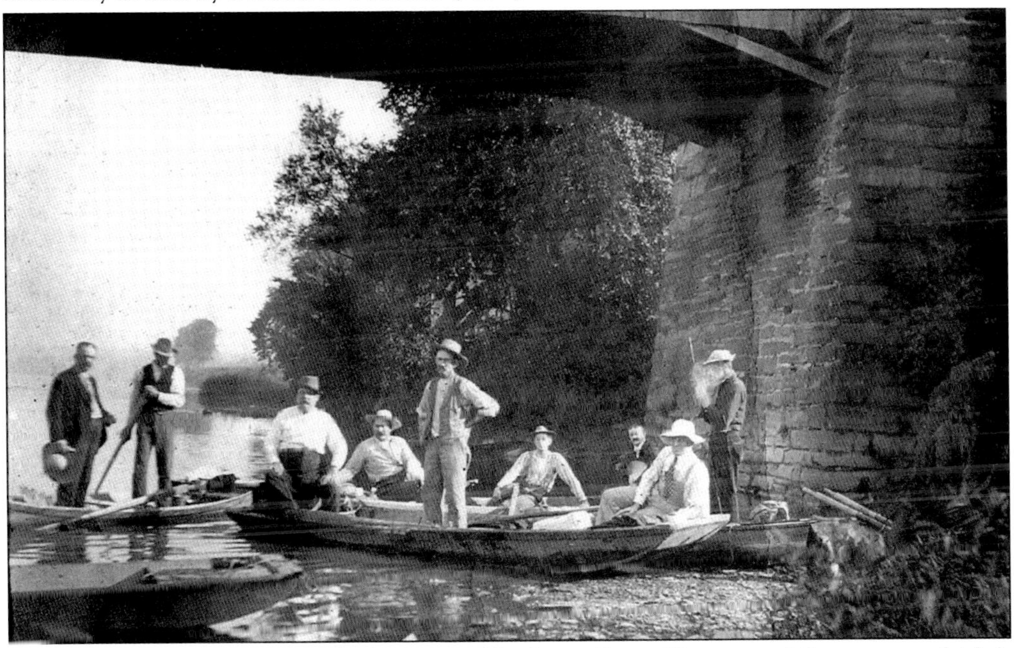

A flotilla of boats rests beneath the covered bridge at Point Pleasant, while one man (right), engulfed in smoke, tends to his fishing rod. The only identified member of the group is Charles Housem, the portly proprietor of the Point Pleasant Inn, wearing a white shirt and seated in the stern of one boat. (KLB.)

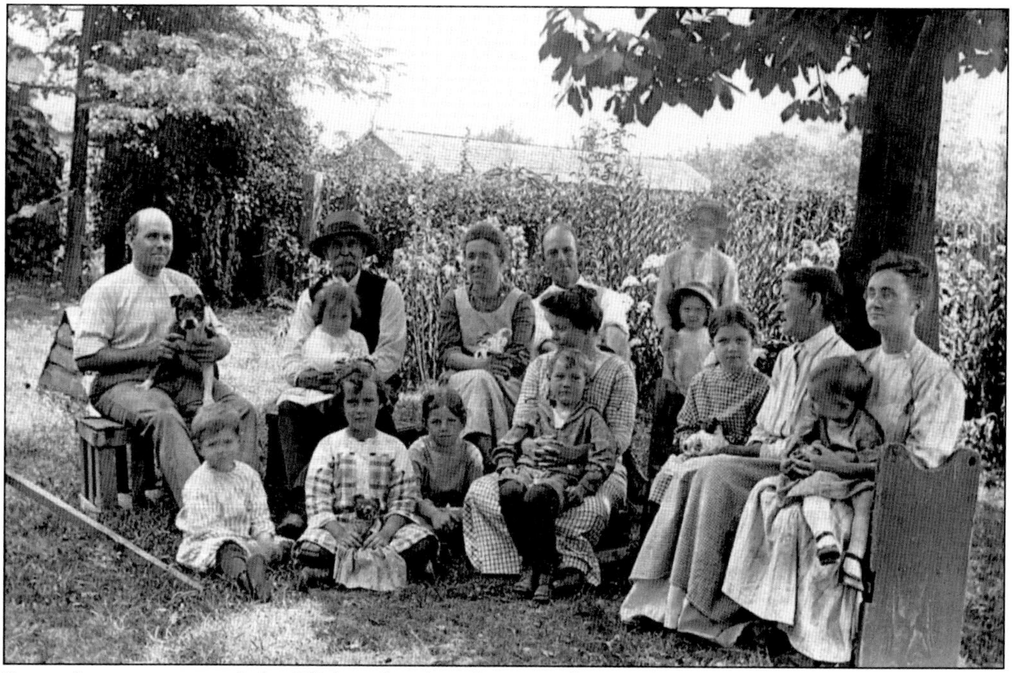

Several generations of the Walter family relax together with visiting relatives from Chester County on a 1912 summer afternoon in Point Pleasant, a time to share refreshments and stories. Identified in the front row, young Helen Walter (second from left) holds her teddy bear, while hostess Mary (Ingram) Walter (center front), wearing a checked dress, holds her son, John Willis Walter Jr., on her lap. (WLT.)

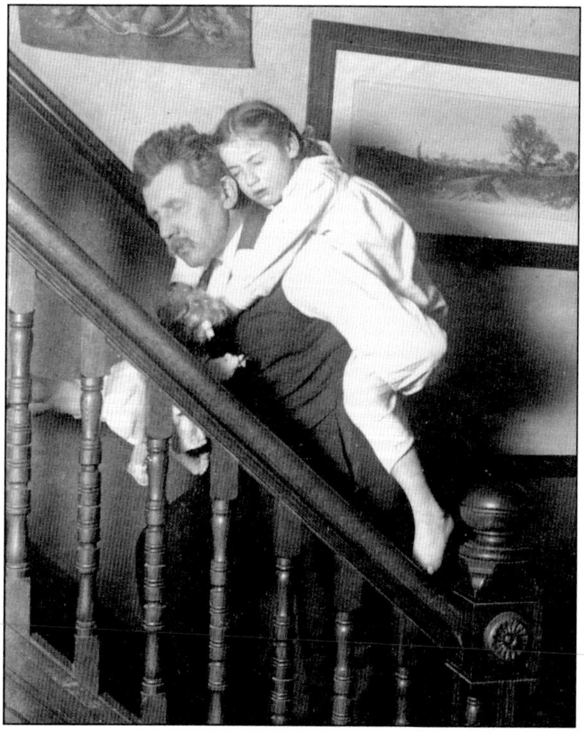

After a busy day of work or play, all ages are ready for a good night's sleep. Paul Krebs carries his daughter, Clara, and her doll upstairs to bed. (EWH.)

Seven

A Heritage Becomes a Legacy

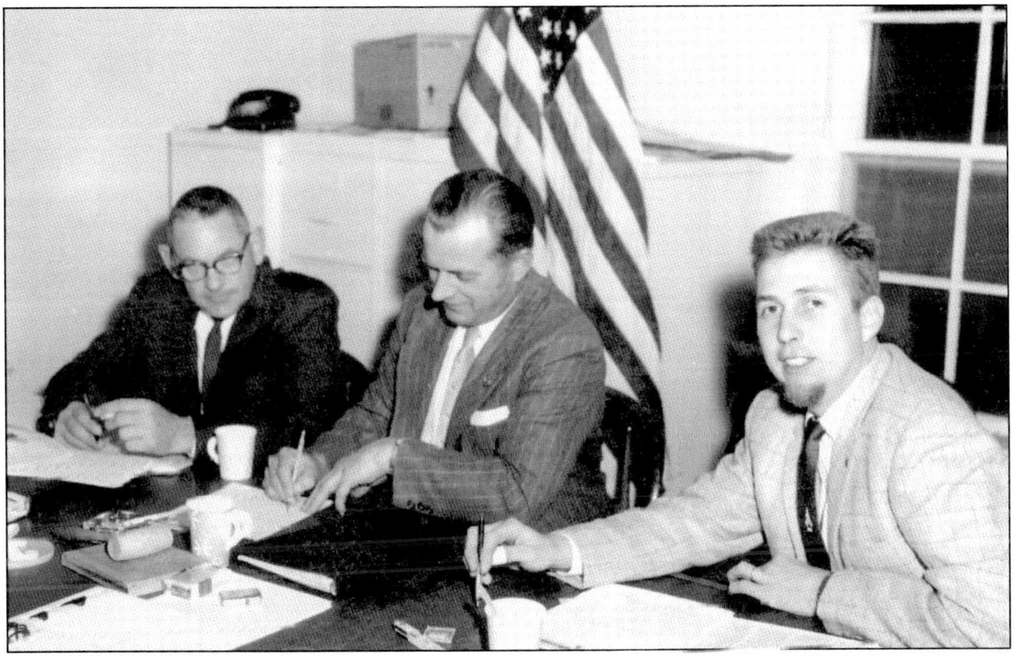

The right to clean air, pure water, and the preservation of natural scenic, historic, and aesthetic values of the environment are guaranteed to the people, including generations yet to come, by the Pennsylvania Constitution. Over time, Tinicum has adopted plans and ordinances to ensure the protection of these vital resources. In this 1963 photograph, from left to right, supervisors Ralph Zemel, Hiram Beer, and John Quinby ponder the future of the township. (QBY.)

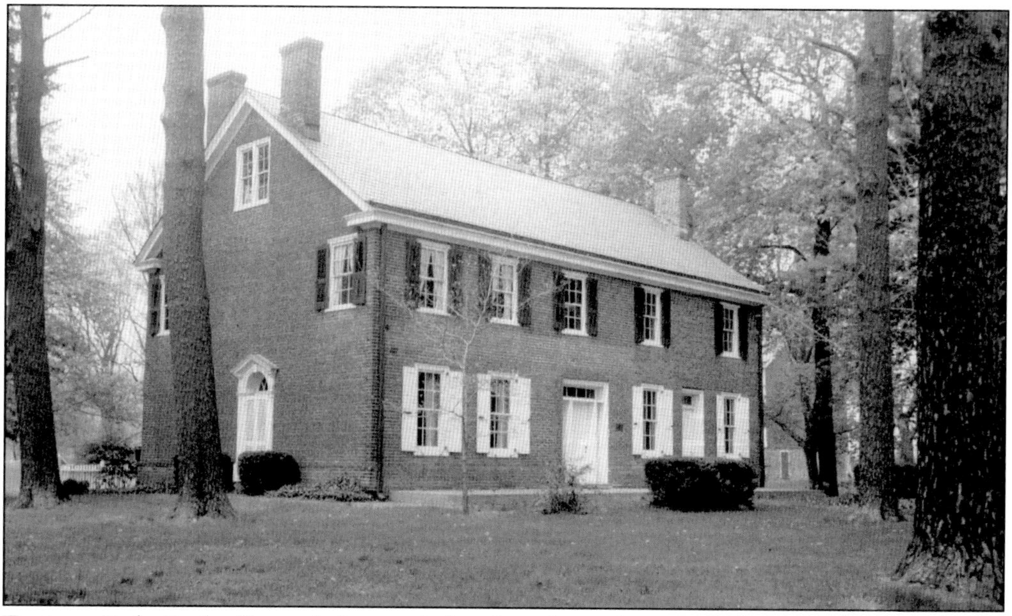

Tinicum Park, Bucks County's first park, has long been the site of the annual Tinicum Arts Festival and numerous other events. In 1846, Henry S. Stover, founder of the Stover family in Tinicum, bought the 125-acre Erwin farm, extending from the Delaware River to the canal. His grandson John J. Stover gave the property, with this handsome brick Erwin-Stover house and large barn, visible on far right, to the county in 1955. (BCP.)

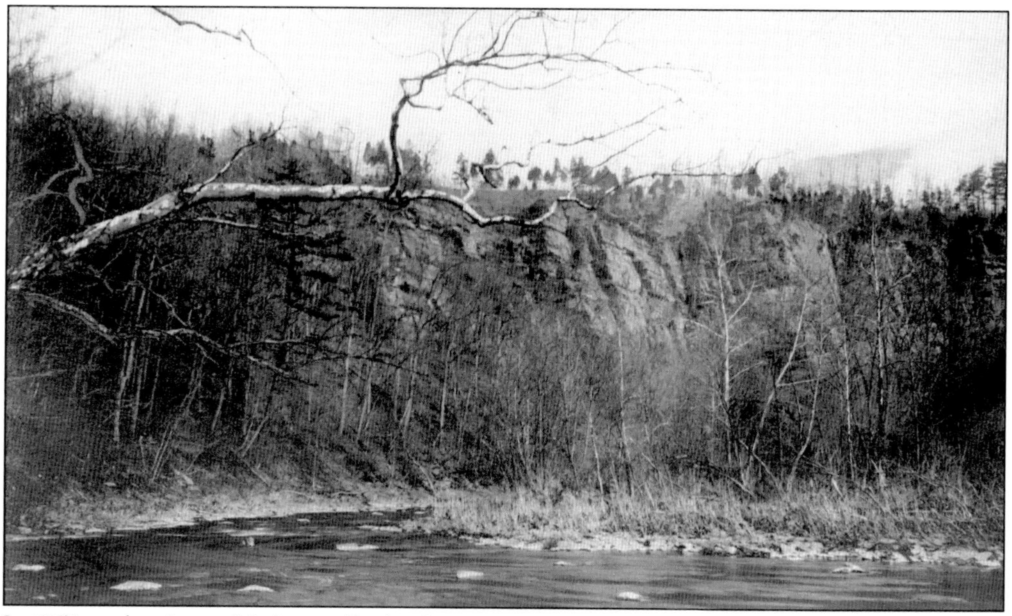

In 1952, author James Michener, Bucks County native and Tinicum resident, donated the seven acres overlooking Tohickon Creek, known as Indian Rocks, or High Rocks, to be added to Ralph Stover State Park. The sparse vegetation atop the Tinicum cliffs in this *c.* 1925 view, from the Plumstead Township side of the creek, has since matured to forest. (LDV.)

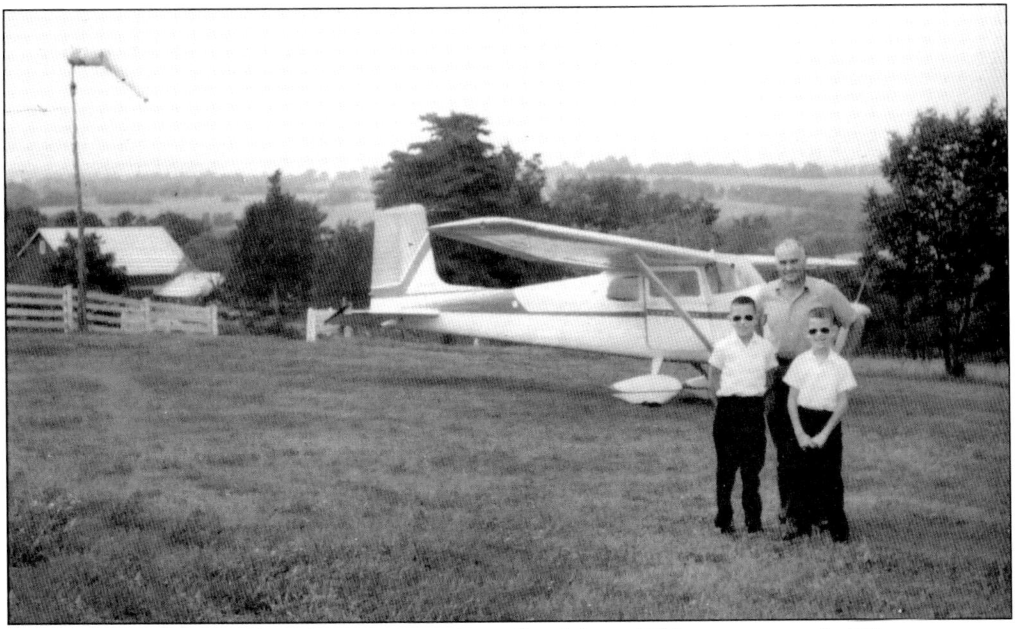

The airport established by John Van Sant above Sundale in 1954 is now part of a 296-acre county park. With its collection of still-operational historic aircraft, grass runway, picnic area, and views of distant hills, the park is popular with visitors, who can observe or go for rides in gliders and vintage biplanes. In 1977, John Van Sant stands beside his Cessna 172 with grandsons David Somp (left) and Wesley Hawkins. (VNS.)

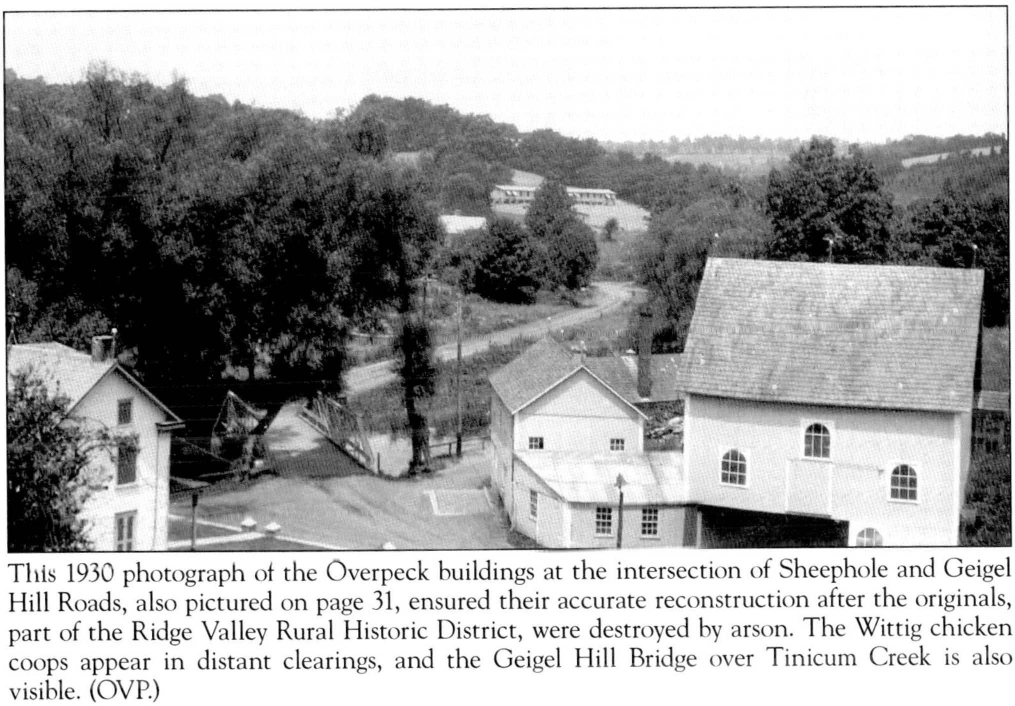

This 1930 photograph of the Overpeck buildings at the intersection of Sheephole and Geigel Hill Roads, also pictured on page 31, ensured their accurate reconstruction after the originals, part of the Ridge Valley Rural Historic District, were destroyed by arson. The Wittig chicken coops appear in distant clearings, and the Geigel Hill Bridge over Tinicum Creek is also visible. (OVP.)

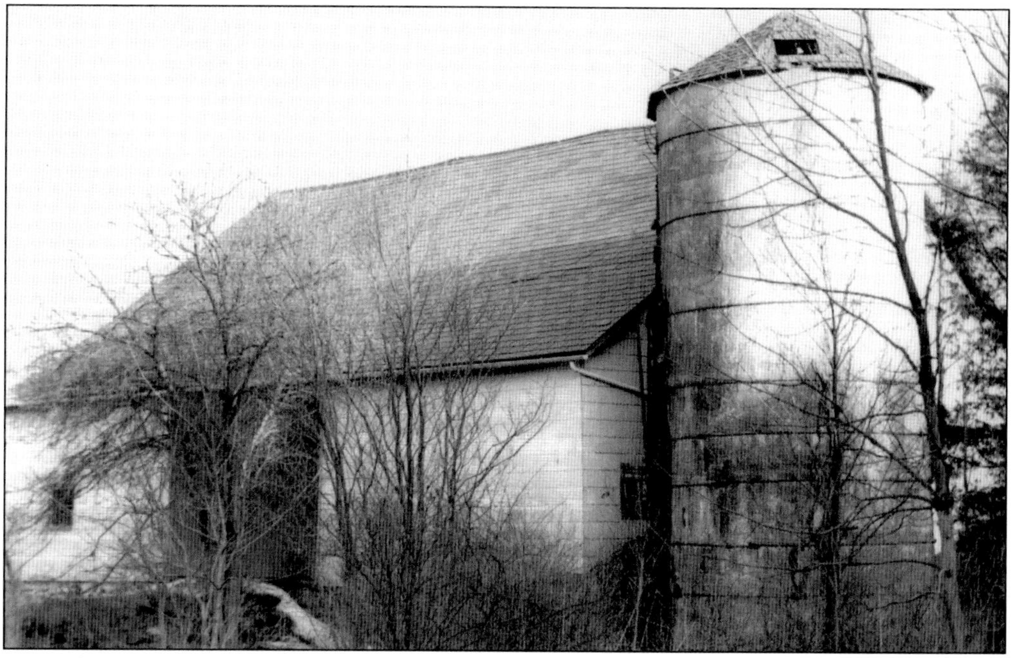

A number of Tinicum's historic architectural treasures are on the National Register of Historic Places. Uhlerstown and Point Pleasant are historic districts, as is the Ridge Valley Rural Historic District. Erwinna and Wormansville have been nominated for inclusion. Individual buildings whose historic integrity has earned this honor include Red Hill Church and School in Ottsville; Stover Mill, Stover Riverside Farm, and Isaac Stover House in Erwinna; Erwinna and Frankenfield Covered Bridges; and Lewis Summers Farm. (TTP.)

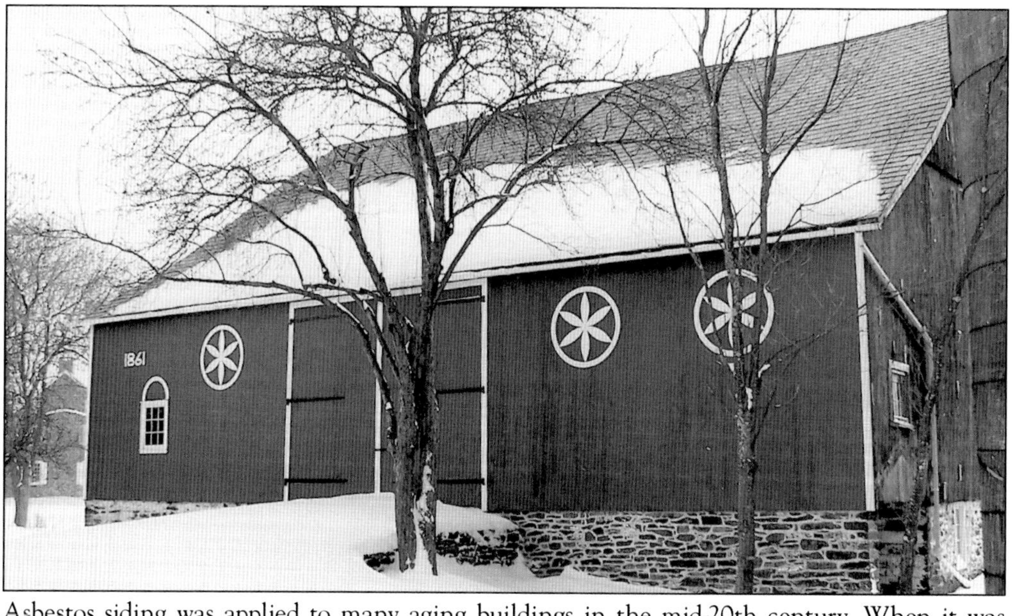

Asbestos siding was applied to many aging buildings in the mid-20th century. When it was removed from the Lewis Summers barn on Headquarters Road near Ottsville, pictured above in 1974, the faded outlines of these six-petaled rosette hex designs, typical in upper Bucks County, reappeared to guide the accurate restoration of the building. (WHT.)

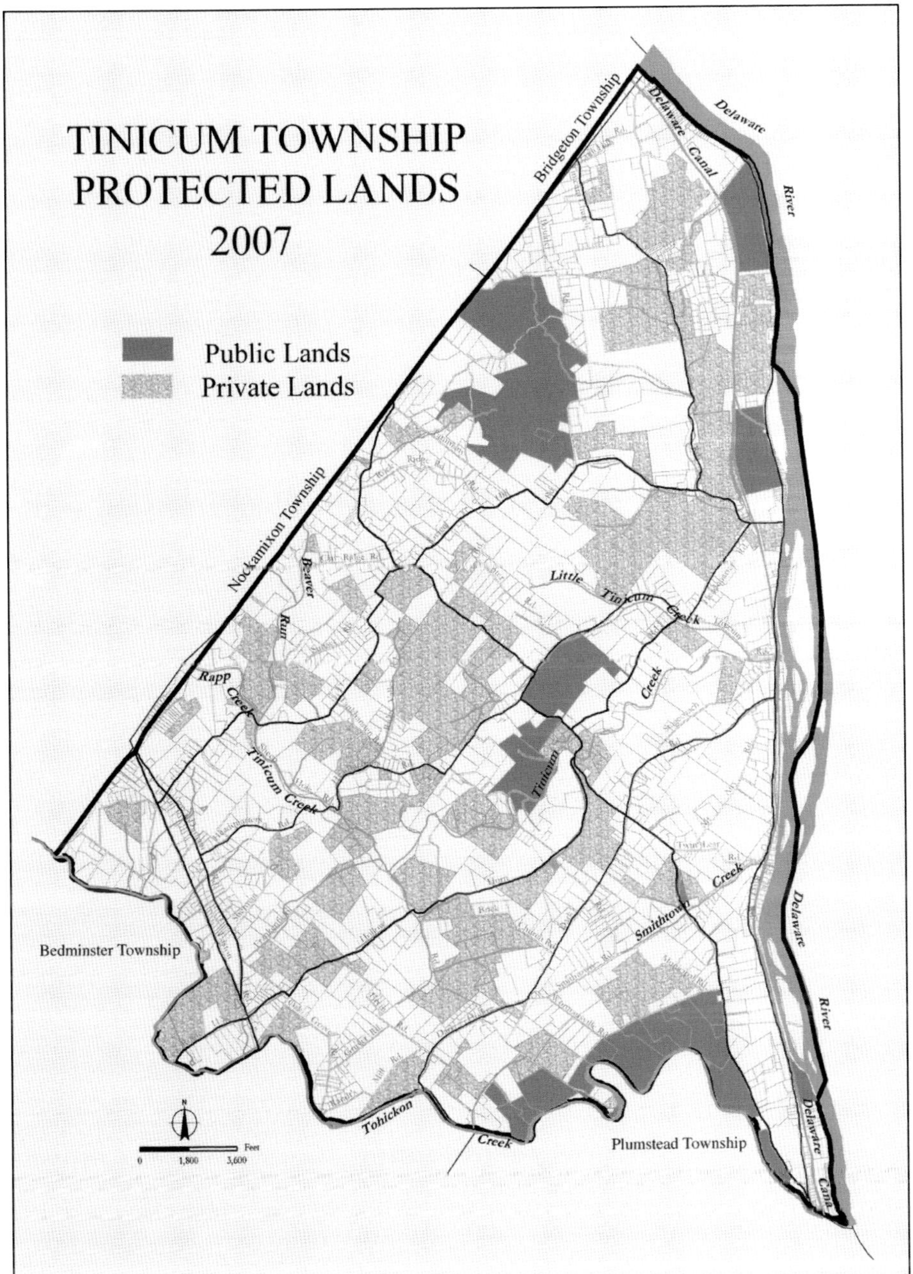

Recognizing the importance of environmental protection and growth management, residents formed the Tinicum Conservancy in 1992 to encourage the voluntary preservation of private lands by permanently relinquishing development rights. Subsequent funding provided by county and township open space bonds has aided in the acquisition and retirement of the development rights on additional private lands. Including state and county parklands, over 6,000 acres, or 30 percent of Tinicum's land, as shown on this map, were permanently protected by December 2007. Lenni-Lenape tradition holds that aromatic cedar boughs give clarity of mind. Perhaps the abundance of cedars in the township has inspired the efforts and generosity of residents to preserve the natural and historic resources of Tinicum. (TTP.)

Consistent with our mission to preserve history on a local level, this book was printed in South Carolina on American-made paper and manufactured entirely in the United States. Products carrying the accredited Forest Stewardship Council (FSC) label are printed on 100 percent FSC-certified paper.

MADE IN THE USA